SLAVE SONGS OF THE GEORGIA SEA ISLANDS

1. *Old Polly Goodwine*

SLAVE SONGS

OF THE GEORGIA SEA ISLANDS

Lydia Parrish

FOREWORD BY
Art Rosenbaum

INTRODUCTION BY
Olin Downes

MUSIC TRANSCRIBED BY
Creighton Churchill and Robert MacGimsey

Brown Thrasher Books

THE UNIVERSITY OF GEORGIA PRESS   ATHENS AND LONDON

Published in 1992 as a Brown Thrasher Book
by the University of Georgia Press
Athens, Georgia 30602
© 1942 by Lydia Parrish, 1969 by Maxfield Parrish, Jr.
Foreword to the Brown Thrasher Edition © 1992
by the University of Georgia Press

Printed and bound by Thomson-Shore
The paper in this book meets the guidelines
for permanence and durability of the Committee on
Production Guidelines for Book Longevity
of the Council on Library Resources.

Printed in the United States of America
96   95   94   93   92   C   5   4   3   2   1
96   95   94   93   92   P   5   4   3   2   1

Library of Congress Cataloging in Publication Data

Slave songs of the Georgia Sea Islands / [compiled by] Lydia Parrish ;
foreword by Art Rosenbaum ; introduction by Olin Downes ; music
transcribed by Creighton Churchill and Robert MacGimsey.
p. of music.
"Brown Thrasher books."
Reprint. Originally published: Creative Age Press, 1942.
Includes bibliographical references.

ISBN 0-8203-2389-6

1. Afro-Americans—Georgia—Music.   2. Folk music—
Georgia.   3. Folk songs, English—Georgia.   4. Spirituals
(Songs)—Georgia.   5. Work songs—Georgia.   6. Slaves—
Georgia.   7. Islands—Georgia.
I. Parrish, Lydia.
M1670.S6   1992   91-22948
                                                          CIP
                                                            M

British Library Cataloging in Publication Data available

CONTENTS

Contents

MUSIC

ILLUSTRATIONS

Bilali's "Diary"

Foreword

In 1976 on my first visit to Sapelo Island off the Georgia coast, Ronister Johnson, a resident of the black Hog Hammock settlement, described a scene from his youth: Mrs. Parrish, the wife of the artist Maxfield Parrish and a long-time resident of the Georgia Sea Islands, had arranged for several older black men to demonstrate the art of shanty singing for Mr. Coffin, the owner of Sapelo's "big house," and his guests. The men tied a rope to a tree, and at Mrs. Parrish's signal they pulled as they sang the sailors' work songs of their youth. Johnson did not reveal whether the men might have felt pride in their venerable tradition, annoyance at having to entertain the white folks, or a combination of the two. But the vignette showed Lydia Parrish in action, actively encouraging both the continued performance of folk songs by African-Americans and the interest and support of whites.

Nearly half a century ago, when she published her important collection of African-American folk songs from the coastal regions of Georgia, Parrish believed that their survival over the preceding thirty years had almost entirely been due to her "persistence, plus a little money" as well as contributions from other white admirers of these folk traditions. Not only did she plumb the memories of African-Americans—though her word was inevitably "Negroes," the term then in use—for songs originating in slavery and record them in their contexts as much as possible, but she offered the African-Americans financial rewards and the opportunity to perform for visitors in "the cabin," a building constructed especially for that purpose near her home on St. Simon's Island.

In 1965 the folklorist Bruce Jackson wrote a foreword to *Slave Songs of the Georgia Sea Islands*, and while he recognized the value of Mrs. Parrish's collection, he maintained that her interest in African-American folklore had been mainly sentimental and stated that we "should not join her in lamenting the demise of the order that produced it."[1] Jackson believed that the traditions recorded in the book were "historical folklore . . . of collateral current interest," though African-American folklore changes as social, political, and educational conditions change. Even if what Jackson believed is true, this

[1] *Bruce Jackson, in his foreword to Lydia Parrish*, Slave Songs of the Georgia Sea Islands (1945; reprint, Hatboro, Pennsylvania: Folklore Associates, 1965), p. xi.

xiii

collection is still of great value as evidence of African tradition on the North American continent, of new hybrids that arose in the Gullah areas of Georgia, and of cultural roots that nourished the African-American and larger American culture.

In the 1980s and 1990s we have witnessed the persistence of even the oldest forms of slave traditions. Though sometimes performed for the bigger society in the manner Mrs. Parrish initiated, these folk songs are maintained primarily by the communities along the coast, far from the sentimental paternalism of the whites who Jackson supposed were the only reason the "old folklore" could have survived the conditions of its creation. This new publication of Mrs. Parrish's book is even more welcome as it becomes clear that the rich folk culture it documents continues to live and function.

Separated from the mainland by salt marshes and mangrove swamps, the rice and Sea Island cotton plantations of the coast were relatively isolated. A portion of the slave population along the coast came directly from Africa and the West Indies, and Mende slaves from Sierra Leone in West Africa were imported to Charleston to provide the rice-cultivation skills the European-American planters lacked. Consequently, the string of barrier islands along the Georgia coast and the adjacent mainland areas were home to traditions bearing stronger evidence of African origin than those customs found in areas farther inland.[2] After Emancipation many freed slaves came to own the land of former masters and remained in tight-knit communities.

In the 1960s Alan Lomax recognized that coastal African-Americans "kept to the speech of their ancestors and, in some places, still speak dialects in which many African words and syntactical features survive. Their folk and animal tales show a rich admixture of European and African traits at an early stage of blending. Their funeral customs, their religious ceremonies, indeed, their whole way of life bear the stamp of ante-bellum days. Yet this is no decadent culture. It has simply grown strong around a conservative base that is part pioneer, part planter gentility, and part African."[3]

Today Interstate 95 cuts through the salt marshes from Savannah to Brunswick, fishing and agriculture are in economic decline, and condominiums and shopping centers mar the region. Still the strains of the Gullah speech are heard, and the Bolton Community in McIntosh County celebrate Watch Night by welcoming in the New Year with the ring-shout of their slave ancestors.[4]

---

[2] *Tim Carrier (producer)*, Family Across the Sea *(South Carolina Educational Television, 1990)*.

[3] *Alan Lomax*, Georgia Sea Islands, *volume 1 (Prestige/International LP 25501, 1961)*.

[4] The McIntosh County Shouters: Slave Shout Songs from the Coast of Georgia, *recorded and annotated by Art Rosenbaum (Folkways LP FE 4344, 1984); and, Georgia Public TV, Down Yonder(The McIntosh County Shouters, 1987)*.

Lydia Parrish was born in Salem County in southern New Jersey in 1871. It was there that she first heard black folk songs sung by descendants of runaway slaves harbored by the area's Quaker population. Bruce Jackson attributes to aspects of southern New Jersey political and social history both Mrs. Parrish's relatively liberal feelings and her less tolerant attitudes toward African-Americans and their culture.[5] Yet it is clear that she had a keen interest in the songs of the Georgia African-Americans from her first visit to the Sea Islands in 1909.

During the many years she lived on St. Simon's before the publication of her book, Parrish won the confidence of many African-American singers and collected not only the songs but other elements of traditional culture that were the context of the folk songs. "Amateur folklorist" though Parrish may have been—Jackson faults her for mixing prejudices, and at times shaky scholarship, with her valuable first-hand observations— she painted a richer picture of the interweavings of music with oral lore, language, religious and social customs, foodways, and aspects of material culture than was usual for the time, even in the work of many professionals and academics. In this way she anticipated what has come to be called "folklife studies" by modern folklorists.

The African-American linguist Lorenzo Dow Turner met Mrs. Parrish during his travels through the coastal regions in the 1930s while studying African survivals in speech and song. He helped interpret her collected material and made sound recordings of the services at the cabin. It is from these, presumably, that the musical transcriptions in her book were made. Turner reported to Jackson that Mrs. Parrish was "a very enthusiastic and stimulating person, and she was highly respected and well liked by the many Negroes with whom she had dealings."[6]

Given the complexities of African-American traditional singing styles, which Parrish acknowledges, the musical transcriptions appear to be trustworthy—free from impositions of fine art music conventions that mar some collections of African-American folk music. The texts as well seem authentic, though both text and tune transcriptions may have been collated from several performances. Parrish occasionally identifies her informants but never indicates times and places of the performances. We can assume she gives us typical versions of songs that often varied considerably from performance to performance, although the modern practice of indicating what was sung by a given singer at a given time and place would have provided a more telling document.

Mrs. Parrish worked to recover all categories of traditional song from the region,

---

[5] *Jackson, op. cit., pp. ii-iv.*
[6] *Ibid., personal communication with Bruce Jackson, March 13, 1965.*

sacred and secular. Most unusual are the "African" songs, unique except for the Mende texts that Turner found in Georgia. While we would be grateful for interpretations of the African words and even a skeletal transcription of James Rogers's "astonishingly strange" vocal performance of "Freewillum," these remarkable survivals take their place alongside Siras Bowen's abstract wooden grave markers at Sunbury Baptist Church and "Stick Daddy" James Cooper's hand-carved walking canes as monuments of African culture in coastal Georgia.[7]

Parrish recognized the importance of the ring-shout, the "holy dance" that early outside observers and present-day participants in the tradition understand as being of African origin. While some scholars, including Robert Gordon early in this century, did not distinguish between the shout songs and other spirituals, Mrs. Parrish notes the difference and contributes the interesting information that shout songs in earlier times did double service as rowing songs. Early observers such as the pioneer slave-song collector William Francis Allen recognized that the shout was the dancelike movement rather than the vocal part of the performance, but Lorenzo Dow Turner was the first to relate the word itself to the Arabic *saut*, meaning a dance around the Kaaba;[8] and Parrish reports this connection. Mrs. Parrish expresses surprise that her African-American friends on St. Simon's were at first secretive about their knowledge of the shout, yet there had been a long history of suppression or, at best, disapproval by white missionaries and some black clergy of the practice of ring-shouting.[9] She seems to have had mixed feelings about the shout, appreciating the artistry of the pantomime, the difficult footwork, the "Egyptian" stances, and the moving poetry of some of the songs; yet she was embarrassed by erotic movement when her former servant Margaret "wiggled her hips shamelessly" as she moved around the circle. This is in line, however, with African fusion of the sensual and spiritual and is what today's shouters call the "rock" movement, though they make the distinction between shouting (for the Lord) and dancing. Somewhat inconsistently, Mrs. Parrish also calls the shout an "innocent performance." The shout, however, is a powerful combination of call-and-response singing, dramatic movement, and polyrhythmic percussion, exemplifying what Robert Farris Thompson has called

[7] *For more information on Bowen's grave markers and Cooper's walking canes, see Georgia Writers' Project,* Drums and Shadows: Survival Studies Among the Georgia Coastal Negroes *(1940; reprint, Athens: University of Georgia Press, 1986), pp. 25, 116–17.*

[8] *Lorenzo Dow Turner,* Africanisms in the Gullah Dialect *(1949; reprint, Ann Arbor: University of Michigan Press, 1974), p. 202.*

[9] *Parrish does not group "Aye Lord, Time Is Drawin' Nigh" with the shout songs, although I have noted its continued use for the ring-shout in McIntosh County.*

"*songs and dances of social allusion* (music which, however danceable and 'swinging,' remorselessly contrasts social imperfections against implied criteria for perfect living)."[10]

Mrs. Parrish also worked assiduously to collect secular songs of many types: ring-play songs (what would be called children's game songs or play parties elsewhere); solo dances, including the singular Buzzard Lope; and antebellum frolic and fiddle tunes. She considered Green Harris's verses "harmless," even though the well-known "Raise a Ruckus" lines sardonically comment on the futility of waiting for the mistress to fulfill her promise of freedom. Jackson chided Mrs. Parrish for her obtuseness in asserting that the words of "Ball the Jack" are "of no particular moment," missing the Freudian significance[11] (though she did note that an African-American nurse clearly felt that the hip movements associated with the song were not to be seen by white children). Shanties, the work songs of river and deep-sea sailors and port stevedors, were collected along with other work songs, rowing songs, and rice-fanning songs, in which the wind was called up to blow the husks from the grain. As much as possible these are described in context, as are the religious songs. While most collections present spirituals as text and melody alone separated from their function in practice, we learn from Mrs. Parrish that "May Be the Las' Time" was used at communion, "One-a These Days" closed prayer meetings, and "Ride On Conquering King" was sung while "settin'-up" with the dead. It is no surprise that the well-known spiritual "Wade in Nuh Watuh" was sung at baptisms, but Mrs. Parrish's vivid description of a baptism on a cold February morning on the Frederica River is an enduring record of the fusion of song and ceremony. Later Mrs. Parrish lamented that "cement tanks are built in the yards of conventional churches, and another picturesque custom will soon be a thing of the past." If this is the sentimentality that for Jackson flawed Parrish's work and rendered questionable her organization of groups dedicated to preserving authentic songs and performance styles, then what of Jim Cook, the centenarian African-American deacon of Adox who complained forty years later of "dead churches with a concrete floor" where the ring-shout could not be held?

The older traditions have persisted and held value for many coastal African-Americans. Lawrence McKiver has told me why he and others in Bolton continue to perform the ring-shout: "We're proud of what we're doing because it come from our poor parents." He describes seeing the remains of irrigation ditches dug by his slave grandparents on the land he still lives on and feels that the shout honors his forebears who labored and suffered in slavery. Similarly, Frankie Sullivan Quimby of today's Georgia Sea Island

[10] *Robert Farris Thompson,* Flash of the Spirit *(New York: Random House, 1983), p. xiii.*
[11] *Jackson, op. cit., p. vii.*

Singers, a continuation of the "star songsters" that Lydia Parrish organized, will show a visitor to St. Simon's the "Ibo Landing," where Ibo captives marched into the water to drown rather than submit to slavery.

Parrish certainly knew that not everything was being revealed to her by her informants, though she attributes this somewhat patronizingly to their innate reticence. Jackson takes her to task for assuming that "if a Negro tells nothing to a white he has nothing to tell anyone? She doesn't realize that the slave and former slave might have been loath to offer the white southern plantation owner or manager information for the same reason a convict does not chat freely with the warden or a union organizer with the company lawyer."[12]

Times have changed, and Frankie and Doug Quimby are eager to share with European-Americans and a new generation of African-Americans the hidden meanings and subtexts in the slave songs that were not revealed to or understood by Parrish. From Chatham County to California, the Quimbys tell audiences that "ham bone, ham bone, wha's you been? / All roun' the worl' an' back agin" in the well-known patting rhyme was not nonsense or simply a reference to the thighs of the performer, as Parrish has it, but rather the bitter commentary on a ham bone, having been stripped of its good meat by the masters and making the rounds of the slave cabins to impart a bit of flavor to rations of peas or beans. They also reveal "Ragged Leevy" as a many-layered and pithy social commentary by slaves and "Ole Tar River" as an Underground Railroad map. This lore was passed down among the organized Georgia Sea Island singers, gradually surfacing in their public performances. In Bolton it is still understood by the McIntosh County Shouters that "kneebone bend" in the shout song "Knee-bone" refers to their slave ancestors kneeling to pray in the wilderness when they found themselves slaves in a strange continent, and "shout, Daniel," in a shout song not published by Parrish, was a pantomimed and sung directive to a slave, Daniel (not the biblical Daniel), on how to elude the master who was pursuing him for stealing meat from the smokehouse. When I asked Lawrence McKiver in the early 1980s, shortly after he and his group began for the first time to perform the ring-shout for outsiders, why he was willing to tell anyone the heretofore hidden meanings of the songs, he answered simply, "Now we can spit it out."

Beyond the explicit and encoded meanings in the texts of the slave songs, the style of performance holds a key to the cohesiveness in group, family, church, and community. Call-and-response was not limited to African practice (many of the shanties sung by coastal blacks were sung as enthusiastically by white British and American sailors), but it

[12] *Ibid., pp. vii-viii.*

is central to the slave culture of the Georgia coast. The shout, in particular, is a clear continuation of the social African tradition and anticipates its use in later work songs, spirituals, modern gospel, and secular musical idioms. Robert Ferris Thompson has pointed out that "call-and-response goes to the very heart of the notion of good government, of popular response to the actions of an ideal leader."[13] Though her appreciation of the beauty and richness of African-American performance styles was certainly genuine, Lydia Parrish seems to have been unaware of how crucially important these traditions were in sustaining the slaves and their descendants through incredibly adverse conditions—or that they would persist within and beyond the close-knit communities of the coast as an assertion and reinforcement of cultural values.

It is important to understand that folk traditions continue to exist in the communities that sustained them *and* in new interactions with other groups through live performances and mass media. Folklorists have been wise to point out the pitfalls of what David Wisenant calls "cultural intervention" and European folklorists have called "folklorism": essentially the changing or utilization of folk traditions through the intervention of a third party for reasons of nationalism, chauvinism, tourism, or any other motives. Yet, are new channels for old traditions always to be disdained? I recall a folklorist at an academic meeting speaking of "taking folklore out of context"—he was called on this by a colleague who said there is no such thing as "out of context," there are only *new* contexts; and the point was admitted. Surely there is a significant difference between the Watch Night shout at Bolton and the ring-shout performed by Lawrence McKiver's group at Emory University, or between the Dawson, Georgia, setting for ring-plays of Bessie Jones's girlhood and a Cambridge, Massachusetts, schoolroom where she now teaches children these games. Yet the traditions live; they illuminate history and the ongoing processes of cultural and social change.

Bruce Jackson wrote in 1965 that "there is yet much old Negro folklore on the Sea Islands, but not very much."[14] This may have been true then, and may still be true today, though one wonders how even a professional folklorist can define "much" and "very much." Surely Lawrence McKiver would agree that the old ways are less central to the way of life of today's generation than to that of his grandparents, but he and his kin and friends still sing and shout the New Year in with songs collected by Lydia Parrish in a vastly different time. Sister Ruth Cohen's demonstrations of singing and beating and

[13] Robert Farris Thompson, *African Art in Motion (Los Angeles: University of California Press, 1974), p. 27.*
[14] *Jackson, op. cit., p. xi.*

fanning the rice and the Quimbys' singing of the stevedor shanty "Pay Me My Money Down" serve a different purpose than the performances of slave songs in an earlier day in farmyards, or on the docks at Darien, but the perpetuation of these songs through the years has led to their cultural conservation.

These African traditions surely owe something of their survival to Lydia Parrish's work and vindicate her effort and her mission—perhaps even the row of former sailors on Sapelo singing and pulling the rope tied to a tree would seem less stilted now. Despite enormous economic and social change on the coast of Georgia, its African-American communities are mixing and gaining recognition with national and world culture: the McIntosh County Shouters perform at the Smithsonian Institution, and Gullah Georgians, South Carolinians, and their "black Seminole" kin from Oklahoma journey to Sierra Leone to meet and sing with the people from whom they and their culture sprang.[15] Today Lydia Parrish's book continues to be a cultural touchstone for a changing African-Atlantic culture and for us all.

                                                                    Art Rosenbaum

1991

[15] *Carrier,* Family Across the Sea.

Acknowledgments

In the twenty-five years of research represented in the collection of slave songs, from which the comparatively few examples in this book have been culled, aid has been given me that words can never repay. Without the help of its many friends, this music of the Georgia Sea Islands could not have been preserved. Two of its admirers gave generous support in the four frightening years following 1930. One provided the funds needed to continue the work when the chastened Negroes would do for a quarter what they will not do today for a dollar; the other contributed her time, thought and general assistance.

I wish that the names of all who have shared in this work could be given, but over a period of years I have become indebted to so many associates that it is inadvisable to mention more than those whose coöperation has produced far-reaching results.

Mr. and Mrs. Joseph Parsons of Lakeville, Connecticut, and Wassaw Island, and the late Augustus Oemler of Savannah and St. Catherine's Island, gave me in February, 1909, my first opportunity to hear the singing of primitive slave songs on the coast of Georgia.

In later years the hospitality of Mr. and Mrs. Alfred Jones, of Sea Island, furnished an opportunity to hear similar songs on Sapelo Island.

The friendly interest of the late Mrs. Clifton of The Ridge, McIntosh County, made me acquainted with the "ring-shout," which is so rarely seen, even by Southerners, that few realize "shouting" is a religious dance of African origin, and not a loud cry.

The Misses Dent, of Hofwyl Plantation, on the mainland in Glynn County, generously shared their knowledge of the songs that descendants of their family's slaves have been encouraged to preserve.

In Camden County, Mr. Chacey Kuehn, of Satilla Pines and New York City, gave valuable help in locating the best singers in the neighborhood of Tompkins, Burnt Fort, and Jerusalem.

The late Howard E. Coffin never lost an opportunity to share with others his delight in the slave songs. The applause of the cosmopolitan audiences he assembled at

The Cloister, on Sea Island, did more for their prestige than years of single-handed effort.

On St. Simon's Island, Emma Postell Shadman was an unfailing source of inspiration and information. Her death is an irreparable loss.

In the work of bolstering up the waning authority of the religious slave songs, it was necessary to take various steps that could never have been carried through without the assistance of the following friends and acquaintances. To them I wish to express my gratitude.

Mr. and Mrs. J. Franklin McElwain, of Sea Island and Boston;

Mr. and Mrs. Eugene W. Lewis, of Hamilton Plantation, St. Simon's Island, and Grosse Pointe, Michigan;

Mr. and Mrs. A. L. Kuehn, of Satilla Pines, Camden County, and Oak Park, Illinois;

Mrs. Henry Hodge, of Savannah;

Mrs. Burwell Atkinson and Mrs. Charles T. Nolan, of Incachee Plantation, Camden County, and St. Simon's Island;

Mrs. Kenneth Berrie, of Brunswick;

Mrs. George W. C. Drexel, of White Oak, Camden County, and Bryn Mawr, Pennsylvania;

Mr. and Mrs. Grainger, of Colesburg, Camden County;

Mr. and Mrs. Robert Pettigrew, of Dauphin Plantation, Fort Liberté, Haiti, gave the opportunity in a never-to-be-forgotten month to hear repeatedly the primitive drum rhythms of Haiti;

Thanks are due Mrs. W. K. Bunner, of St. Catherine's, Ontario, for first-hand information concerning the music of Africa's Gold Coast Negroes;

To Margaret Davis Cate, I give special thanks for help in uncovering certain particulars concerning life on Georgia's coastal plantations.

To Lucile Bruce Brown, of Sea Island, I am greatly indebted for constructive criticism of different sections of the manuscript.

The publishers of *Country Life* courteously permit me to include the article on slave songs which I wrote for the issue of December, 1935.

I owe much to the information given me by Melville J. Herskovits and Joseph Greenberg, of Northwestern University, and Dr. Lorenzo D. Turner, of Fisk University. The results of their research in various aspects of Negro history have been most helpful.

Through the kind offices of Chalmers S. Murray, of Charleston and Edisto Island, South Carolina, and Albert H. Stoddard, of Savannah, Georgia, and Daufuskie Island, South Carolina, the doors of their respective islands were opened to me. Their generous assistance will never be forgotten.

To Foresta Hodgson Wood, I am deeply grateful for the many photographs she has generously contributed. To Clara E. Sipprell, Ralph Steiner, Dr. Orrin S. Wightman, Maxfield Parrish, Jr., and others I also give thanks for the use of various pictures.

To Creighton Churchill I am under obligation for his inspiring coöperation and sustained interest.

But for the help generously given by Mary Burnet, of Athens, Georgia, I doubt if this book would ever have been finished. My debt of gratitude to her is immeasurable.

Thanks due these and other friends must not, however, obscure the fact that without the coöperation of the colored singers—the only people qualified through their racial background to present properly the traditional songs—there would have been no occasion for this book or these acknowledgments.

Although Julia Armstrong, of the singing Proctor family, has never told me the half of what she knows, particular thanks are due her for the help she has given since 1915. Her husband, Joe Armstrong, her brother, Willis Proctor, Cornelia and Edith Murphy, and others at the South End of St. Simon's have all aided in resurrecting old songs. Ben Davis, of the North End, comes of another family of singers, and special mention is due him for his loyalty and dependability. Bessie Cuyler, Catherine Ramsey, Peter Davis, Alec Stewart, and Mansfield Jackson have demonstrated the fine spirit on which the successful presentation of this type of music depends. There are other first-rate singers on the island, but the foregoing are singled out because they recognize that the requirements of the group take precedence over those of the individual.

When a causeway was put across the marshes in 1924 and St. Simon's Island was connected with the mainland, we were able to include other Glynn County singers in our "Spiritual Singers Society of Coastal Georgia." Among those who have proved their devotion to the slave songs are Jeffry Union and Susyanna Vallion. Several of the children in the Broadfield contingent, trained by Susyanna and her assistants, Clara Roberts, "Coots" Hightower, and Gertrude Cohen, now sing at the Cabin on St. Simon's with the older group. In McIntosh County, Josephine Young is an able exponent of the old-style singing: so are Henry Shaw, Rosa Sallins, Julia Walker, Nancy and Alphonzo Thorpe.

Camden County, too, has many excellent singers, but proximity to Jacksonville, Florida—as is the case with the section south of Savannah to the Ogeechee River—has not increased the popularity of the old-time music. Outstanding among those who sing in the traditional manner are "Major" Harris, Will Harrell, the Lukes, the Gibbses, and several other singing families that appear to have inherited the gift. There are hundreds of others listed in the membership book of our Society. Unfortunately it is impracticable to name them all, though their devotion is the only safeguard against oblivion that this music possesses.

Formerly the allegiance of the singers to the slave songs was supported by religious fervor and by the authority of the praise-house and the church, but these strongholds are now given over to Europeanized book versions and vapid sacred hymns. Neither possesses the power to stir the blood, and in many churches—even where a vested choir sits in smug self-possession beside the pulpit—the congregation sings the traditional songs when collection time comes around: the deacons know from experience that the old tunes are potent money-getters, while the book songs are not. It is well to recognize, however, that in a materialistic world loyalty needs something more solid to stand on than religious exaltation. For this reason the help of the white friends who have given their moral and financial support to the preservation of the slave music is beyond price. To them this book is gratefully dedicated.

An Explanation

There are certain matters connected with the singing of these slave songs that should be cleared up in the very beginning. First and foremost, however, it may be well to give my credentials. I am frequently asked: "How did you—a Northerner—come to interest yourself in this music?" The question is legitimate, and deserves an answer. In fact I have a fellow feeling for the Atlanta gentleman who said: "What right have you to know anything about it?" I always wish to put just these words to writers who grow authoritative on the subject—and, as we all know, what is sauce for the gander should be sauce for the goose.

I was born in a Quaker community, thirty miles south of Philadelphia,[1] where descendants of slaves—and some ex-slaves themselves—were the only singers. Theirs was the only music worthy of the name that I heard in my youth. In those days members of the Society of Friends were not the liberal people they are now. They had no "hireling ministers"; their meetings were silent until the Spirit moved one of the older—and approved—members to speak. All forms of art, including music, were taboo among the overseers of our meeting,[2] and none was heard in the Friends' Academy I attended up to the time I was sixteen. Paradoxically enough, their abolitionist views attracted a singing race into their midst.[3] Their tolerance was such, however, that as far as I could see they never attempted to curb its musical exuberance in the kitchen or in the fields. Perhaps, with them as with me, the Negro's music filled a real need.

For many generations prior to the War Between the States, colored people—mostly from tide-water Virginia—had secretly crossed the river from Delaware into

[1] One of my ancestors, John Pledger, was the first of the Salem Quakers to reach America. He arrived, via Maryland, in January, 1674-5. His wife and small son came with the founder of the colony, John Fenwick, in September, 1675.

[2] The stand taken by the Quakers represented a reaction from the frivolity of Charles II's day.

[3] Their opposition to war created still another anomalous situation: Lincoln emancipated the slaves, yet he did not keep the country out of war. In my family, the feeling against him was bitter on this account. My mother took the stand that killing was a far more serious offense than holding a race in bondage. In consequence I saw Lincoln in the same light as did the Southerners—but for a different reason.

Salem County, New Jersey, where they found sanctuary among the Friends.[4] One of the stations of the underground railroad was located in our community, and the consideration shown the runaway and manumitted slaves caused them to settle there in such numbers that by 1840 they needed, and built, a large two-story church, and, after emancipation, still another. In my childhood they so greatly outnumbered the white voters that we had a colored overseer of the roads. At that time there was no lack of spontaneous music and laughter among them. However, in the late eighties, when a railroad was put through their village, the sophisticated Philadelphia Negroes were enabled to show the country cousins that they were hopelessly out-of-date. Then it was that the dull but stylish hymns of the white man supplanted those of the old régime, and standardized behaviour became the rule.

I did not hear the slave songs again until I visited the coast of Georgia in 1909. As we all know, opportunity rarely knocks more than once, and this time I took steps to insure that the songs should not escape me. Herein, I believe, rests my right to know something about them.

The Negroes frankly say that it was a good thing I arrived on St. Simon's when I did, and I know that if I had been there years earlier I could have saved many priceless songs which are now lost. These primitive songs—like the carvings of Africa —had been ridiculed, and the Negroes were ashamed to sing them in the presence of strangers. It took considerable brain-cudgeling to find a way to overcome their feeling that the traditional mode of expression was peculiar and old-fashioned, and to show the singers that many white people recognized its beauty.[5] As can be seen from the photographs illustrating this book, these colored people have regained faith in their birthright—and I hope it will last.

Another question asked me is the reason for avoiding the term "spiritual." Today it is applied to almost any religious song in Negro dialect, regardless of its age or

[4] *From the probated will of the Quaker, John Fenwick, it is evident that in 1683 there was one "Black" too many in our settlement. He disinherited his "grand childe Elizabeth Adams totally . . . except the Lord open her eyes to see her abominable transgrescen against him, me & her poore father, by giving her true repentance & forsakeing yt Black yt hath beene the ruine of her . . ." About 12 miles south-east of Salem is a town called Othello and a few miles farther east is Gouldtown where Elizabeth and her "blackamoor" are said to have located.*

[5] *For years I tried to think of a way to rekindle interest in the old songs. In the dark of a wintry four A. M., I awakened with the full-blown answer: form a society and admit only those who could sing in the old way. The plan was nothing but good common sense—and it has worked.*

origin, and because of its indiscriminate use I have suppressed it whenever possible.[6]

I notice that the only writers who used the term "spirituals," prior to 1909, were those who collected the bulk of their material in South Carolina. References were made to Georgia "spirituals," but Georgia was off the beaten track and, in consequence, few examples were given. In such collections as Hampton's *Cabin and Plantation Songs*, in editions up to 1909, no mention is made of "spirituals"—the songs are called "slave hymns." Nor does the name occur in Barton's *Old Plantation Hymns*, published in 1898. Our Negroes in southern New Jersey, who had come from Virginia, never used it. The first time I heard it applied to a Negro song was in 1909 on St. Catherine's—a sea island half way between the Savannah River and the Altamaha. I was told by Old Quarterman, born in Liberty County, and by Julia, born on St. Simon's Island, that they always called their own songs "spirituals," although one old grandmother called them "ant'ems" to the end of her days.

But why was the name adopted by the slaves of South Carolina and Georgia and not by those of the states to the northward? A bit of early history may perhaps supply the answer. When a band of Puritans who had settled at Dorchester, Massachusetts, in 1630, heard of the need of work among the Indians of South Carolina, they migrated with their pastor in 1695 and settled at a spot they named Dorchester, on the Ashley River, about twenty-six miles from Charleston. Here they stayed until 1750, but the unhealthy location caused them to move on to St. John's Parish in Georgia. There, they established another Congregational church which they called Midway. At this church the Negroes sat in the gallery as was the custom in various other places.[7] Olmstead in *A Journey in the Seaboard Slave States* (1853–54) gives an account of the concern shown by members of this Midway community for the moral enlightenment of their slaves and says, "I heard them spoken of even so far away as Virginia and Kentucky. I believe that in no other district has there been displayed as general and long-continued an interest in the spiritual well-being of the Negroes."[8]

[6] *Ben Davis told me the way he knew the age of a song was by the way it made him feel. "The old ones make you feel good, the new ones don't make you feel anything." I know of no better test.*

[7] *Where there was no gallery they sat in the rear of the church—if a separate service was not held for them.*

[8] *Olmstead also tells of a religious service held by the crackers in an isolated section south of Savannah. To this day such a service can be seen and heard in conservative Negro churches. It is significant that in the North white people were never encouraged to go into a Negro*

These transplanted New Englanders were outstanding people, and undoubt-edly made their influence felt in South Carolina just as it always has been in Georgia. The center of Revolutionary ideas was in their community at Midway. It sent two signers of the Declaration of Independence to Philadelphia, and among its notables were six foreign missionaries and eighty-two ministers. When the British burned their church, during the Revolution, the members built another—in 1792—that was a replica of the Congregational churches seen throughout New England; and, when the parishes became counties after the Revolution, they called theirs Liberty County. Although the members of this church—organized in Massachusetts, re-moved to South Carolina, and then to Georgia—had been in the South for genera-tions, their sympathies were clearly with their Northern co-religionists: their pastors came from New England and one of them was the Calvinist, the Reverend Abiel Holmes, father of Oliver Wendell Holmes. Under these conditions it is unlikely that they omitted the use of the *Bay Psalm Book*, published in Cambridge, Massa-chusetts (1640), of which the revised and enlarged edition of 1651 was called the *Psalms, Hymns and Spiritual Songs of the Old and New Testaments*. The first edi-tion having been adopted by nearly every congregation in the Massachusetts Bay Colony, there is no reason to believe that it was any less popular with the God-fearing colonists who went to the Southern outposts. The slaves of the group of Puritans who had settled on the Ashley River probably sang *Spiritual Songs* [9] with their owners just as the slaves of their descendants at Midway undoubtedly did. In all likelihood the name "spiritual" struck the fancy of the Negroes, and accounts for its application to the songs of their own composition. Naturally enough these songs had little in common with the hymns sung with the white people, and were used only at such services as took place—apart from the slave-owners—during the week at prayer meeting held at the praise-house or the cabin of a deacon, or at a "settin'-up" or a funeral.

Before the year 1800 the old hymn book, which had gone through more than

---

church, but in the South, they have always been welcomed—a survival of an earlier custom. If I had known this when I first went to St. Simon's I could have learned what I needed to find out without the delay to which I was subjected. But I was from the North—and was told nothing about the Negro. Before the first World War pushed the War Between the States into the background, anyone who hailed from New England was suspect if he showed an interest in the colored people. This attitude still exists in certain places on the South Carolina coast. To those who know the unsavory record of Northern carpet-baggers, such a situation is not surprising.

[9] Before 1743, Spiritual Songs for Children, by J. Wright, was published by John Newbery.

fifty editions in less than a hundred years, gave way to the newer versions by Tate and Brady and by Isaac Watts. Although I have been unable to find any points of resemblance between Negro songs and those contained in the older collection, I have found traces of the influence of Dr. Watts—but only in word combinations. A Watts hymn, sung to long metre, runs as follows:

> Broad is the road that leads to death and thousands walk together there
> But wisdom shows a narrow path with here and there a traveller.

Katie Brown on Sapelo sings the following version—but to a tune that bears no relation to any I have ever heard:

> Narrow road is Heaven road
> Believer I know
> With here and there a traveller
> Believer I know
> The broad road is Hell road
> Believer I know
> Thousand walk together there
> Believer I know.

It is self-evident that the Negro borrowed a word here, another there, whenever it pleased him, and he probably did the same with a musical phrase. But as is said by those who heard his songs at their best, soon after the Civil War, the creation for the most part was his own. The surprising thing is that so much of the traditional music has survived.

It is just possible that the almost human will to live displayed by many of the old songs has something to do with it. Frequently persons, who have heard the singers the night before, telephone for the words of a song. The tune haunts them, but without the verses they cannot give it expression. They have my sympathy. I, too, have suffered in the same fashion, and been obliged in self-defense to learn the songs. When I complained to Julia, my cook, of their torment, she answered: "They do us that way too, until we learn them." Susyanna, in teaching me "A'n' Jinny Hoe-cake," looked at me knowingly, and said: "You'll be singin' this tomorrow." I was. Cha'lotte, from Ragged Island—one of the Bahama group—also told me they got in her mind "like a worm" and gave her no peace. As can be seen, these songs have no regard for color.

Unfortunately our system of notation is inadequate to interpret the Negro's traditional music. For this reason the writers who work in libraries and not in the field, and base their claim of preponderant white influence on book versions and on the singing of students in Negro schools, have the best of the argument. No matter how skillful a musician may be, he is hampered at the start because his interpretation is conditioned by his training and by the limitations imposed by our form of notation.[10] As for the singing of Negro students, it is a known fact that education and folk-music have never been compatible. Under such circumstances the advice given by Thomas P. Fenner in his preface to *Cabin and Plantation Songs*, written in 1873, is the best I know. He tells us "tones are frequently employed which we have no musical characters to represent. . . . It is of course impossible to explain them in words, and to those who wish to sing them, the best advice is that most useful in learning to pronounce a foreign language: *Study all the rules you please, then—go listen to a native.*" In addition to listening to a Negro, I would suggest writing down the words as sung—not as recited. With the best intention in the world the Negro

[10] *N. G. J. Ballanta, in an explanation of his idea of the need of a seventeen-tone octave to correctly express African music, tells us why the Western scale is unfit for use in African melodic expression. He believes that "a different system of tuning should be adopted to satisfy the demands of African musical expression, as the values given to notes tuned to equal temperament of twelve divisions to the octave, however much they may be of advantage to the western musician for his system of harmony, do not at all agree with the values given to those same diatonic steps when sung by the African. The same thing is true of Negroes in the United States whose singing of their native songs has a better effect when unaccompanied by the piano than when accompanied. . . .*

"Theoretically speaking, Western musicians agree that there are seventeen different sounds in the octave to be provided for; but, by the system known as 'Enharmony,' two sounds are represented by one key known as the sharp and flat to adjacent keys."

Mr. Ballanta goes on to say that "the Africans employ Septimal Harmony in a great majority of cases and there is no reason why they should be made to give way to the Western system of tertian harmony by employing the present tuning of the piano."

In an address made some years ago, Mr. Ballanta stated that "The æsthetic value of the Spirituals arises from the fact that they are conceived and sung in harmony. This fact has baffled many musicians, as the folksongs of other peoples are conceived in unison. The reason is that the Negro in singing, as his African brother, thinks not of a scale which is simply a succession of individual tones, and which forms the basis of the folksongs of other people, but of a chord where there are three distinct and individual tones sounding at the same time, and in combination producing a harmonious effect."

This interesting explanation agrees with what W. E. Ward tells us in "Music of the Gold Coast" concerning the African's amazing ability to carry on "five simultaneous rhythms, the melody and four percussion parts." On St. Simon's Island, three simultaneous rhythms are quite common—the melody, hand clapping, and tapping of the feet or heels on the floor.

never speaks the words of a song as he sings them.[11] To catch what is sung is diffi-cult, but it is the only way that the tricky rhythm of a song can be learned. Any per-son who wishes to give an authentic presentation must be respectful of the older Negroes' disregard of our rules of spelling, pronunciation, and punctuation, and above all resist the temptation to use a formula. As the editors of *Slave Songs of the United States* say in their preface: "The remarks upon the dialect which follow have reference . . . almost exclusively to a few plantations at the northern end of St. Helena Island [South Carolina]. They will, no doubt, apply in a greater or less de-gree to the entire region of the southeasterly slave States, but not to other portions of the South. It should also be understood that the corruptions and peculiarities here described are not universal, even here. There are all grades, from the rudest field-hands to mechanics and house-servants, who speak with a considerable degree of correctness." These words apply perfectly to the types of dialect found on the Georgia coast, and explain the lack of consistency in the songs of this collection.

Few people realize that the slaves—like their African cousins—sang on every possible occasion. Religious ceremonies, as well as work and play, were all conducted to music. Naturally there were times when singing was a solo matter—as over the wash-tub—but the Negroes have always been gregarious (private life as we know it has never been popular among them), and it is no wonder their singing reflects this characteristic. In consequence it is particularly important to know how each of the two or three outstanding singers handles his contribution to the effect produced by the group. It seems to me that Creighton Churchill has succeeded admirably in con-veying this idea—but as he frankly says, the whole problem is one of approximation. When it comes to reproducing peculiarities of African music and tones for which we have no symbols, we are out of luck. As Fenner indicates, the best we can do is to listen to an accredited singer.

Those who sing in the traditional manner never appear to take breath when

---

[11] *Syllables are frequently divided arbitrarily to suit the rhythmic needs of a tune. Sometimes the last syllable of a word is attached to the one-syllable word that follows, and whole syllables are occasionally omitted. The slave disliked certain sounds in the English language. Th was difficult for him to pronounce, so was final g, and he dropped an r whenever it interfered with fluency. It is no wonder that a white man cannot compose an authentic slave song, for the transplanted African thought in the speech pattern of his native land, and employed his limited English in that fashion. He also disregarded genders as he did in Africa. On Hilton Head, South Carolina, the dialect of the Negroes sounds—at a little distance—like a foreign tongue because of its curiously different emphasis and intonation. Close at hand, however, the meaning becomes clear enough.*

leading a religious song; a fact which makes it advisable, in writing down the words, to use as few punctuation marks as possible. The effect of an inexhaustible supply of breath is achieved through the simple expedient of the "basers"—as members of the chorus are called—"spelling" the leader, who gets his breath at the end of a narrative line while the chorus sings the response or the next line. In the old days, here, as in Africa, the virtuoso did not exist, and the basers played as important a part in group singing as the one who sang the leading lines. Now, however, there is a tendency to disregard the customary technique, which demands that the basers remain silent until the last word or two of the leader's narrative line is sung. In authentic slave music no nuances are observed,[12] but the absence of any variation in tone is not conspicuous when alternation between leader and chorus produces changes in volume. When the whole group sings in unison, however, the effect is extremely dull and monotonous.

One of the few trustworthy writers on the subject of Negro spirituals, Jeannette Robinson Murphy, could also sing them. It is regrettable that her book *Southern Thoughts for Northern Thinkers* (1904) is out of print. In the section on "The Survival of African Music in America," she tells us: "During my childhood my observations were centered upon a few very old negroes, whose mothers and fathers came directly from Africa, and upon many others whose grandparents were African born, and I early came to the conclusion, based upon negro authority, that the greater part of their music, their methods, their scale, their type of thought, their dancing, their patting of feet, their clapping of hands, their grimaces and pantomime, and their gross superstitions came straight from Africa." Even at this late date, it is possible to find ex-slaves in remote spots on the coast of South Carolina and Georgia who can—if their confidence is won—substantiate practically every one of her conclusions. It cannot be done, however, by sitting peacefully in a library chair or spending a comfortable summer vacation on the campus of a Negro school. Writers from New England who have studied the songs of the Negro, mostly in libraries, are prone to emphasize the importance of book evidence. They do not appear to realize that their conclusions are valueless without work in the field among the children and grandchildren of native Africans—who are our only authorities.

As Carter Woodson truly says, the proof offered by the writers who claim a white origin for the Negro spirituals "would not pass the test of any research depart-

[12] *A Negro quartet that sings in a staccato fashion, or renders the last verse of a song pianissimo shows clearly that it has taken its cue from the white man.*

ment of a real university." Mrs. Murphy goes on to say that "Some of their later songs, it is true, we must technically call 'modified African,' but how far the original song elements have been altered (and usually not for the better) by contact with American life is a question of fact, and can only be settled by a careful comparison of the songs as sung among the natives of Africa and the changed forms in which their modified ones are found today in the South. It must be determined in each case, and cannot be settled by any general theory or formula. . . . The stock is African, the ideas are African, the patting and dancing are all African, and those who study this weird music at short range have no difficulty in recalling the . . . conditions that gave it birth."

Mrs. Murphy stresses the fact that the traditional way of singing slave spirituals must be learned in childhood when the voice is flexible, and—if you are to become proficient—you must listen to the older Negroes, preferably ex-slaves. Every characteristic she mentions is duplicated in the singing of the Negroes of the Georgia coast. As in South Carolina, they break every law of musical phrasing and notation, yet there is nothing to be found on the printed page to show how this is done. For instance, a prominent note is embellished with a variety of small notes which used to be called "trimmin's," tones are sung not found in our scale, humming is employed that is not easily transcribed, emphasis is placed—according to our ideas— where it does not belong, and one note is not left until the singer has a firm hold on the next—a method which produces the undulating effect that characterizes the genuine spirituals. The appearance of never taking breath,[13] already described, is another characteristic that must be observed in singing songs of this type. Unfortunately, the trick of dropping from a high note to a low one on a prolonged one-syllable word is less common than in my youth, but the arbitrary division of a monosyllable, and the placing of emphasis on the second half, are as popular as they ever were.

In our music, the accents generally fall on the stressed syllables of the spoken word and on the regular beats of the music, but as Natalie Curtis-Burlin tells us in *Negro Folk Songs* "the accents fall most frequently on the short notes and on the naturally *unstressed* beats, producing what we call 'syncopation' of a very intricate and highly-developed order. The peculiarity of this syncopation is best explained to the layman by drawing attention to the way in which the natural rhythms of the

[13] As Mrs. Murphy says, the breath should be carried over "from line to line and verse to verse, even at the risk of bursting a blood vessel."

English language are distorted to fit the rhythm of Negro music: where the white man would sing, 'Go down, Moses,' the Negro chants, 'Go *down, Moses*' . . . .These identical accents are found in even the wordless vowel refrains of native African songs."

Many more questions will crop up than have been touched upon in this section, but I hope that the most important are answered in these explanatory words.

Lydia Parrish

St. Simon's Island, Georgia
December 1, 1941

Introduction

This book of Mrs. Parrish's is a singularly sincere and valuable contribution to the subject of Afro-American song. It is first-hand work with an excellent background. The data are the result of personal experience of Negro song at its sources. The approach is that of a writer who by fortunate circumstance was peculiarly equipped for her studies. Her first experience of the Negroes and their music was that of the girl in a Quaker community whose Abolitionist tendencies had made their locality first a station of the Underground Railroad in slave times, and later a haven where ex-slaves gathered and sang. The vitiating influence of the white teacher bent upon uplifting and de-racing the Negro was not to be felt where the blacks greatly outnumbered the whites, and where the whites, being Quakers, gave music a wide berth in their religious services, permitting the Negro to sing his songs in his own native and unashamed way. Nor, until the eighties, were these singers made self-conscious or musically corrupted by the sophisticated Negroes of the near-by city. They were heard by a young girl at the most impressionable period of her life. The quality of the original songs and the way they were sung left indelible memories.

Many years later, Mrs. Parrish found herself the chatelaine of a home on St. Simon's Island on the coast of Georgia, in a district which proved a veritable sanctuary of Afro-American music, and from which her investigations branched out into neighboring territories of the coasts and islands of Georgia and South Carolina, eventually reaching the Bahamas and Haiti. It is probable that the first slaves transported to America were landed near the place which became her Southern home. The beginnings of one of the most mysterious and fruitful amalgamations of racial musical elements that music knows may well have been here.

How old are these folk songs? And are they still being produced? This last is a question of great importance, and not only where this one issue is concerned. The answer concerns the entire evolution of the musical art. Mrs. Parrish believes that the body of the American Negro's music accumulated within a period, roughly, of one hundred and fifty years. There are those who would dispute this statement, since allegedly new "spirituals" keep turning up in many quarters. (Mrs. Parrish's theory of the origin of this word is worthy of remark: that it was bestowed as a result of the proselytizing of Puritans from Dorchester, Massachusetts, who brought the Bay Psalm Book with them to Dorchester, South Carolina, with ensuing consequences.) But are these fresh creations? Repeatedly, songs believed to be new have proved to be songs well-known in some other place than the one in which they were found. Thus it transpired, in the case of a certain "new" American Negro song, that it was the precise equivalent of a chant well-known and still heard in Africa! In this connection the background of African origins of American Negro song, dance, religion, and ceremonial is of special interest, and a further testimony to the soundness and the zeal with which the author has conducted her investigations. Is it, then, that the singer who improvises, as he believes, in reality draws subconsciously upon a deep well of racial experience and memory? The idea is extremely suggestive. And if this should be the case, how far does the identical principle apply to the acts of individually developed composers? Thus the peasant Dvořák turns with much simplicity to Czech folk song for a musical expression which is natural, rather naïve, and fresh and eloquent; while a Sibelius, a composer of more subjective and complex mind, composes, as a young man, the *Kullervo Symphony*, and then goes into the forests of Karelia and hears the Finnish peasants singing the runes of the Kalevlaka in phrases similar, in spirit and contour, to the ones from which he has made his score. One goes farther up the creative spiral, and discovers the stylistic and spiritual qualities of the folk songs of races transmuted in the music of a Mozart, a Beethoven, a Verdi, or a Wagner. In this sense the folk song of a race is all-inclusive. It would then appear that however highly developed the individual speech of a great composer, his expression, in proportion to its sincerity, is in essence that of his forebears and his environment. It is important to bear this aspect of Mrs. Parrish's studies in mind—important not only as it bears upon her earnest and greatly needed effort to restore to its proper place in art the uncorrupted song of the American Negro, but also in its bearing upon the cultural present and future of the American people.

How significant the relationship is can be realized if in the first place we dispense with the misleading and ridiculous theory that Negro religious music is an imitation or variation of the hymns of the white. That is a most unfortunate product of pedantry, sophism, or racial prepossession, as the case may be. It is a nonsense which should long since have been dispersed by the plain evidence of ordinary human ears and the simplest intelligence. But it has stuck in various quarters, and been echoed by those willing to sit between library shelves—or not even in such learned quarters—and fit facts to prepossessions, or let others do their thinking for them.

Now if this were merely a doctrine and refuge for the narrow-minded, it would have done no particular harm to anyone but themselves. The unfortunate thing is the manner in which the doctrine is inculcated, in the name of education, in the mind of the Negro, and especially in the mind of the Negro teacher who must lead his own people to "enlightenment." What is to be said, not of that teacher, but of those who have taught him, or her, to say that, of course, if the Negro students in the class can't learn to sing their songs as they should—i.e., as ancestral tradition and spirit and style dictate—they must be "corrected." Anyone who has listened, first to the singing of Negroes naturally and inimitably expressing themselves in song, and then hearkened to the vitiated and Bowdlerized versions of these same songs, conventionally harmonized, rhythmed, and performed by a frocked Negro choir, will know without further inquiry the profound and inescapable difference between Negro folk music and the material it is supposed to emulate, and will say amen to the indignant words of Mrs. Parrish, to the effect that, while slavery of the body is terrible enough, slavery of the mind may be an even deeper wrong and a greater destruction.

One wonders, indeed, if the Negro composer can ever arrive who will reveal in an individual way the genius of his race, under these well-nigh insuperable obstacles to sound education and a liberating development. How is that composer to be freed, instead of inhibited, in the expression of what is within him? If such a development ever does occur, we as the American people will have evolved, for at least one phase of our expression, a music of new potencies and horizons, of which, as the author of this book observes, there is crying need in the whole world of sophisticated modern composition today. In the meantime, for the white musician as well as his darker colleague, it is of the utmost importance to realize the strength that there is in the product of Afro-American folk music, to conserve it in its original essence, and to understand its real values.

One can go farther. One can say that the principle involved has a vital bearing upon future cultural developments of the world after the present war. The optimists among us—and the writer is one of them—see in this conflagration, not only an end of at least some of the terrors which have held back the social development of

the entire human race and the nations thereof, but a burning up of the rubbish of
an ideology based upon the conception of racial ascendency. That dark and medieval
doctrine is not as new as it may seem, or as old as to have faded from the subcon-
scious of the most advanced peoples today. In a large degree, at least, it is going to
go. It is going by the board, as these lines are written, in February of 1942, after
Pearl Harbor, and after the fall, so perilously near extinction of white supremacy in
the Far East, of Singapore. Other peoples than the English-speaking nations, with
that hitherto immovable conviction of superiority—which they shared with western
Europe—are going to take a hand, and a powerful one, following the debacle of
totalitarianism, in the liberated expressions of peoples. That is going to affect art,
greatly to its advantage. The deep, but narrow, chauvinistic, and exhausted cul-
tures of a few small nations have come to the end, at least temporarily, of their
creative resources. New blood, new spirit is needed, and history is seeing to it that,
under the most tragic circumstances, it is being supplied. These processes will also
apply to America, and to the very essential broadening of our perspectives, and our
half-conscious, extremely costly emergence from slavery of many kinds—and perhaps
to confinements of mind, which have made so difficult and so rare American creative
achievement in music. Let emancipation, of a real and not an affected or sentimental
kind—but a real emancipation of ideas and of culture—begin at home.

It is, however, not to be assumed from the foregoing, any more than from Mrs.
Parrish's pages, that in acknowledging the unique and unparalleled contribution of
the Negro, we can overlook or minimize the white influences which have contributed to the quality of his song. Clearly and incontrovertibly, the "spiritual"—as
other types of Afro-American folk music—is of Negro origin. No white composer or
hymnal has produced anything like it. At the same time, such a music would never
have come into existence if the Negro had not been brought here in bondage, with
all the concomitant emotional, religious, and artistic consequences of that tragic experience. Here is a fusion of spiritual and musical forces not to be duplicated in the
music of any other land—and this though all folk music, as it evolves through the
centuries, is to be found to consist of the interweaving of various racial and melodic
elements. But in no other folk music than America's is there to be discovered such
a collision of dissimilar forces as in this American blend. Nor has there materialized
such a product in any other country where whites and blacks assembled. Special
types of folk song predominate in the most isolated communities, just as the folk
songs of the British Isles have existed, uncontaminated, and for centuries, in isolated

mountain districts of America. In other lands a long evolutionary process of centuries shaped melodic idioms that sprang from the soil. In America a special thing happened, which neither scientist, anthropologist, nor music critic has ever explained. The phenomenon is not to be dismissed as either accidental or unimportant, but to be studied in all its bearings upon our progress.

This is a direction in which the author of the following pages is working with a modesty and unassuming conviction and purpose which need no praise. She is materially aided in her research by Mr. Churchill's transcribing of the songs. He has worked with a fidelity to the originals only conditioned by the limitations of our standardized scale and the inexactitude of our notation. The songs cannot be put down, exactly as they are sung, on paper. But these are the songs, as near as may be. They offer highly illuminative exposition of the various balances and amalgamations of racial elements of both African and American origin. Some of them are more than a little barbaric. In others the white influence is clear, if not predominant. In sum, these notations represent a fragment of a song literature that is unique among the expressions of mankind.

The rest is for the reader. The quality of this book, not that of a partisan, or reformer, or *ex cathedra* musicologist, is that of a seeker of the truth through the human contacts which lie at the basis of living art.

Olin Downes

New York City
February 16, 1942

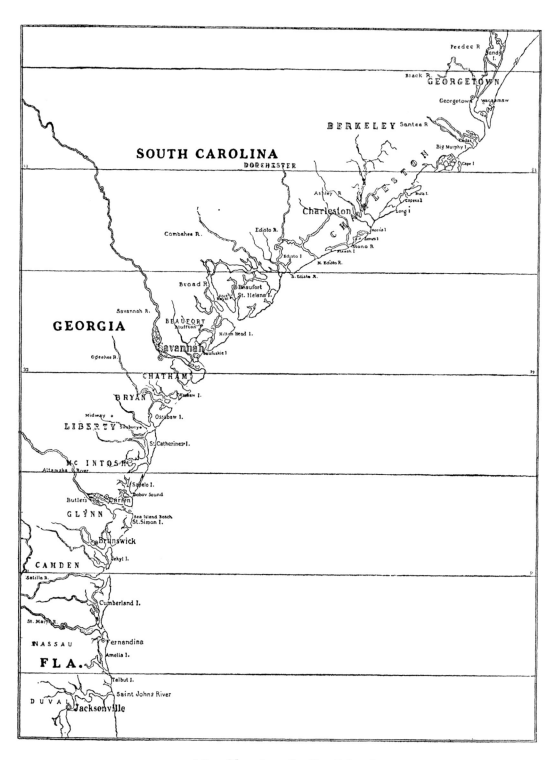

3. *Map Showing the Sea Islands*

SLAVE SONGS OF THE GEORGIA SEA ISLANDS

CHAPTER ONE

Concerning Slave Songs and Their Preservation

Where did they come from? Who composed them? How old are they? These are the questions repeatedly asked by Northern guests on hearing the little-known slave songs. But I have searched libraries, North and South, without finding the answers. The reason is simple: no one knows enough about the African side of the songs to write authoritatively concerning it, and their beginnings in this country are so obscure that one man's guess is as good as another's. This lack of knowledge, however, does not prevent guesses—both good and bad—from being made.

The birthplace of the songs is conceded to be the Old South, and they are found nowhere else except where introduced—as in the Bahamas—by the slaves of loyalists from the mainland; [1] but the honor of their creation, as indicated in the first half of their name, Afro-American, goes definitely to the Negro, for they represent the genius of the early slaves who combined the complicated rhythms of Africa with the more highly developed melodies of the Colonial planters.

To be sure, native Africans studying music in this country question the justice of the share of credit allotted them by the hyphen, for they consider the songs to be preponderantly Negro. Nordics are no better satisfied. They as firmly believe that the slave composers were nothing more than plagiarists—and in the way of phrase-lifting, they were. These alien people were under the necessity of learning a foreign language in a few months, but it is a recognized fact that no white man can turn a phrase with the same pithy economy as the Negro, and none has ever composed—to my knowledge—a successful imitation of a Negro song. What neither claimant appears to recognize is this: without the remarkable musical gift and deeply religious nature of the African slave, there would have been no soul-stirring sacred songs. On the other hand, without the contact with Western music and the inspiration provided by the Bible—at the hands of the slave-owners—these selfsame songs might

[1] *In all likelihood they were also carried to Liberia in 1820 by the transplanted American slaves.*

3

never have come into existence. Like those that accompany the primitive African dance called the "ring-shout," they might have continued to be primarily concerned with rhythm, which represents Africa's idea of music, just as melody represents ours. Rhythm, in fact, may well be called the heart-beat of true Negro music, for it is based upon the natural beat of the pulse and its even division of tempo.

The question as to the identity of the composers of these songs lends itself to a more definite answer, from the accepted fact that folksongs everywhere represent the voice of a people rather than the creation of any one person. Those of the Negro are no exception.

Many Negro preachers and evangelists claim the composition of certain modernized "ballets" [2] and spirituals, but, on investigation, their assertions prove to be based upon the composition of new verses rather than new tunes—all of which fits the idea that folk melodies are traditional, and are looked upon as common property. The African technique may also account for the inability of the white man to sing like the Negro. The latter clearly possesses an intuitive knowledge of the song-form of Africa which enables him to weave polyphonic effects into familiar songs, and to follow acceptably a leader in those he has never heard before. In the old days his gift was such that he could sing extemporaneously—like a bird—on any and every occasion. Without a system of notation, however, we have no means of knowing how much credit was due the creative ability of the individual singer, and how much belonged to communal tradition. The word of white musicians who have recognized in Africa the ancestors of such songs as "I Ain' Got No Fr'en' in This Worl' but the Lord" and "Swing Low, Sweet Chariot" also obliges us to be skeptical of claims of any kind—oral or printed, individual or sectional—as to their composition.

A few years ago a Northern Negro composer made the assertion that "new spirituals are born every day." The news was widely publicized, but he was unfortunate in his choice of an example: the words he gave in illustration belonged to a song that was popular on the coast of Georgia long before he was born. Recently I saw in print that "Ride on, Conquering King" was first sung on St. Helena Island, South Carolina. Perhaps it was, yet the fact would be difficult to prove for the song is known throughout the southeastern states and in the Bahamas. Until we are more familiar with the distribution of these songs, and until we know more about the great store of folk music said to exist in Africa, it behooves us to be wary of making positive statements, unless we deliberately choose this method of getting at the truth

[2] Ballads. *In the seventeenth century, the two words were often confused.*

through the corrections that are likely to follow—which may perhaps be a quicker way.

As already mentioned, the lack of a system of musical signs is a serious handicap which interferes with a better knowledge of the authentic slave songs, and makes any estimate of their age pure guesswork. Nevertheless, we do know that twenty blacks from Guinea were sold from a Dutch man-of-war to the tobacco planters of Jamestown, Virginia, in 1619. Sometime between that date and, let us say, 1760, these songs probably assumed the characteristics they now bear, for they appear to have become as crystallized by 1776 as folksongs ever are. But unless old church or family records turn up describing the musical reaction of the slaves to their owners' interest in the salvation of their souls, we are unlikely to find out when, how, or where the songs originated.

The slave songs or "ant'ems," [3] as they were sometimes called in Georgia before the Civil War and are called in the Bahamas to this day, may have resulted from a spark of divine fire; and the blacks, like so much tinder, may have carried them far and wide through the agency of the slave markets or the removal of the planters from one state to another. Then again, they may have been the outcome of nothing more than an elaboration of simple African themes under the influence of the richer harmonies of the Colonial planters. In other words, the tunes may represent a gradual development over a period of a hundred and fifty years, rather than a full-blown inspiration.

For all we know, the songs may have originated in Virginia, for there were two hundred thousand blacks in the state at the time of the first census in 1790. It is possible, however, that South Carolina provided the nursery, as the majority of the Negroes in the coastal section of that state and Georgia who today sing primitive "shout" songs and spirituals are Baptists, and Charleston was one of the first proselyting centers of that denomination in the Colonies between 1684 and 1746. It is on record that the zealous efforts of William Screven caused the Baptist principles to be "widely disseminated throughout that region" and the preponderance of Negro Baptists in all the Low Country of South Carolina and Georgia indicates the success of his activities. But we have only historical data to bolster up any of these suppositions, and the chances are that details concerning the origin of the songs will never be learned.

[3] *Old English for anthem. Diana, from Turk's Island, B. W. I., snorted when I called "Study War No Mo' " and "Who Built the A'k?" spirituals. "Them's not spirituals, them's ant'ems!"*

Evidence of their pre-Revolutionary existence found in Professor C. L. Edwards' *Bahama Songs and Stories* led me to several of the out islands for the purpose of verification. I discovered that Professor Edwards' book included many tunes and verses still sung, though not consecutively, throughout the "Black Border" of South Carolina and Georgia—a fact explained by the author when he says: "The first settlements were in some cases made by families of loyalists who fled from the American colonies during the Revolution." Miss Mary Moseley, in her *Bahama Handbook*, states that the number of whites and Africans was about equal before the arrival of the American loyalists with their slaves—an influx which doubled the white and trebled the Negro population. Elsewhere, Miss Moseley tells us that the slaves numbered from six to seven thousand, and that the Caicos Islands were originally settled by loyalist refugees from Georgia. Stark's *History of the Bahamas* gives further information about the Georgia contingent: "At the close of the American Revolutionary War, twelve families of loyalists settled here with from two to three hundred slaves; previous to that time there was not more than thirty acres of land cleared in all the Caicos." [4]

Such references explain why "much community of both poetical and musical phrase" came to exist between the songs given in Professor Edwards' collection and those found in sections from which the loyalists fled at the time of the Revolution. In H. E. Krehbiel's *Afro-American Folksongs*, their common origin appears to be overlooked in the assertion that the Bahama songs "show a higher development than do the slave songs of the States"—a fact which is undeniably true of those found in books, but not of those that have escaped, through isolation, the corrupting influence of such Western music as the Negroes usually hear.

The remoteness of the Bahama out islands accounts for the preservation of the genuine eighteenth-century Negro melodies; and on one of the islands may still be heard the tune that accompanied the "ring-play" called "Emma, You My Darlin'," done on their knees—forty years ago—by the barefooted Negro children of St. Simon's Island. How this game song as well as many of the religious songs given in *Bahama Songs and Stories* came to exist on such widely separated islands as those of the Bahama group and St. Simon's may be explained by local history in two ways.

---

[4] *Diana, from Turk's Island, told me one of the Caicos Islands was near her old home. Her sister lives there, and I could get plenty of "ant'ems" from her. Bethell, in* The Early Settlers of the Bahamas, *lists the names of one quarter of the two thousand loyalists who took up land on the various islands of the group.*

The first possibility is that they arrived in both places from the mainland of South Carolina. In 1795, a few years after the exodus of South Carolina and Georgia loyalists to the Bahamas, Major Pierce Butler gave up his estate on the Ashley River near Charleston and established about eight hundred slaves on his rice plantation on Butler's Island and his near-by cotton plantation on the "North End" of St. Simon's. Or the songs may have come from Savannah, via Nassau, with the entourage of Captain Alexander Wylly, a loyalist, who was obliged to flee from Georgia to the Bahamas immediately following the Revolution. However, when England began to consider the abolition of slavery in her colonies, this gentleman—who apparently had slaves to lose—became indignant and returned to Georgia. After he had fought against his friends and relations and suffered exile, it seemed outrageous to him that he should be robbed of his property. The fact that a thriving trade existed at that time between Nassau and Darien, only a few miles—by water—north of St. Simon's, and the ease with which he could transport his family and his belongings to this island, probably account for his choosing it as a final resting-place.

In addition to the circumstantial proof of the age of the songs given by history, there is also evidence of continuity of development in the singing of such old Bahama Negroes as Elvira Albury of Harbor Island, born in 1849, and Isabella Bean of Eleuthera, born before 1860, and of such centenarians as Liverpool, born on St. Simon's in 1828, and Janey Jackson, also born on St. Simon's in 1826—to say nothing of Old Quarterman, born in Liberty County in 1844. At the same time it would be reassuring to have more references in books concerning the character of the songs of the slaves. William Bartram provides in a brief passage in his *Travels* the only eighteenth-century description of Negro music I have been able to find.[5] Apparently he was favorably impressed with what he heard and saw on a model plantation in Georgia, on the banks of the Savannah River. In a description of life on board a slave ship that occurs in *Captain Canot, or Twenty Years of an African Slaver* (1827–1847), there is presented in the following words a pleasanter picture of the Middle Passage than is usually given us: "During afternoons of serene weather, men, women, girls, and boys are allowed while on deck to unite in African melodies which they always enhance by an extemporaneous tom-tom on the bottom of a tub or tin kettle." This short paragraph contains the only admission I have seen in ante-bellum books that the slaves brought their "melodies" with them. (Illustration 6).

[5] "The sooty sons of Africa, forgetting their bondage, in chorus sung the virtues and beneficence of their master in songs of their own composition." (April, 1776)

Of all the descriptions of slave music that have come down to us, there is none to equal in closeness of observation those given by Fanny Kemble in her *Journal of a Residence on a Georgia Plantation*. The fact that she was a musician as well as an actress no doubt accounts for the keenness of her perception.[6] The lines that follow have been so widely quoted that I hesitate to give them again, yet it would be unfair to leave them out of such an account as this, since they apply so perfectly to the singing of the descendants of the very slaves who inspired them.

"The high voices all in unison, and the admirable time and true accent with which their responses are made, always make me wish that some great musical composer could hear these . . . performances. With a very little skillful adaptation and instrumentation, I think one or two barbaric chants and choruses might be evoked from them that would make the fortune of an opera."

Although Liverpool, the last of the Pierce Butler slaves, claimed to remember his former mistress, her anti-slavery views [7]—voiced to the slaves and the free alike—clearly fell on deaf ears, for the patriarchal Negro lost no opportunity to tell what a fine master he had, and when explaining that he was "Butler born," he invariably added, "an' Butler I shall be until I die." Seated on the whiffletree bar of his ox cart, (Illustration 4) accompanied by a few descendants of other Butler slaves, this Negro with the courtly dignity of the Old South gave such a dramatic demonstration of ante-bellum singing for the benefit of his Maussa's granddaughter, Lady Butler, as the actress herself would have approved. With whole-hearted fervor and more accuracy and sweetness of tone than one would have expected from a centenarian, Liverpool proved what I have so often noticed: that primitive Negro music is more dependent upon the perfection of its rhythm and the precision that a good leader can inspire in the responses of the chorus, than upon the virtuosity of the individual.

In the Negroes' lack of concern for mere sweetness of sound as an end—with their major interest invariably shown in rhythm, in the melodic balance of a song, and in the performance of the group as a whole—can be seen the same fundamental approach as is displayed in primitive African sculpture. Some examples, dug up by Leo Frobenius at Ife, on the Niger River, are believed by him to belong to the tenth century. This date is of interest in giving an idea of the age of the African cul-

---

[6] *It is unfortunate, however, that her capacity for self-identification led her astray when the atrocity tales told by her husband's slaves aroused her emotions.*

[7] *Her* Journal of a Residence on a Georgia Plantation *in 1838–39, was first published, for purposes of propaganda, in 1863.*

tural movement and its works of art which have had such profound influence upon the art of the West in the last thirty years; which produced the talking drums, and developed rhythm to a point "two centuries ahead of Europe." [8] It is also significant that the art critics who write concerning the primitive sculpture of Africa call attention to the manner in which the best examples conform to canons that are universal and, according to Louis Carré, apply with equal force to European classic art. It is clearly no matter of accident that the Negroes who composed the Afro-American slave songs came from the very section of Africa which has yielded the finest specimens of sculptural art. Nor can it be considered a coincidence that musicians trained in the tradition of the "three B's" should marvel at the extraordinary feeling for rhythm and musical form shown in the slave compositions—"built on a foundation as solid as that of Bach," as one of them remarked after hearing the Negro singers of St. Simon's.

There seems to be no answer to the question of where the race got its intuitive knowledge of music (which musicians admit is acquired by white students only after years of study) unless we accept the theory advanced by Gobineau, the celebrated French Orientalist, that "the source from which the arts have sprung is concealed in the blood of the blacks"—with the concomitant conclusion that Ham must have been the musically gifted member of Noah's family.

So much for an historical outline of a form of music that is said by Franklin Harris, the composer, to be as distinctive and individual as any in the world.[9] But what of its status today and its chance of survival?

Thirty years ago, when I first visited the coast of Georgia, I would have said it hadn't a ghost of a chance. But now, after seeing what persistence, plus a little money has accomplished, I am not so sure—although I am still certain that those with any interest whatsoever in this music must do more than they have in the past to keep it alive.

When I arrived on St. Simon's in 1912, the stillness of the Negroes was puzzling until questioning brought out the fact that the island was a summer resort, and contact with city whites and their black servants had had its numbing influence; that the old-time singing had gone out of style, and spirituals weren't sung any more. After three musically barren winters I discovered, however, that a few Negroes

---

[8] *In the words of W. E. Ward. For the complete quotation, see page 19.*
[9] *Call it "hybrid" if you will—but a name cannot alter its right to recognition.*

remembered their old songs and could be induced to sing for me if I would make it worth their while. This was in 1915, and, ever since, I have been doing just that: making it worth their while. During the bleak winters of the depression, some of the singers literally sang for their supper—which, they thankfully observed, the Lord had provided. In 1929 it was found expedient to put a cabin at my "Corner," and ever since overflow audiences from the resort hotel at Sea Island have worn a path to its door.

All of which goes to prove that this exotic music need not be given up for lost so long as a few singers live to teach the traditional technique (Illustration 13) to the younger generation—on whom its survival depends. Long ago the need of training the children seemed to me particularly urgent, and six groups in two counties were taught by older singers, until hard times put an end to the undertaking. In the last few years the value of such instruction has been proved in the help the young people have given their groups at the "sings" on St. Simon's. (Illustration 25.) Where death has thinned the ranks of the older singers, the younger ones have filled the gaps with distinction.

But genuine Negro music is confronted by a real menace in the scornful attitude of those Negro school-teachers [10] who do their utmost to discredit and uproot every trace of it. Instead of being inordinately proud of their race's contribution to the music of the world, as they have every right to be, too many of them treat it like a family skeleton. In the schoolroom, even in sections where spirituals may be said to be indigenous, they are suppressed, and the supposedly "more artistic" Europeanized book versions are laboriously learned. This misplaced zeal even follows the pupils into the school yard. Such musically commonplace English game songs as "The Farmer Takes a Wife"—although I admit the action is picturesque—are substituted for such joyous Afro-American melodies as "Go roun' the Border, Susie" —for all the world like carrying synthetic coals to Newcastle! It must be remembered, however, that the teachers cannot be blamed for the harm they do the musical taste of their pupils: they only reflect the type of training imposed upon the race since 1861. No one quarrels with any system of education that helps the Negro to hold his own in a white man's country; but when a system is employed which causes him to despise everything African, and to throw away his birthright at a time when

[10] *At Hampton Institute, when I protested at the way the old tunes were altered, a music instructor loftily informed me: "When they are wrong, of course they must be changed."*

many authorities encourage him to believe in its value, it is evident that such a system stands in need of drastic revision.

In an address delivered in Philadelphia some years ago, Carter Woodson, the Negro historian, frankly said that the average American Negro is the victim of traditional teaching in Northern white schools; that his people are becoming a race of imitators; that not until they study their African background, react to it, and interpret it, can they hope to come into their own. A lifetime of contact with ex-slaves and their descendants, and of observation of the deleterious effects of the present-day system of education upon the younger Negroes, has convinced me that Woodson's arraignment is entirely merited. America has splendid material—and see what we do with it! Slavery of the body is bad, but I am positive that mental slavery does more harm to the race than physical bondage ever did.[11]

If ignorance of the history, dialects, art, music and literature of Africa—due probably to the ignorance of the educators themselves—can be remedied, and these educators can be made to appreciate the value of African art and music, then undoubtedly the race can once more contribute its quota to the art of the world. But such a right-about-face cannot take place until the Negro gets rid of the idea that all culture is vested in the white man's viewpoint. From the fact that Broadway features Negro actors, dancers, and musicians as never before, and that the producers of a Negro opera attempted to teach the Harlem blacks to speak and sing like their primitive Southern cousins, it is clear that this is no time for the race to be disdainful of its African heritage. In 1934, the most exacting New York critics applauded *Kykunkor*, the West African dance-drama, and made it the talk of the town—although some of us deplored its Europeanized singing. At about the same time, exhibitions of primitive African art were accorded such recognition as to fill the classicists with definite alarm.

Such is the precarious position in which the slave music finds itself today. While it is not hopeless, it is none too encouraging. Jaunts up and down the coast of South Carolina and Georgia, to the out islands of the Bahamas, and to Haiti, in search of African art survivals of all kinds give proof that they still exist, but the white man's drive against illiteracy is enabling the Negro school-teachers to make a drive, at the same time, against all things African.

According to Reuben Tolakele Caluza, the same situation exists in Africa,

[11] *J. A. Tillinghast says, in* The Negro in Africa and America, *that American slavery, in effect, was a vast school, in which all the pecuniary profits went to the teachers.*

where records of London music-hall ditties are preferred to the folksongs of the native. It is a discouraging sign of the times to find quantities of sentimentalized spirituals listed in foreign record catalogues side by side with songs of African natives. It does seem as though we have come to a pretty pass when the Negro, who sings a spiritual as only a Negro can, is determined to sing "Nearer, My God, to Thee," and the white man, who sings a Brahms song to perfection, is equally determined to sing "Roll, Jordun, Roll." What a contrary world we live in!

But a clue to the solution of the problem is found in the fact that the rural Negro has always taken his cue from the white folks at the "Big House." If they favor and enjoy the slave songs, it may be that he is not so far wrong after all, in cherishing his heritage in the face of jeers from the "style" leaders of his community. Such being the case, the future of the old-time music evidently rests in the hands of the landed gentry of the South. Their influence is quite as potent as it was in the days "befo' de wa'," and in view of this fact and the known conservatism of the majority of the middle-aged rural Negroes, the prestige that plantation owners can give means the difference between extinction and conservation.

In consequence, I never lose an opportunity to beg the coöperation of those who are in a position to lend an encouraging hand. There is no need to do more than allow the Negroes to provide entertainment in the manner that was usual on many ante-bellum estates. The justification for such a positive statement is found in the efficacy of this very method on the coast of Georgia. No one has better reason than I to know what the interest of certain plantation owners has meant in the preservation of Negro music. For years the "Big Boss" of Sapelo Island [12] did much to increase its prestige. At Hofwyl Plantation, the devotion of the owners to the religious slave songs has made their neighborhood a veritable oasis of Afro-American music; and at The Ridge, "Miss Sis'," [13] as she was affectionately called, did splendid work in encouraging the survival of the ring-shout—although she characteristically disclaimed any credit. In addition, the applause of Northern audiences at Sea Island and at the Cabin has produced a striking change in the attitude of our Negroes toward their music.

If you are interested in African survivals and have a Negro community on or near your property, all you need do (provided you live in a remote district and are generous with your silver) is to let it be known that you wish to see such solo

[12] *The late Howard E. Coffin.*
[13] *Mrs. W. E. Clifton*

dances as "The Buzzard Lope," "Juba," "The Mobile Buck," and "The Mosquito Dance" (accompanied by an occasional exclamation of "Slap 'em! Slap 'em!") — and they may be forthcoming. Another interesting dance, done to the tune of "New Rice an' Okra," is used to scuff off the outside husks of the rice and to prepare it for beating in a hand-hewn mortar exactly like that used on the West Coast of Africa (Illustrations 7 and 8). The pestles are heavy, and, to be wielded effectively, require the aid of rhythmic songs.

There are also the ring-play dances, which appear to be a combination of African play songs and the old English play-party or ring games. In most of them, the action reflects white influence; but to have a variation of the Virginia Reel done to an ominous African tune, with the threatening words, "Lawyer's suit!" repeated after and overlapping each narrative phrase, indicates such a fifty-fifty division as is often found in the religious songs.

One ring-play song uses "Sangaree" for its refrain, and in so doing gives a clue to its age. Few people today know that ante-bellum planters were refreshed by this West Indian drink which consisted of a chilled mixture of wine, sugar, nutmeg, and water.[14]

In the coastal section of South Carolina and Georgia, the ring-shout, a semi-religious survival of African dancing—not a vocal performance as the name implies—is accompanied by a melodious chant which generally concerns itself with the simplest of Biblical narratives and admonitions, as in

> O Eve, where is Adam? O Eve—
> Adam in the Garden pickin' up leaves.

In "Knee-bone I Call You, Knee-bone Bend," tones are used that baffle any transcription; and the leader frequently drops a whole octave in singing the rhythmically prolonged *You*, to the wonderment of white musicians unused to the trick so often employed by the old-time Negroes. In this musical chant warning is given that on Monday morning, and all other days of the week, the Lord calls upon you to get down on your knees and pray. On one of the old Heyward plantations bordering on the Combahee River there occurs a dance (clearly an African survival) which, from its description, seems similar to one I saw performed by primitive Negroes in the north of Haiti. There is another exotic performance on St. Simon's

---

[14] *"Julep sangaree" was in use before 1840. Dr. L. D. Turner believes, however, that the song got its refrain from the African word sangari, meaning a ring dance.*

Island, called by the incongruous railroad term "Ball the Jack." [15] A few years ago I saw it demonstrated by an old resident of Eleuthera, in the Bahamas, and its portrayal in the film *Sanders of the River*—for which "background shots" were made in villages along the Congo—indicates the region from which it originally came.

These dances, and such plantation activities as beating and fanning rice in the traditional African manner, provide effective material for those in the family group who are moving-picture addicts. It is also possible that such survivals persist on our plantations as are not to be found elsewhere in America this side of Haiti or Dutch Guiana; but do not be discouraged if they do not come when you call. It took years for me to see the ring-shout and the Buzzard Lope, and to see and hear the ring-play dances and songs, and the songs in an African dialect. It is a curious fact that the Negro rarely volunteers information—on the sound principle, perhaps, that if you tell nothing you have nothing to regret; and this is my reason for giving so many identifying titles and lines. If you know what to ask for, the work is half done.

For the plantation owner who cares to take the trouble, a barbecue provides the quickest route to results. If the procedure is not already known, an old resident will tell how one should be conducted, and who is competent to do the work. Both whites and blacks remember with nostalgic regret the days when a barbecue celebrated the end of the plantation harvest. For the sake of the picture, if dancing takes place after the feast instead of before, a generous fat-wood fire should be built as close to a spreading live oak as is safe, and a few prizes of old-fashioned white aprons, gilt hoop earrings, gay handkerchiefs for the heads of the women, and red bandanas for the necks of the men should be supplied. A temporary platform of broad boards laid—on two-by-fours or on any firm foundation—under the oak tree will repay the extra trouble. If the plantation is not too near a city, there is likely to be such dancing and entertainment as would make a Broadway producer green with envy. An occasion like this brings out the best—also the worst—in the way of talent, and gives an opportunity to evaluate what is to be found at the back door.

Old songs like "O de Robe" and "Norah Hist the Windah" are suitable for a restful evening; but let it end with shouting, as was customary at the old-time prayer meetings, and the whole atmosphere will change. There will be an inner

---

[15] *I am told that the action employed in "Snake Hip" is similar to that used in "Ball the Jack."*

excitement that may lead to such exaltation as few white people ever see. It is an unforgettable experience, rare in these days of practical religion when all miracles are scientifically explained.

I notice that men are particularly partial to the work songs, of which the shanties [16] of the black stevedores are the most amusing. When a plantation is near a navigable river or salt water, songs like "Stevedore's in trouble, Carry 'im to the Aly-mo," and "Sandyanna" may possibly be heard. Both carry in their titles the date of their inception, and obviously hark back to the period of the Mexican War. Others bring in Australia and Rio along with "Go 'round the Horn, Yalla Gal—Go 'round the Horn" and suggest the period of the windjammer.

At The Mills on the west side of St. Simon's—in the eighteen-eighties—the Inland Waterway was filled with sailing vessels from all parts of the world.[17] These were loaded with lumber that had been floated down the Altamaha; but, as Cap'n Joe, the crew leader, says, so little lumber moves these days that the songs that helped the stevedores to handle the great "sticks" are well-nigh forgotten. A pity to let *one* of them be lost.

Then there are the "rags," the "fiddle" or "sinful" songs. These may be plentiful in the interior; but on the coast, where the Negroes are apparently more religious, they have been the most difficult to locate.

Where there are wide fields, musical half-yodeled calls often bring " 'sponses" from laborers a mile away. When a field needs to be burned over, a sail is flapping idly, or rice is to be fanned, you may hear a Negro "calling the wind": "Co' win'! Co' win'! Co'! Co'!" A prolonged whistle follows:

—in the African manner of calling the rain.[18]

If a plantation is sufficiently remote, and the owner is ultra-modern in his taste, such a jazz band may be organized as has not been heard in many a year. It is only necessary to call for the services of those who can still "rap the bones" (real bones, of a thickness and length suitable for manipulation between the middle fingers,

[16] *Or chanteys—as some prefer to call them.*
[17] *Julia Armstrong tells me they were lined up "like sardines in a box."*
[18] *A gramophone record of a Togoland rain invocation is astonishingly similar.*

which produce an effect similar to that of castanets), or play upon the well-seasoned and polished "old jawbone" of some ox, horse, or mule [19] with the aid of a black-smith's rasp or a large key (a rhythmic tooth-rattling performance), or extract music (of a kind) from the U-shaped iron clevis used for hitching horses to the old-fashioned plow—which, when suspended by a string and beaten upon with its pin, makes a very fair "tr'angle," as the ante-bellum Negroes called it. If you live in the neighborhood of a cane-brake, there may be an old Negro who can demonstrate the kind of music to be obtained from a set of reed-pipes, called "quills," made from graduated lengths of cane tightly wedged into a frame. On occasion, a washboard—played with a thimble—and a frying pan may be added. Now and then a fiddle, "box" (guitar), mouth-organ, or jew's harp is heard in rural districts, but rarely a drum—except in the hands of musically illiterate members [20] of the Sanctified Church who have done as much real harm to the Negro's innate gift of rhythm as have the white man's hymn books.

In New Orleans, wooden horns and home-made drums (made out of nail kegs), with skin tightly stretched over one end, were used in olden times, but were forbidden on plantations where the blacks outnumbered the whites. Planters were well aware of the ability of some of their slaves to use them in the same manner as we use the Morse code,[21] and it was not considered safe to risk the general uprising which might have resulted.

The good-natured ingenuity of the Negroes in circumventing plantation rules speaks well for their ready wit, and it always rouses my admiration to see the way in which the McIntosh County "shouters" tap their heels on the resonant board floor [22] to imitate the beat of the drum their forebears were not allowed to have. Those who hear the records of the musical chants which accompany the ring-shout —made for me by Dr. Lorenzo D. Turner—cannot believe that a drum is not used, though how the effect is achieved with the heels alone—when they barely leave the floor—remains a puzzle (Illustration 24).

[19] *It may even be decorated with ribbons, as in the old days.*

[20] *Joe Loman once said, "The Sanctified people must think God is deaf, they make so much noise."*

[21] *In 1740, following the Stono uprising of 1739, the great slave act was passed. One section prohibited the beating of drums or the blowing of horns, although in cities this provision was not rigidly observed.*

[22] *I am told, however, that in South Africa the natives use their heels on the sun-baked clay of the village square in precisely the same manner.*

If the black tenants on a plantation surprise its owner with the finish of their performance, he may feel inclined to organize a society, put the entertainments they give on a more permanent basis, and hold singing contests between members of different churches, denominations, communities, plantations, or counties, as was done in our section.

Years ago I found it expedient to form the Spiritual Singers Society of Coastal Georgia, and in 1934 to organize another society, called The Plantation Singers, which specializes in secular songs. This was done to help restore the prestige which the slave songs once enjoyed. Friends generously gave trophies for each type of folksong, and both societies have accomplished precisely what it was hoped they would. Only vouched-for singers of the old songs are eligible for membership, and their names are enrolled in a record book. Buttons, with the name of the society around the rim, have been given out to well-nigh a thousand singers along the Coastal Highway, from the Ogeechee River to the Florida line. These buttons proclaim to the world that the men, women, and children who wear them are proud to sing the old songs. There is nothing like the weight of numbers to add importance to any movement! Big "Star Singer" buttons distinguish the leaders, and provide the incentive needed to overcome shyness, and to bring them into the limelight. Incidentally, in the division of the proceeds—every penny of which goes to the Negroes—the leaders are given twenty-five or fifty cents more than the basers.

The particular value of our "sings" lies in the likelihood of impressing a large number of Negroes with the high regard in which their music is held by white people of importance. In 1934, the annual festival at the Sea Island Casino brought out an audience of over three hundred. It is readily seen that one hundred and twenty-five singers, from Negro communities a hundred miles apart, can act as missionaries in carrying word to their neighbors of how the white folks behave when they want a song repeated, of how they sometimes yell: "Bravo! Bravo!"—whatever that means—and that they pay real money to hear Negroes sing.

Except on one occasion, it has always been possible to send the singers home with a dollar in the hand and their transportation paid. At the festival, held during the dark days of the bank moratorium of March, 1933, the singers were thankful to get fifty cents, food, and all expenses. That was a memorable night. A tall Negro from Broadfield—making the "Sign of the Judgment" with uplifted arm—led the sixty swaying singers in the shout: "Can't Hide." They began to move quietly, as in a trance, and it was soon evident, from a peculiar heart-clutching quality in the rhythm, that they were "possessed" by it. Song followed song, and the spell was not broken. Some in the audience wept, others applauded, but the Negroes appeared unaware of their surroundings. Several middle-aged Southerners said it was the first time they had seen the Negroes "get happy." Although the performance was strictly decorous, I was frankly relieved when the participants came to earth, after a third call for:

> My God is a rock in a weary lan'
> A weary lan', 'n a weary lan'
> A weary lan', I know He's a rock 'n a weary lan'
> Shelter in a time of storm.[23]

What the future holds for this music—the only distinctive form, besides that of the Indian, that has been developed in America—remains to be seen. If plantation owners will lend a hand and provide the rural singers with appreciative audiences, the chances are that it will survive and enable the younger generation of composers—to whom I notice it has a particular appeal—to utilize it as a stepping stone for further development. Melody and harmony, instead of being stressed as they now are in Negro colleges, will fall into line with rhythm and architectural form which formerly characterized the music of the slave. The result may perhaps be a new type of music—of which there is serious need. The classic system, through being confined to the development of one musical form to the exclusion of all others, is clearly in need of rejuvenation. Such was the case with the plastic arts in the first two years of the twentieth century, when the primitive sculpture of the African Negro provided the necessary stimulation. It is freely admitted that there is a cloud over the music world today; and writers of music, in their struggle to create something original, are moving from the library to the laboratory in search of new notes, new scales, new tonalities, new harmonies. I would suggest going farther afield, and trying out what Africa has to offer. It is a curious fact, however, that musicians are not adventurous, and few wander far from the beaten track. According to W. E. Ward, who has lived for years in Africa and has made a particular study of its music, that of the West Coast has many more tricks than the one or two obvious ones which have been utilized by Tin Pan Alley. Present-day composers might advantageously follow the lead he indicates.

[23] *An indication of the chastened spirit of the audience.*

In a series of articles on Gold-Coast music in the *London Musical Times* (1932), Mr. Ward says:

Africans are at least as musical as any race in Europe, possibly more musical than any. . . . Their harmony is as far developed as European harmony in the sixteenth century; it sounds very different, but it is not inferior. And in rhythm Africa is two centuries ahead of Europe. Their music is the most alive of any of their arts, and shows no sign of dying; new songs are constantly appearing, and quickly spread over the country. Whether it will survive the attack of bad Western music and the sapping of tribal institutions and religion, with which it is intimately connected, remains to be seen; ultimately music is threatened by the same dangers as other African arts, though it seems likely to resist more strongly. But if it could learn from Europe modern developments in form and harmony, African music should grow into an art as magnificent as any that the world has yet seen.

The relationship of our slave music to that of the African Negro is such that what is said of one applies in the main to the other. This fact gives particular weight to the authoritative words of Mr. Ward.

It seems to me that the ultimate fate of this music rests with the owners of Southern plantations and with those who mold public taste through radio programs. Within the last year, there are indications that up-to-date young Negroes are beginning to appreciate the authentic slave songs; and the increasing popularity of exotic African tones and rhythms among white people leads me to believe that the pendulum of taste is swinging toward the music of Africa and away from the European preponderance of melody and harmony. In this trend lies a ray of hope for the survival of the contribution made by the Afro-American slave.

CHAPTER TWO

African Survivals on the Coast of Georgia

There are survivals of African songs on the coast of Georgia. But let no outsider imagine they can be heard for the asking. From experience I know this to be
true. It took me three winters on St. Simon's to hear a single slave song, three times
as many winters to see the religious dance called the ring-shout, still more winters
to unearth the Buzzard Lope and similar solo dances, and the game songs known
as ring-play. It may be only a coincidence, but the "funny songs" with African
words, translated by Dr. Lorenzo D. Turner, have been the last to be found. They
were discovered about the time Negro educators began to teach their pupils that
the term African was not synonymous with barbarism, and that Africa had a culture of its own.

The secretiveness of the Negro is, I believe, the fundamental reason for our
ignorance of the race and its background, and this trait is in itself probably an African survival. Melville J. Herskovits bears out such a conclusion when he quotes a
Dutch Guiana Bush Negro as saying: "Long ago our ancestors taught us that it is
unwise for a man to tell anyone more than half of what he knows about anything." [1]
It is amusing to question Southerners as to the number of times they remember
hearing Negroes volunteer information. Not one so far has recalled an instance
in which something has been told that was not common knowledge.

This inborn reticence, coupled with the fact that natives of Africa remember
little about their forebears farther back than their grandparents,[2] is undoubtedly
responsible for the race's lack of a past in either the Old World or the New. It is
possible, however, that there may be a cause for their apparent forgetfulness of
which the white man is unaware. On Sapelo I got the distinct impression from two
descendants of Old Bilali, the famous Mohammedan slave, that the dead were dead,

[1] *Handbook of Social Psychology.*
[2] *Mentioned by Clement Egerton in African Majesty.*

20

and that it was safer to let them lie. If you talked about them you might be stirring up trouble for yourself. In Maeterlinck's *Blue Bird* the grandparents came to life when memory recalled them; it may be that the West Africans entertain something of the same belief.

Only by fitting together apparently unrelated parts have I been able to advance a reasonable explanation for our ignorance of the Negro's history and of his private life. He has been in America nearly as long as the white man, yet how much do we know about him? Precious little. We learn of his migrations by inference. Where the pioneering white man went—first South, then West—there went the Negro slave to break the ground.[3] He is mentioned—that is all. From accounts given by travelers in Africa, it is evident that they find out no more about the home life of the native than the interpreters choose to have them know, and in America this same reserve is as persistent a characteristic as is the color of the race or its frizzy hair. Southern planters grow up with certain trusted Negroes, without dreaming that they may be skilled in some particular direction. It was interesting to watch the face of one of them, Uncle Scotia, when he saw the Buzzard Lope—for the first time in his life—done by a Negro woman he had known for more than fifty years. If he had heard about the dance and inquired—as I did—"Can you do it?" she would undoubtedly long before have obliged him. I must reiterate that the importance of knowing what questions to ask cannot be overestimated.

How much of the hands-off policy of the early plantation owners was due to their own lack of initiative, and how much to the silent pressure which the black race knows so well how to employ, had best be left an open question. Southerners say that a college education is of no avail when pitted against the cleverness of the Negro; and I know of too many instances in which the colored man has outwitted the white, to doubt that assertion.[4] But whoever originated segregation [5] and the regime described in 1829 by Captain Basil Hall in his *Travels in the United States*, the Negroes' passion for secrecy was fostered. Captain Hall quotes the owner of a rice plantation on the Combahee River as saying: "We don't care what they do when their tasks are over—we lose sight of them till next day. Their morals and

---

[3] *In considering the distribution of the slave songs this historical fact must be kept in mind. The Negro carried his songs with him, and I am convinced that they did not return against the tide of migration to any great extent.*

[4] *Just as in the Uncle Remus tales, Brer Rabbit always outwits Brer Fox.*

[5] *Mary H. Kingsley, in* West African Studies, *tells us that among the Bantus the slaves live in villages apart from their masters.*

their manners are in their own keeping. The men may have, for instance, as many wives as they please, so long as they do not quarrel about such matters." And, I notice, Southerners on our coast still tacitly observe this tradition.

When I began the work of actively retrieving slave songs, and instituted "sings" at the Cabin in front of my cottage, I found it expedient to follow the same procedure. The group—silently, be it remembered—made it clear that such matters as jail sentences and surplus wives were their affair, whereas my concern was limited to their music, although anything—such as drinking, "soldiering," or insubordination—which interfered with its proper presentation was distinctly within my province.

As a concrete example of the lengths to which the Negro carries his reluctance to give information, I can do no better than tell how Julia taught me a valuable lesson: never take anything for granted. After being my laundress for three winters, she became my cook in 1915, and for the fifteen years in all she enjoyed a precious secret. With her as intermediary I was able to hear the slave songs. She never sang a note on my place, and I assumed that she could not. But in 1927, at Mrs. Arnold's funeral, her dramatic moment arrived. With the group she had brought to my door, she stood beside the open grave, and she sang as well as the others. When I periodically ask why, in all those years, she never told me she could sing, she smiles quizzically, but says nothing. Perhaps she does not know herself.

However, it is just possible that an age-old compensation complex explains the situation. I am convinced that the average Negro enjoys intensely knowing something that the white man does not, and the exquisite delight he derives from realizing that the white man has been bested in a little game makes up for any loss or indignity he may be obliged to endure. Julia's game was innocent and her loss was financial, but that such tactics may have a less pleasant side—aimed at the eventual discomfiture of an exacting employer—it may be well to remember.

Before leaving the subject of the Negro's secretiveness, it may be well to consider this racial characteristic in relation to another that is quite as often mentioned by travelers in Africa: dread of derision.[6] It seems to me that the attitude of the whites toward the blacks has never been calculated to encourage the latter to parade their Africanisms. The slave trader's need of justification, and our ignorance of Africa and its culture, enabled him to persuade us that Africans were barbarians in

---

[6] *Fear of ridicule enables African blackmailers with a gift of clever improvisation to collect tribute from their thin-skinned brothers—for the songs they do not sing.*

need of our "civilizing" influence.[7] The success of his propaganda is reflected in the words of Fanny Kemble, who wrote in her *Journal* that "all tongues—the most vulgar, as well as the self-styled most refined—have learned to turn the very name of their race into an insult and a reproach." Evidence of its pernicious effect on the Negroes themselves is also given by Sir Charles Lyell in his *Second Visit to the United States (1845–1846)*. He asserts: "It is a good sign of the progress made in civilization by the native-born colored race that they speak of the Africanians with much of the contempt with which Europeans talk of Negroes." To the truth of these statements I can testify. I was cautioned as a child never to use the term African in the presence of our colored people for fear of hurting their feelings. Need we be surprised that the Negro denied all knowledge of Africa—even as Peter denied all knowledge of Christ!

Colored people are not the simple-minded, insensitive individuals (Illustration 9) that certain Southerners lead us to imagine when they jauntily say: "Negroes are like children and must be treated accordingly." As in every race, there are immature minds, but in my experience they size us up far better than we do them. I am inclined to agree with an observant Georgian who told me: "They know us better than we know ourselves." In consequence it seems to me advisable to make no definite assertions about the race, yet we do need every hint which will enable us to avoid such pitfalls as trap those unsuspecting souls who believe what they are told. Since Fanny Kemble's time we have seen in print all too many instances of the way the psychic Negroes obligingly tell unsuspecting listeners exactly what they wish to hear. Also, like their African cousins, our colored people are born actors; and an outsider with a pet theory about them can find ready confirmation of almost any notion.[8] The inquisitive college professor is particularly vulnerable, and when he becomes authoritative he is giving the Negro the opportunity he relishes above all things to laugh up his sleeve at the white man's gullibility.

Not all Negroes are like this. Some are loyalty itself; others hold themselves

---

[7] *As late as 1902, Joseph A. Tillinghast, in* The Negro in Africa and America, *speaks of the "benighted savagery" of the African Negro and stresses the vast superiority of European culture. In the light of what is happening in Europe today, it seems to me wiser to say little about the blackness of the pot.*

[8] *From Fanny Kemble's account of her contact with her husband's slaves, it is ironically evident that they were the better actors. Their performance was so perfect that it carried conviction, and added to the difficulties encountered by Pierce Butler in his attempt to make a living out of his plantations.*

aloof, and never lose a chance to mislead and to poke fun at the white man behind his back. But I have noticed that they often reflect the treatment meted out to them in slave days. Geoffrey Gorer, in *Africa Dances*, calls attention to this fact: "If you can watch a man dealing with negroes you have no need to ask his opinion about them; and if you can watch a man's negroes you will know the chief points of his character. They mirror their masters faithfully and terribly." This approach has always interested me, and I have traced the ancestry and former ownership of many of our Glynn County Negroes. Cusie [9] Sullivan provided me with a striking exemplification of Gorer's statement. His good manners excited my curiosity, and when I encountered his father, Ben, at a Negro funeral, they were explained. Mrs. Shadman, who had known Cusie's grandfather, Bilali, gave me his history. He was the butler at the Couper plantations, at Cannon's Point on St. Simon's, and at Hopeton on the Altamaha River. The courtesy of the three generations of Sullivans known to Mrs. Shadman is a tribute to the genuine distinction of the Couper family.[10]

However, the self-respecting dignity [11] of this group of Negroes undoubtedly had its roots in Africa. Sir Charles Lyell devotes considerable space to a description of life on Hopeton plantation and to "African Tom." [12] Lyell tells us: "Under the white overseer, the principal charge . . . is given to 'Old Tom,' the head driver, a man of superior intelligence and higher cast of feature. He was the son of a prince of the Foulah tribe [West Soudan], and was taken prisoner, at the age of fourteen, near Timbuctoo. The accounts he gave of what he remembered of the plants and geography of Africa have been taken down in writing by Mr. Couper, and confirm many of the narratives of modern travelers. He has remained a strict Mahometan, but his numerous progeny of jet-black children and grandchildren, all of them

[9] *In* West African Studies, *Miss Kingsley says that among the Fanti Negroes a boy born on Sunday is called Quisi.*

[10] *By the same token, one of my most helpful singers—Ben Davis—who was trained from early childhood by Mrs. Shadman, mirrors the thoughtful dependability of her character.*

[11] *Egerton, in African Majesty, makes it very clear that he was impressed with the great dignity and presence of the uncle of the King of Bangangté in the French Cameroons. The many wives of the King also excited his admiration: "They were dignified, self-possessed and definitely regal."*

[12] *Professor James A. Grant of Darien, tells me that his great-grandfather, Thomas (called Carcastone among his own people), was a driver on the Couper plantations. In his youth he had heard his grandfather, Thomas (brother of the Couper's Bilali), say that he was named for his father who was an African prince and a Mohammedan. Apparently "African Tom" and Bilali's father, Thomas, were one and the same.*

marked by countenances of a more European cast than those of ordinary negroes, have exchanged the Koran for the Bible. . . . During the last war [1812] when Admiral Cockburn was off this coast with his fleet, he made an offer of freedom to all the slaves belonging to the father [John Couper] of my present host, and a safe convoy to Canada.[13] Nearly all would have gone, had not African Tom, to whom they looked up with great respect, declined the proposal. He told them he had first known what slavery was in the West Indies, and had made up his mind that the English were worse masters than the Americans. About half of them, therefore, determined to stay on St. Simon's Island, and not a few of the others who accepted the offer and emigrated had their lives shortened by the severity of the climate in Canada."

Z. Kingsley, in his *Treatise on the Patriarchal Form of Society*, published some time before 1829, cites "two instances to the southward [of Charleston], where gangs of negroes were prevented from deserting to the enemy by drivers . . . and what is still more remarkable, in both instances the influential negroes were Africans, and professors of the Mohammedan religion." It is clear that Kingsley had John Couper's "Old Tom" in mind, and that the other Mohammedan was Spalding's Bilali,[14] whose so-called *Diary*, written in Arabic, on Sapelo Island, is now in the possession of the Georgia State Library in Atlanta.

This manuscript has aroused keen interest among anthropologists, and the photostatic copy I sent to Melville J. Herskovits has been translated by Joseph Greenberg.[15] During the summer of 1939 Mr. Greenberg visited Northern Nigeria, under the auspices of the Social Science Research Council, and through his fluent knowledge of Arabic won the confidence of educated Malams in the city of Kano. They assisted him in deciphering certain parts of the "diary" and in locating the places in an important Mohammedan legal work[16] from which most of the manuscript derives. It is amusing that the first result of Mr. Greenberg's study was to

[13] *Admiral Cockburn harried our coast during the War of 1812, and as late as January, 1815, destroyed the orange orchards on Cumberland Island.*

[14] *Charles S. Wylly, in Seed Sown in Georgia, tells us how, in 1813, his grandfather, Thomas Spalding, relied upon Bilali to aid in the protection of his property on Sapelo with its "five hundred slaves, many fresh from . . . Africa."*

[15] *A résumé of the results of his work has been published in the Journal of Negro History, July, 1940.*

[16] *The Risala of 'abu Muhammad 'abdullah b. 'abi Zaid 'alquairawani.*

show that the "diary" was in reality not a record of Old Bilali's life. Disappointing as this discovery may be to those who are primarily interested in his history, it is still possible, according to Mr. Greenberg, to draw certain conclusions about him from the character of the manuscript.

He was apparently a fanatical Mohammedan, for the "diary" consists mainly of descriptions of "ablutions and the call to prayer." Mistakes in the Arabic script,[17] along with "repetitions, incorrect word divisions, and incorrect arrangement of the excerpts," indicate that he was trying to reproduce what he had learned orally. Since "books are first taught by oral memorization," Mr. Greenberg conjectures that "at the time of his departure from Africa the writer was still a young student."

It was reassuring to find that Mr. Greenberg's deductions tallied with what Katie Brown, Bilali's great-granddaughter, had told me about him years before. According to her, he was captured when not fully grown, and went to Sapelo from Nassau with his wife and children. Where he spent the intervening years no one knows. Both Katie and her cousin, Shadrach Hall, tell me that the three oldest children were named Margaret, Hester, and Charlotte (Cotty). The others bore African names: [18] Fatima (Shad says she was named for her mother), Nyrrabuh or

---

[17] *Concerning the possibility "of discovering the origin and status of the writer" through the character of the script he used, Mr. Greenberg says: "The fact that the Arabic script was of the Maghrebine, or Western variety, and that the Risala is a legal work of the Malekite school, which is dominant in appproximtely the same regions as the Western style of writing, would seem to indicate that the writer came from some part of northwest Africa (Morocco, Algeria, Tunis) or from the Western Sudan. The confusion of 'd' and 'l' in several cases points strongly to the Sudan, since this pronunciation is unknown elsewhere. It is doubtful whether local varieties of the Maghrebine script in the Sudan can be distinguished at the present state of our knowledge; at any rate, no attempt has hitherto been made to do this, and therefore, this approach would seem to be closed to us pending further research."*

In Notes on Northern Africa, the Sahara and Soudan, by W. B. Hodgson, the birthplace of Bul-ali is established in a letter from James Hamilton Couper of Hopeton plantation, Georgia. This letter is given in full, and states that his "driver Tom" and Mr. Spalding's Bul-ali were intimate friends. Both spoke the Foulah language, and were from the Kingdom of Bambara. Tom was born on the Niger River in Kianah, between Jenne and Timbuctoo, but Bul-ali was from Timboo.

[18] *Lyell mentions the singular taste displayed by Negro parents in naming their children: January, April, Monday, and Hard Times. He did not know what Dr. Turner has discovered: the slaves followed a West African custom in naming their children according to the time of birth, conditions surrounding it, or the temperament of the child. Bad Boy, Peanut, Blossom, and July are names found on the Georgia coast. In West African Studies Miss Kingsley tells us that soon after a child is born it is given "the name by which it is to be called. A second name which the child usually takes is that of the day of the week on which it is born."*

Yarrabuh, Medina, and Binty (probably Bintu), the youngest, who was the only one of the family group who could not speak French. The others spoke English, French, and their native tongue. Why was it that Binty spoke only two languages? This fact raises still another interesting question.

Katie's grandmother was Margaret and Shad's was Hester. Both were apparently Mohammedans, since Katie and Shad remember fragments of their prayers and, in particular, the rice balls which the half-famished children were given when the sun went down on a certain fast day. They were vague about the time of year, but both gave me the identical recipe for making this ceremonial food. Katie said they got a peck of white rice from Darien and soaked it overnight. In the morning surplus water was drained off and the rice was put into the well-washed mortar. All the larger children were set to beating it. When it was fine, enough white sugar was added to make it taste like white loaf-sugar candy. Unlike a similar West African rice ball,[19] this type was not cooked. Shad said the pieces were made into dumplings, and that his grandmother used syrup if she could not get sugar. But Katie particularized and said the paste was rolled into balls "the size of small fowls' eggs" which were then put on a fanner and set aside to harden. When the children lined up to receive the rice balls, which were called "sarika," [20] the grandmother's eye was on the lookout for grimy hands. Any child whose hands were not perfectly clean had to leave and do a good job while the others waited. As she handed the sarika to a child she would say either "Sarika dee" or "Ah-me, Ah-me."

Portions of the prayer used by Bilali and his wife as they "got down flat," when it came time to pray, were remembered by both descendants. The two Mohammedans would hold a long string of beads. As Bilali moved a bead along he would say "Karo baro." Fatima would say: "Ah-me, Ah-me." When he moved the next bead he would say: "Saka baro" and again she would say: "Ah-me, Ah-me." Shad says he remembers hearing that Bilali ended his prayers with "Mohammedoo." According to Charles S. Wylly, in *Seed Sown in Georgia*, his grandfather, Thomas Spalding,

---

She gives the names of the days in the Fanti language, and it is interesting to find that a boy born on Monday is called Kujot—probably Cudjo—and on Tuesday, Quabina, which was the name of a faithful slave at Retreat Plantation. Friday's child was called Kufi, and it is now easy to see where Kuffie Jones got his name.

[19] Described by M. J. Field, in *Gold Coast Food* (The College Press, Pamphlet No. 3).

[20] *Dr. Turner attributes the name sarika to the Bambara tribe, which inhabits the greater part of the French Sudan. This tribe is said by Geoffrey Gorer to be fanatically Mohammedan, and reared in a warlike tradition.*

had slaves of "Moorish or Arabian descent, devout Mussulmans, who prayed to Allah . . . morning, noon, and evening." Wylly adds in a footnote that three times each day Bilali faced East and called upon Allah.[21] When he died his Koran and praying sheepskin were buried with him.

Other details concerning Bilali are given by Georgia Bryan Conrad in her "Reminiscences" which appeared in the *Southern Workman* in 1901. She tells us that "On Sapelo Island, near Darien, I used to know a family of Negroes who worshipped Mahomet. They were all tall and well-formed, with good features. They conversed with us in English, but in talking among themselves they used a foreign tongue that no one else understood. The head of the tribe was a very old man called Bi-la-li. He always wore a cap that resembled a Turkish fez. These Negroes held themselves aloof from the others as if they were conscious of their own superiority." [22]

Bilali's descendants on Sapelo have given me much interesting data on old notions which probably came out of Africa. To avoid collusion I never question two Negroes together, and always check the material given by one with that from others. Several Sapelo Negroes have told me that red was such a popular color with the Africans that many were captured by slave-ship captains hanging red cloth on the deck of a ship. When the Negroes unsuspectingly came aboard, they took a long

[21] *Thomas Astley in Vol. II, of his Collection of Voyages and Travels, 1745, gives extracts from the writings of various African explorers. Their observations on the Mohammedans of the Senegal and Gambia region throw some light on the religious customs of the Mohammedans on Sapelo. One said: "the natives along the Gambia worship the one true and only God, whom they call Allah." Another remarked that "Mohammedanism found among these people is very lame. . . . It consists in . . . two or three ceremonies as the Ramadhân, or Lent, The Bayram, or Easter, and the practice of circumcision." Francis Moor made explorations in the same section in 1730 and Astley quotes him as saying: "they [the Fuli] are much like the Arabs, whose language is taught in their schools . . . they are generally more skilled in the Arabic than the Europeans in the Latin; for most of them speak it, though they have a vulgar tongue of their own, called Fuli. . . . Their humanity extends to all, but they are doubly kind to their own race . . . support the old, the blind and the lame. . . . They are rarely angry and the author could never hear them abuse one another. . . . They are always very clean. . . . They are strict Mohammedans and only a few drink brandy." Another explorer specified the time at which the Mohammedan Negroes said their prayers: "at Day-break, Noon, and at Sun-set." Sieur Brûe reported that "they keep standing a considerable time, looking . . . towards the sun-rising; then they advance two paces, muttering something between their teeth: Then they lie flat on their faces: next rising on their knees . . . and afterwards they kiss the earth, several times."*

[22] *It is estimated that Mrs. Conrad saw the Sapelo Bilali shortly before 1860.*

voyage from which they never returned.[23] Ten years ago Katie told me that the Sapelo Negroes never swept dirt out the door at night if they could help it. If they did or were obliged to throw out water, it was important to say, "Move on, fr'en," or " 'Scuse me, brother." Otherwise they were in danger of offending some of their kinfolk who might be passing by or "visitin' aroun'." On St. Simon's I was told if it were necessary to sweep at night you must first throw out a live coal, to make sure you did not sweep away the spirit of some member of the family.

On Sapelo if a hag torments you at night you put a knife, or a Bible, under your pillow. Glasgow says that a man he knows would cry out in his sleep and could get no peace until he tried this remedy.[24] Katie told me that when you had occasion to speak of the dead, you made the sign of the cross on your forehead. At a funeral on St. Simon's an old woman went to the fireplace and, with a sooty finger, made the same sign on the forehead of a little child. The next day, when asked why she did this, she explained that it was to keep the spirit of the dead man from troubling the youngster.[25] Katie also told me that passing the child over the coffin to someone on the other side afforded the same immunity.

I have never been convinced that the reason given by our Negroes for holding funerals at night was unimpeachably true. The answer I usually get, when I question them, reflects on the generosity of the slave owner. It seems unlikely that any master as kindhearted as the one described by Susan Dabney Smedes, in *A Southern Planter*, would begrudge the time it took from the daily "tas' " for the funeral of a beloved slave. Night funerals were apparently an established custom in Virginia in 1835, the time the Dabneys left for Mississippi. Mrs. Smedes tells us that she re-members the death of Grannie Harriett, born in tide-water Virginia long before

[23] M. Andanson is quoted in Astley's Collection as saying that the "Bristol and Liverpool ships were the worst offenders." It is also reported by Miss Kingsley, in West African Travels, that red was a favorite color of the spirits ("spirits always like red") and the most frequent charm-case was of that color "to flatter and please" them.

[24] Miss Beckwith mentions the same inclination to ascribe supernatural powers to objects used in Christian religion; "hence a [Revivalist] preacher always held a Bible, although he might hold it upside down." On the coast of Georgia this custom is the rule, but it is from an unwillingness to admit illiteracy and to depart from a convention. But Miss Beckwith tells of other superstitions that are surprisingly similar to those found on our sea islands. They were in all likelihood carried to Jamaica by the slaves of the loyalists who settled there following the Revolutionary War.

[25] A curious instance of Catholic influence on an African superstition. Lampblack was used to darken coffins in the old days, and a finger rubbed on the coffin was as effective as one dabbed in soot.

her master, Thomas Dabney, who was born in 1798. Grannie had been given to him by his mother with the words: "You can trust her in everything." When he went to Mississippi she went along with his other slaves, but apparently the journey was too hard, and Grannie died soon after their arrival. "The master himself led the funeral procession, and all his children followed the coffin as mourners. He ordered out the whole plantation, every one who could walk, and every man, woman, and child carried a torch. The sound of the funeral hymn and the blazing of the many torches, as we wound down the road to the dark shades of the burying-ground, made a painful impression on me as a child and caused many a secret tear." In her *Journal* Fanny Kemble describes another night funeral on Butler's Island, to which she reacted in a similar manner—except that she did not shed her tears in private.

In describing an African burial, Mungo Park mentions that the body is dressed in white cotton, wrapped in a mat, and then "carried to the grave in the dusk of the evening, by the relations." From this I am led to believe that the custom may have originated in Africa. Further evidence to support such a view is furnished by Monroe M. Work, who says, in an article in the *Southern Workman* (1907), that it was an old Hamarian practice to bury the dead in the dark. It may be that our Negroes carried out some such traditional observance when they threw their pine torches beside the grave and went back without them. We know the belief in spirits is strong, and it is possible that in this way the spirit of the dead man was prevented from following the living to their homes. Be that as it may, the pine torches were never removed, and the nearest I have come to an explanation of why they were left was given me by Katie Brown: They belonged to the dead. You must not take away a thing that is theirs. If, at the burial, a button falls to the ground from your dress, you must not pick it up. Bad luck follows you if you do.[26]

A nephew of Katie's gave me an instance of what happened to a Sapelo colored man he knows, who helped clean up the graveyard. After he had put the brush in piles to burn, he thriftily changed his mind and brought in his ox and cart to carry it away. Instead, he had to back his "team" into the fence and leave in a hurry when attacked by an immense dog—as big as a yearling calf—that had never before been

---

[26] *If you start to do something for the dead—whatever it is—you must carry it through. Laura never reached the grave of her son with the flowers she had apparently gathered for it, and in a few months she died in an asylum. The headstone carved out of the marble top of a washstand by young Aaron for his father's grave is still in the Cabin. He has been in serious trouble ever since he left it there.*

seen on the island. Later he returned with three men to get his ox. This time the dog did not appear—but the cart went back empty.

In the Sapelo burying ground I have seen many evidences of the African custom of placing useful articles on the tops of graves. The Negroes generally say they are for ornamentation, but on Sapelo I was told that the alarm clocks—of which there were many—are for the purpose of waking the dead at Doomsday. At the Petersville graveyard, lamps and electric-light bulbs are as popular as cups and pitchers.

Work also tells us in the above-mentioned article that "Among the Zulus, pottery is broken by the widow over the grave," [27] and René Maran, in *Batouala*, speaks of the same custom, specifying that the dead man's pots are placed upon his clothing. With his easy chair on top of everything, he is prepared for living the life of the dead. The pictures that accompany an article on "Fetishism in Congo Land" [28] by E. J. Glave, one of Stanley's pioneer officers, give positive proof of the origin of the custom. One, portraying the grave of a Congo Chieftain, shows the same type of decoration that is in use among our Southern rural Negroes. In addition, the author gives a picture of a distorted "charm root" which explains the use of eccentric wood growths in the decoration of the Negro graveyard at Sunbury. Headstones like the cement work found in the Sunbury yard, are a modern innovation. Mungo Park tells us that he "never observed that any stone was placed over the grave, as a monument or memorial." The noticeable lack of interest displayed by our Negroes in providing any sort of marker for their dead, other than a couple of stakes which soon disappear, may be accounted for in this way.

The custom observed by the men, in walking apart from the women, to a baptism and to a "buryin'," is apparently based on an African tradition. Maran tells us: "It is not right to walk side by side. A custom as old as the Negro, dictated single file." To this day older members of the race walk single file—the men in front. In the old-time funeral processions the women and children followed the men, or else walked on the opposite side of the road—now they ride in automobiles. In many Negro churches, the men sit on the left side, the women on the right.[29]

[27] Our Southern Indians made holes in the bottom of the pots they put in graves, so that the spirit of the pot could accompany the spirit of the dead man to the other world.

[28] *Century*, April, 1891.

[29] In the Friends Meeting I attended in my youth, the women sat on the left side of the meeting-house and the men on the right.

Another custom, more widespread than is generally known, probably originated in Africa. When a new building is completed it is christened with prayer and song, followed by shouting. The afternoon Joe and Clarence finished the Cabin, (Illustration 12) Clarence made a prayer and asked a blessing, Julia put rice in the four corners for good luck, and after a few songs it was considered that the building was auspiciously launched.

The addition to the original Cabin was *not* blessed. It is a curious fact that the roof developed leaks at once, termites got into the floor, and it was necessary to re-build the whole section. If such bad luck continues, it will look as though the Sapelo idea is not far wrong. There, it is considered most unwise to put on an addition to an old house. "You will lose some member of your family if you do."

In the papering of the Cabin, on my own initiative, I took another precaution which has afforded the singers much amusement. The walls of many small cabins are covered with news-print, because the prevailing idea in the old days was that a hag had to read every word before she could work evil on you.[30] I used the financial section of *The New York Times* for good measure. In the accompanying illustration (Illustration 14), it can be seen how this original type of wallpaper enhances the picture made by the singers, and separates them from their background. It was made during the closing song—"One a These Days, My Sister"—when Willis was shaking the hand of Bessie in accordance with the usual custom at prayer meeting in a less sophisticated era.

DeZayas, in *African Negro Art*, tells of an exceedingly sensitive devil at Sierra Leone, who requires the utmost respect, and, if not propitiated by liberal offerings of palm wine, rice, and fowl, will certainly bring trouble to those invoking his intervention. Every time he is consulted, rice flour must first be offered. However, our Negroes disclaim any knowledge of their reason for using rice at a housewarming, except to bring good luck.

Chance often enables us to discover new examples of the general belief in occult forces. Such was the case when a friend and I heard a cracking report in my empty kitchen. On investigation we found that a glass bowl had broken in half. The next day Julia told me it is a sure sign that some member of your family is going

[30] *A similar notion is held in Nassau according to M. Cavel in "Items of Folk-Lore from Bahama Negroes," in Vol. 17 of the* Journal of American Folk-Lore. *"If you think you are being hagged, take a pint of benne seed . . . and guinea corn . . . spill it all in the four corners of your house; that will catch the hag as she cannot leave the house before she has picked up all the seeds, one by one, during the night."*

4. *Liverpool and His Ox-Cart (Born, St. Simon's, 1828–Died, Darien, 1938)*

5. *Bessie Cuyler*

6. *Oscar Massie, an African-born Slave*

to die. But in this instance it was her family, not mine. She had eleven children—now there are only ten. Julia told me later that within a few days of her son's death two lamp chimneys in her house had broken without being touched, and a saucer had broken in half in her hand, one half falling to the floor.

When a letter from Dauphin Plantation, Haiti, reported gloom in the laundry, all because three little stones had been left on the window sill of the cabin of Diana, the black washerwoman, I made inquiries and found that those innocent-appearing pebbles meant something quite as ominous to our Negroes as to Diana. When I asked a couple of colored women if they would mind if such stones had been left on a window ledge of theirs, they made it distinctly clear that they would. To get the better of such an ugly situation, one told me, she would take a piece of tin or shingle, push the stones onto it with a stick, and throw them far away. The other particularized and said you mustn't face the stones, you must approach from the side and shove them from that angle—and it was much safer to throw them into the fire.

I first learned about the dime worn on a string around the ankle—to ward off bad luck—at a little Negro church. The preacher was railing at his congregation for believing in charms: "Right now, I know a lot of you have dimes strung 'round your ankles." Since then I have been on the lookout. Sure enough, they are there. According to Mungo Park, similarly worn charms, or amulets, are common in all parts of Africa.

Kingsley says in his *Treatise* that he purchased Gullah Jack—who was a conjurer in his own country—a prisoner of war, at Zinguebar. "He had his conjuring implements with him in a bag which he brought on board the ship, and always retained them." For the benefit of those who are interested in knowing where "Gullah Jack" was born and to eliminate the idea that he belonged to the Gola tribe living in Liberia, east of the City of Monrovia, I wish to quote Kingsley's statement that Gullah Jack's "own country" was M'Choolay Moreema, where a dialect of the Angola tongue is spoken clear across Africa from sea to sea, a distance perhaps of three thousand miles. These words should establish the origin of the Gullah dialect, but if you have always believed that "Gullah" derives from the Golas of Liberia—Liberia it will undoubtedly continue to be.

Mrs. A. S. Hilsman, who was born on a plantation at Fancy Bluff, tells me there was a witch or goof doctor among her father's Negroes, who had learned his magic in Africa. After "freedom" he took the surname of Polecat, as he wanted one that was distinctive. He taught his wife Milly (Illustration 34) how to make "goof bags." Apparently his magic was no more potent than Gullah Jack's when it came to protecting himself. Gullah Jack was executed in Charleston for his part in the uprising of 1822; and when Jim Polecat was old, decrepit, and a nuisance, his own children pushed him into the fireplace, and burned him to ashes. Milly must have been a peculiar character. She would turn her back on you when she had anything to say. When her cabin was built she insisted on having no windows—a good African mode of construction. She said: "Door's enough to watch." When urged to have them for ventilation, she insisted that "Chimney gives enough air." There were no windows put in. The walls of her cabin were lined with boxes and trunks that had belonged to her children, all of whom were dead or in the penitentiary. It is no wonder she was moody, and that the other Negroes were afraid of her. They might well be, for—in addition to being looked upon as a witch—she was the mother of seven murderers.

In every Negro settlement there are usually frizzled chickens.[31] These curious-looking birds are supposed to be on the watch for goof bags or any "sleight-o'-hand" buried under doorsteps. Josephine tells me that she always keeps one around for such a purpose. If the chicken "come clean" (loses its feathers), it is a sure proof that it has scratched up something intended for its owner's bad luck. So much for black magic. You hear little about it, but the belief in its efficacy turns up every now and then when least expected.

At the risk of being tiresome, it may be well to call attention to various obscure customs among the Negroes that could easily be passed over as idiosyncrasies. From the pulpit of the Jewtown African Baptist Church I heard Parson Joe Lowman say with a weak voice that he was feelin' very po'ly and in no condition to preach a Christmas sermon, but by the grace of God he would do his best. I was astonished to find, as he warmed to his subject, "The Christ Child and the Three Wise Men," that his voice grew stronger and stronger. When his sermon was finished, I realized that I would never hear a better one, and that he had either received supernatural aid or was a consummate artist—perhaps both. Later, I read an article by Morton C. Kahn, on "Adventures in Medical Research among Two Strange Tribes of Dutch Guiana,"[32] in which the author described the greeting employed by the Bush Negroes, the translation of which runs somewhat as follows: "Howdy, white man.

[31] *Captain R. S. Rattray tells us such freakish birds are called* asense *chickens in Ashanti.*
[32] *"Where Black Man Meets Red,"* Natural History, *May, 1936.*

How are you, brother?" The reply is: "So-so, Granman. How are you, brother?" The writer explains that "It does not do to claim that one is feeling too well, otherwise the enmity of the spirits might be incurred." From this it can be seen why there was a wide divergence between Lowman's words and his performance, and also why our older Negroes always appear to enjoy poor health.

Another tradition caused me to be embarrassed for the poor preacher, who seemed to have a strange affliction. I furtively looked around to see how the younger members of the congregation were taking the curious performance. Their matter-of-course attitude should have made me less innocent. However, it was not until I heard other preachers give the same effect—the mewing of a harassed cat combined with the bark of a half-strangled dog—that I realized my ludicrous mistake. At the peak of the preacher's harangue the words pour out so fast that he has no time to get his breath, and his gasping efforts cause the outrageous sounds that appear to have no name with us, but which are described by Martha Beckwith, in *Black Roadways*, under the name of "trooping." [33] She believes that the exercise "if persisted in, will produce that semiconscious condition so favorable to the communication of spirits." But it has always seemed to me that religious ecstasy is itself the source of the strange manifestation. When the preacher has reached his rhythmical best; when an insistent tapping of toes on the floor provides an under-current of sound along with a feeling of uncanny suspense; when the "moaning" (as the peculiarly beautiful humming of the Negroes is called) takes on an elemental quality that comes from everywhere and from nowhere in particular—then the snapping point is reached for someone, and you hear a piercing shriek. A woman stands up with stark, stiff arms stretched high above her head. If she makes much of a commotion she is supported into the open air to recover. When I was a little child I saw a woman who had gone into this rigid state carried to a pump beside the church, where, under the spout, she was quickly brought to her senses. In the House of Prayer in Savannah (where the pillars are thickly padded, and the sawdust is inches deep on the floor) I saw a "lone shouter" fall into a trance that lasted half

[33] *It is possible that the tradition was carried to Jamaica by Elder George Lisle, the former slave of Mr. Sharp, a loyalist of Savannah, who gave him his liberty. Lisle preached in Georgia during the Revolution. At the close of the war he went to Jamaica. Though an ex-slave, he organized, in Kingston in 1784, the first Baptist church on the island, and became "the chief human factor in the salvation of Jamaica." (L. G. Jordan, Negro Baptist History in the United States.)*

an hour. She was covered with a coat and left where she fell until she returned to consciousness.

In *African Majesty* Egerton speaks of the same hands-off treatment, saying: "When persons not given to such behavior fall down in a fit, they are left where they fall, and no one touches them." It is a very easy matter for a Negro—even in this country—to become possessed. I have seen this phenomenon happen too many times among our Georgia Negroes to believe that the Negro patterned his behavior after that of white fanatics.[34] The chances are that the whites copied the blacks, since it is a matter of record that both races attended the same revivals. It is also possible that the whites took over the African song-form, and the system of punctuating the sermon with responses like the Negroes' "Tell 'im!" "Preach the Word!" "Go on!" and "Amen!" I heard a Negro preacher say to an unresponsive congregation: "You gotta help me. You needn't think you can sit back there an' do nothin'." From then on, he held their attention, and received the emotional support that is required to become a successful evangelist. This form of encouragement evidently came out of Africa, for Captain Canot, in his *Adventures of an African Slaver*, tells us that "It is the custom in African palavers to give token of assent by a sigh, a groan, a slight exclamation, or shout, when anything affecting, agreeable, or touching is uttered by a speaker."

Where the "holy laugh" came from I am unable to say, but it is clearly of a piece with the unusual observances already mentioned. I had read about it, but heard it employed on several occasions before I recognized the mirthless staccato "ha-ha" for what it was. It is unobtrusively introduced to carry on a rhythmical phrase, in much the same way as the enclitical *a* helps to fill any gap which may interfere with the undulating flow of a song.

There is far more of tradition connected with the religious observances of the Negroes than appears on the surface. The custom of sending messages by the dying to those who have gone before, moaning, singing, and "hollerin'" while "settin' up" with the dead, holding elaborate funerals, preaching the funeral sermon when it suits the convenience of the pastor—anywhere from one to three months after the "buryin'"—each one has its counterpart in Africa. Egerton, who stayed in one

---

[34] *Melville J. Herskovits says in his* Handbook of Social Psychology: *"The religious hysteria that marks the manner of worship by certain white groups in the United States is so different from the kind of evangelical excitation found in Europe that it can be referred only to influences—in some cases, indeed, two or three times removed—which emanated from Negro religious gatherings."*

spot long enough to find out many fascinating things about Africa's black residents, mentions the fact that "In the cold wet months it is inconvenient to have . . . a [funeral] feast, and if some one dies at that time of year, the feast is often postponed until the dry season."

Negro preachers—particularly those who possess good voices and a store of spicy proverbs—often deliver sermons and offer prayers that stick in the mind. One I heard in Liberty County (the one whom I thought afflicted) expatiated on the subject of sin. He made it clear that certain types were worse than others. "Sin is a mean thing," and his tone was scornful; but when he said: "Self is a terrible thing!" it was thunderous and convincing. In a barn of a church in Camden County the substance of the preacher's prayer was in these touchingly earnest words: "We're down here, Lord, chewin' on dry bones an' swallerin' bitter pills. We can't do nothin' without You." Whatever may be said about the emotional character of the religion of our American Negro, it must be conceded that his sins are of the flesh rather than the spirit. He is generous with his last crust, and there would be no need of orphanages if white people, in proportion to their means, adopted as many children as colored people.

When it comes to terse economy of speech we are obliged to concede that no one can equal the Negro. Mrs. Annie Arnold, born on St. Simon's in 1844, gave me the perfect example of this fact in recounting a bit of local history. A cargo of slaves of the Ebo tribe had been landed at a suspiciously secluded spot on the west side of the island. They preferred death to a life of captivity, and as they walked into the water the leader said: "The water brought us here. The water will take us away." No one but an African could have expressed such poignant unhappiness in so few words. In view of the fact known to traders that the Ebo men made poor slaves and were prone to suicide,[35] the account is probably true. The Negroes believe the story, and to this day they have to be extremely hungry to fish by themselves at Ebo Landing. One night a few years ago some colored boys braved tradition, and went 'possum hunting in the neighborhood. I have my own ideas as to the real cause of their terrifying experience, but the fact remains that no others have been tempted to repeat it.

Sir Charles Lyell tells us that "The slave trade ceased in 1796, and but few negroes were smuggled into Georgia from foreign countries, except indirectly for

[35] *For this reason as few as possible were accepted by the traders.*

a short time through Florida before its annexation [1819]; yet one fourth of the population of this lower country is said to have come direct from Africa." [36] A little calculation indicates that he was misinformed either as to smuggling or as to population. I am inclined to believe it was the former, as the last slaves to be smuggled into Glynn County arrived in November, 1858,[37] on the Wanderer, and the last African of that group died in Brunswick only a few years ago.

Because of the illicit slave trade that continued for economic reasons to such a late date on the coast of Georgia, we probably have more African survivals here than are to be found in sections of the Atlantic coast which were settled before the slave traffic was technically abolished. This may account for the similarity between the proverbs of Africa and those in use among our older Negroes. A few illustrations will suffice to establish the relationship: When I asked Joe—so dark that protective coloration serves him in the shade—why it was that I never had any trouble with dark Negroes, while those of a light color were often a different matter, he explained with a wide grin: "High yalla pizens the stream." On another occasion I asked him what to do about a certain singer who persisted in double-crossing his group. His reply probably had its origin in Africa: "My ole gran'mother use t' say: 'Them's the kind you gotta feed with a long spoon.' " In *Suriname Folklore*, Melville and Frances Herskovits quote a proverb found among the Negroes of Dutch Guiana that is very similar: "When you eat with the devil then you must have a long fork." In McIntosh County I heard a Negro preacher tell his congregation that when a man dug a pit for his neighbor, at the same time he dug one for himself. Another Suriname proverb carries the same warning: "When a person digs a hole to put another in he himself falls into it." Once I said to Bessie that it looked as though she had forgotten me. In disclaiming such a charge she quoted "the old people" as saying: "Never forget the bridge that carries you over." A. F. Chamberlin reports a corresponding proverb from the Yoruba of Southern Nigeria, which warns against kicking away the ladder by which one rose. As can be seen, the advantage of using a proverb lies in its indirection. It allows no accusation to be pinned against the speaker, and generally displays a whimsical humor that is more telling than any literal presentation of facts.

[36] Second Visit to the United States.

[37] J. A. Tillinghast, in The Negro in Africa and America, says that the importation of Negroes from the Guinea coast did not cease until after the Emancipation Proclamation, and quotes Professor W. E. B. DuBois (The Suppression of the Slave-Trade) as saying that the Act of 1807, forbidding the trans-Atlantic slave trade, "came near being a dead letter."

In the employment of a single derisive word the Negro is indeed a consummate artist. I know a cook with a disarming smile who accomplished what lectures never could. All she did was to point humorously to a puddle of clothes left on the floor by an untidy child and say: "Snake." Anyone who knows the snake's habit of shedding its skin in any place where it feels the urge will understand why that child's clothing was ever after left on a chair.

Another example of this knack of using the one right word was furnished me when I gave a "lift" to a Negro going my way. I asked where he wanted to get out. He replied casually: "Oh, jus' let me out at Lord Bing's." Although I use a fictitious surname, there is only one Negro on the island who could possibly qualify for the title.

There is, I believe, a biological reason for Lord Bing's feeling of importance. He is the living image of one of several bronze heads dug up in 1938 at Ife in Southern Nigeria, and believed to be portraits of rulers, kept as a record.[38] William Bascom, who was in Ife at the time of the discovery of these heads, says (in an article in the *Illustrated London News*[39] which should be reprinted in this country) : "It is possible to identify the exact counterparts of these heads among the people of Ife today. Also, interestingly enough, striking resemblances between some of the heads and individual Negroes of the United States have been noticed. A large proportion of the ancestors of American Negroes are, indeed, known to have come from this region of West Africa." Members of Lord Bing's own family exclaim at the likeness (Illustrations 18 and 19), and it is clear that he is a "throw-back" mentally and physically. In addition, the Yoruba tribe, to whom the people of Ife belong, are said by N. G. Ballanta, in "Music of the African Races,"[40] to have the most highly artistic dance songs of all the tribes he investigated from the Senegal to the Cameroon. It is significant that this St. Simon's Negro is a good singer, and belongs to the family that has given me the most help in the preservation of the characteristic African rhythms.

Although the West Africans were not supposed to have a literature because of their lack of a written language—except in a few tribes—the tales brought to America by the slaves have entertained old and young, black and white, whenever and

---

[38] *Others of the bronzes (thirteen in all) are assumed to be likenesses of deities.*
[39] "The Legacy of an Unknown Nigerian Donatello," April 8, 1939.
[40] West Africa, June 14, 1930.

wherever heard. The humor [41] and keen knowledge of human nature they display indicate clearly enough that the Negro realized the necessity of keen wits if the little man was to survive in a world governed by brute force. Ages ago, apparently, the race learned another valuable lesson: to convey an idea by inference rather than to state it baldly. The stories given me by Peter Davis—who learned them from his Uncle John—illustrate this fact, and demonstrate the way scanty training in the sea-island school-rooms was supplemented by older members of such families as had the story-telling gift:

Buh Rabbit an' Buh Wolf in deh Well

One day Buh Rabbit wuz walkin' thru de woods an' 'e met an' ole well. Deh wuz two buckets in it—one went up when de udder went down. Buh Rabbit say to hese'f: "Deh's nice water in dat well. Believe I'll go down an' get me a drink—some ole fool'll come alon' an' pull me up." By an' by Buh Wolf come whistlin' down de road. Buh Rabbit call: "Hey, Buh Wolf, want some cool watah?" Buh Wolf say: "I wouldn' mine!" Buh Rabbit say: "You jes' git in de bucket an' come right on down heah." Buh Wolf was hebbier dan Buh Rabbit, so when he got in de bucket an' start down, he meet Buh Rabbit half way comin' up. Buh Rabbit say: "O boy, dat's de way in dis worl'— some comin' up an' some goin' down. Well, I'll be seein' y'u some mo'."

In her chapter on "Folk Art," [42] Martha Beckwith gives an example of the "so-called animal talk . . . often reported from African fields." Bessie Cuyler, of St. Simon's, gives a good illustration of this talk. She explains that, when the preacher comes for a visit, the poultry gets very excited, the rooster most of all:

He say: Preacher comin', Preacher comin'!
The guinea hen say: I knowed it, I knowed it!
The goose say: Tell it, tell it!
The duck say: Hah, hah, hah!

But the turkey gobbler is a wise old bird, an' he got fussed at all de noise an' when de rooster keep sayin' Preacher comin', Preacher comin', he sputter: "Schu-u-uw!" an' say:

What de hell do I care
You betta look out fo' you' neck!

[41] *An example of Afro-American humor runs true to form: A child calls to its mother "O mamma look dat da fulafafa!" The mother with a superior air says: "Gal, you bin in dis buckle country [buckra is white man] so long, an' can't say wulisāpăpa." The joke lies in the fact that "fulafafa" and "wulisāpăpa" both mean woodpecker in an African dialect.*

[42] Black Roadways, a Study of Jamaican Folk Life.

Miss Beckwith is evidently right in assuming that this form of amusement represents "the breakdown into sport of an outworn belief in the claim by sorcerers to a knowledge of the language of beasts."

Discovering an unsuspected connection with Africa in words which sound as though they might be English, but really aren't,[43] provides almost as much satisfaction as finding new songs or dances. Conservative Negroes still retain many of these words—particularly in the old songs—and such are passed on to Dr. Turner in the hope that he may know their meaning. From his *West-African Survivals in the Vocabulary of Gullah* I have learned much that has been an enigma to me in the past, but even Dr. Turner is puzzled by "giffy," which on Sapelo means damp. Years ago I heard the great blue heron in the marshes called "Poor Joe," and judged his lean body had given him his name. Not at all. *Podzo* is the name of a similar heron in Africa. We call a certain type of southern tortoise a "cooter." In the neighborhood of Timbuctoo its near relative is called a *kuta*. When I first visited the Georgia coast I heard the name "tackies" applied to the small wild horses found on the salt marshes of the sea islands of South Carolina and Georgia.[44] Now I find that *taki* is the West African name of a horse. The same with the "tabby" houses built for the slaves out of old oyster shells, sand, and cement (made from burning live oyster shells in pine cribs built for the purpose). In Africa the name for a house of similar construction is *tabax*. When a Southerner hears the word "tote" he knows that it means to carry; a very similar word, *tota*, from the Congo, means to pick up. Southern children know the "joggle board," or see-saw, but they do not know that the name comes from the West African word, *dzogal*, meaning to rise. In the old days you asked a colored woman where to find her husband. If she said at the "jook," it meant that he was in the rather ungodly place where drink was sold and good women were not supposed to go. According to the *Vocabulary*, *dzug* means "to misconduct oneself" and it is easy to see how "jook house," in the Gullah dialect, derived its name. In *Gentlemen, Be Seated*, Dailey Paskman and Sigmund Spaeth tell us that Africa possessed an instrument known as the *banjar* made of a large gourd

[43] *By this time I should be wary of laughing up my sleeve when the Negro uses such words— but white people are like this. My last nugget was found through Mrs. Cate's keen sight. I had told her of the amusing application of the horse breeder's term "in foal" to the condition of one of my singers. With a fresh eye, she spotted in Dr. Turner's Gullah Vocabulary the word "en(in)fo le" meaning "pregnant."*

[44] *These hardy little horses are said to be descendants of those left by the Spaniards in the sixteenth century.*

with a neck of wood attached, and fitted with four strings.[45] A Georgian I know called her devoted colored nurse "Dah," which means mother in an African dialect. Many Southerners are familiar with the odd word *swanga* as applied to a proud, boastful Negro. They probably assume, as I did, that it is a corruption of "swagger," but like the word "shout" it is another African word that happens to sound something like one of ours. For the same reason such African names as *Sandi, Suki, Aba, Bina,* and *Beti,* that are quite similar to our diminutives, have passed unnoticed, while such names as *Pinda, Mandigo, Dembo, Sambo, Cudjo, Quash,* and the Arabic names on Sapelo arrest our attention.

The survival of African food names such as *gumbo* or okra (famous in New Orleans), *benne* [46] (that figures in Charleston's special candy), goobers or peanuts, suggests that African cooking methods as well as names survive in Southern kitchens. Much interesting material on this highly controversial subject has been furnished by Herskovits in an article entitled "What Has Africa Given America?" [47] Of all who write about the Negro, I find the conclusions of this well-known anthropologist the most convincing. What he says on the subject of Negro music, on certain "musical" aspects of Southern speech, the survival of African idioms and pronunciation, and the impress on Southern white children of the courtesy instilled into them by their colored nurses ties up with my years of experience with the Negroes.

It may be only a coincidence, but *mpinda* and *nguba* are both Congo names for peanut, and the Cater family, of Kelvin Grove, had a slave called Pinda, who was the daughter of their faithful Dembo.[48] Dembo's father was an African prince, to whom a gun was of greater value than a son—probably there was a surplus of the latter and a shortage of the former. At any rate Dembo was sold into slavery for a

[45] *Cable tells us in "The Dance in Place Congo" that "for the true African dance . . . a sensual, devilish thing tolerated only by Latin-American masters, there was wanted the dark inspiration of African drums and the banjo thrump and strum." Perhaps this accounts for the banjo not being heard in Georgia—with its strictly English background.*

[46] *The tradition on St. Simon's is that once you plant benne, you must keep it up. "Old man Death'll catch you if you don't." If you are ill, you can at least throw it out the window and give it half a chance to grow.*

[47] New Republic, September 4, 1935.

[48] *Dembo was the "driver" who had charge of the other slaves under the white overseer. When the overseer killed his master, Thomas Cater, in the neighborhood of 1805, Dembo saved the life of Thomas' only son, Benjamin, and looked out for his young master's interests so whole-heartedly that he earned the hatred of the other slaves. When he died they buried him on the North Boundary of the plantation as far from their own graveyard as they could place him.*

gun. Mrs. Arnold, who was the daughter of Captain Stevens, of Frederica, told me how her father's slave, Old Grace, had been captured in a "goober patch" in Africa. Old Grace and some members of her tribe had made a stealthy night raid on the stockaded garden of a neighboring village. Although Mrs. Arnold told me the story over twenty-five years ago, I can still see Old Grace trying to climb the fence when she and her companions were discovered.

We are supposed to dig our graves with our teeth, and inferentially Grace's appetite for peanuts was her undoing, but no grave was dug for her, if the story of her end is true. Mrs. Stevens always cautioned her children to keep away from Old Grace's cabin, for she boasted that she had eaten pickaninnies in her native land, and "the meat was sweet." She was also reputed to be a hag and many a "marsh tacky"—found in the morning with a matted, tangled mane—was she supposed to have ridden. When the Federal forces—followed by an iniquitous carpet-bagger [49]— took over St. Simon's, Captain Stevens, although a Dane and a non-combatant, was sent to Fort Delaware, where he died. His widow and children were sent to Savannah. After the war was over, they returned to Frederica and found that Old Grace had disappeared. No one would talk about her, but the story got around that her own people had grown tired of her wicked ways, and had staked her out at low tide in one of the salt-water creeks. If the water rose above her head, that was an act of God, and was no concern of those who did the deed. In Miss Kingsley's *Travels in West Africa*, I have lately found that this mode of drowning was one of the popular methods of disposing of African witches. [50]

Besides survivals of language, customs, and beliefs, we have survivals of particular skills. Such useful ones as carrying unwieldy bundles on the head, making canoes and mortars by hollowing out logs, weaving baskets—particularly the flat type used for fanning rice—are a commonplace in the South, and may not on this account

[49] *His name was Eaton, and he is said to have come from Maine. He purported to be a minister and insisted on remarrying the Negroes at twenty dollars a pair. Although the price was high, they were enabled, through his assistance, to occupy the homes of the refugee planters. Before Mrs. Stevens was out of her house the Negroes came in and made their choice of rooms—generally a family to a room. When the Postells returned to Kelvin Grove Plantation after the war there were ten Negro families in their house. Not a shutter was on it. Every one had been taken down to make corn bins in the basement, and every pane of glass had been shattered by the gun-boats. Can we wonder that the Southerners called us "Damyankees"?*

[50] *Miss Kingsley believed that the black man recognized "in a dull sort of way" that witchcraft meant the same thing as poison. She tells that he very generally regarded "the best remedy for witching as being a brisk purgative and emetic."*

be recognized as African. However, the æsthetic taste of the race, which expressed itself in Africa in ceremonial dances, in song, and in carvings, had less opportunity for expression in the utilitarian lives led by the slaves.

Olmstead reports that "it is interesting to find in what ways the creative instinct continued to manifest itself," and goes on to quote a prominent Virginia planter as saying that his Negroes "never worked so hard as to tire themselves—always were lively and ready for a frolic at night." As in Africa, every possible piece of work was done to song; and it probably did not take the slave-owners long to discover that the output was greater when leaders with a gift for rhythm were appointed to regulate the work of gangs of laborers. Nor is it surprising that the slaves were expert blacksmiths, when it is remembered that Africa since time immemorial has worked in iron. Her deposits were so rich and so near the surface that comparatively simple methods were required to make the ore available. On this account certain tribes have always been skilled in iron-work, and the reason for the excellence of the famous grilles, balconies, and railings made by the slaves of New Orleans is obvious.

George D. Lowe, editor of the *Baxley Banner*, tells of a Georgia slave who could take a blackgum log and cut from it a perfect screw for the old-type cotton press, and also cut the opposite thread for the follower block—all this without laying out a line on the log, just using his eye. Mr. Lowe says: "There was another Negro slave owned in Twiggs county who was a famous stairbuilder, and his owner rented him out to men building fine homes as far away as Mississippi. . . . I have heard it said that he built at least one hundred stairways, never using a plan, but producing curved lines that no modern builder has approached in graceful beauty." At Incachee Plantation there is a wrought-iron basket made by a colored blacksmith for holding flaming fat-wood (pine) knots. I am covetous every time I see it. And in the plant of the Brunswick Marine Company, I am told, there are several mechanics trained in the old school who show unusual skill in metal-work.

During the last depression, when there was no work for the Negro cabinetmakers and carpenters, whittling was the inevitable pastime for Willy Rogers, of Darien and Lonnie Davis, of St. Simon's. (Illustrations 20 and 21). Both made a number of canes which were ornamented with alligators climbing their length. These wood carvings are obviously in line with West African tradition, and indicate that the sculptor's art is only dormant in the race. Given leisure, enough to eat, and greater respect for his own mode of expression, the Negro might again take to the forms of art in which his African forebears excelled. However, it must be kept in mind that *Art for Art's sake* never existed in the life of the African natives. Their dances and their music were not separated from daily life, and until about 1900 this attitude persisted among our Negroes in the rural sections. Now it is the fashion to imitate the white man, and the results are unspeakably dull.

Survivals, such as these I mention, have come to light—more or less as a side issue—in searching for links connecting the dances and songs of our Georgia Negroes with those of the African natives. As far as the songs are concerned, it would be gratifying to be able to say definitely what proportion of African influence is shown and what should be attributed to America. Unfortunately the methods of research employed today by most musicologists do not produce results that can be considered reliable. I would not accept as authoritative the findings of an anthropologist who based his conclusions concerning the African food tabu found in Georgia on what he learned from me. And I am no more willing to accept the word of the musicologist who depends on transcriptions found in books, and on inadequate phonograph records, to decide what the slave music owes to Europe.

In my experience transcriptions and records are both too susceptible to the biased interpretation of musicians trained in the European idiom. Far too many know nothing about African music, and do not care to learn anything about it at first-hand from the ex-slaves and their children. When they stop voicing the suspicion that the Negro spirituals derived their syncopation from Europe, probably from the Scottish folksong—then, and not before, shall I be ready to take their pronouncements seriously.

African Songs

FREEWILLUM

James Rogers (born in Liberty County) tells me this song, and the one following, were sung by Dublin Scribben. To use his own words: "Ole man Dublin he belong' to de Andersons o' Sunbury an' every day or two Miss Bertha would sen' me ober fo' him—to talk de ole African talk. I heered him, but I was too small to remember what he said, but I remember de songs 'cause I always p'int it on my mind about de t'ing." [51]

The first song did not sound like English, but when Rogers divorced the words

[51] *Tunes mean far more to the Negroes than words, I notice, and are not easily forgotten.*

from the tune (all but the exclamatory phrase show the influence of the white man's hymns), this is what I got:

Freewillum!
   Gwine home to sine de *oshun.*
Relig-jun to-d'-New Jerusalem-I-bring-good-news-a-tatta-ho!
   My soul sine de *oshun.*

The third line is extraordinary. Following fast on "New Jerusalem," the words run together up the scale into a falsetto squeak ending abruptly on "ho!" exactly as would be expected of songs from Africa. When a group of Negro school-children heard Rogers sing it, they went into spasms of laughter—and they had good cause, for the song is astonishingly strange.

2. ROCKAH MH MOOMBA

The second of Dublin's songs has few words that could pass for English, but, like several of the shouts, it ends with a stamp. The tune is not so wild as "Freewillum" and has not its distinctly primitive character. The last time I saw Rogers he told me that I was right in imagining it was a dance song. "When de ole man Dublin and his daughter Bessie get togedder she [52] shouted; when she say 'quank' de ole woman jump way over, and den de ole man jump, and den turn back again. Do de same t'ing ober, ebery time":

Rockah mh moomba
Cum bo-ba yonda
Lil-aye tambe
I rockah mh moomba
(Cum) bo-ba yonda
Lil-aye tambe
Ashawilligo homasha *banga*
L'ashawilligo homasha *quank!*
Ashawilligo homasha *banga*
L'ashawilligo homasha *quank!*

[52] *One gender did duty for all in the old days, and the first "she" undoubtedly stood for* "they," *and the second "she" for "he."*

Allegro

Rock - ah - mh moom-ba   Cum bo-ba yon-da

lil -   aye tam-be   I   rock-ah - mh moom-ba

(Cum) bo-ba yon-da   lil -   aye tam-be

L'ash-a-will-i-go   hom-ash - a bang-a

L' -ash - a - will-i - go   hom-ash - a quank

C.C.

This song and the one following evidently had a common origin. Perhaps "Ole Dublin" and "Gullah Ben" came from the same part of Africa, or were friends in Liberty County. Both songs are suggestive of the rhythm of the "ring-play":

Wa'k [53] Bil-le Au-ba
Be bul-o
Pretty fine lady
Be bul-o

I WOK OM A MO-NA

The following song was sung by Gullah Ben, who—like Dublin—came from Africa. He taught it to Ben Delegal, who in turn taught it to Amelia Dawley:

Cum bul-le al-le
Lilli—quam-be
I wok om a mo-na
Cum bul-le al-le
Lilli—quank.
Hassa willigo sehowyh bunga
Lilli hassa willigo dwellinda quenk.
Hassa willigo sehowyh bunga
Lilli hassa willigo dwellinda quenk.
I wock om a mo-na
Cum bul-le al-le
Lilli—quam-be
I wock om a mo-na
Cum bul-le al-le
Lilli—quank.
Hassa willigo sehowyh quenda here
Hassa willigo dwellinda quenk.
Hassa willigo sehowyh quenda here
Hassa willigo dwellinda quenk.

[53] Pronounce "Wa'k" to rhyme with "rock."

7. Pounding Corn in West Africa

8. *Beating Rice in Darien*

3. I WOK OM A MO-NA

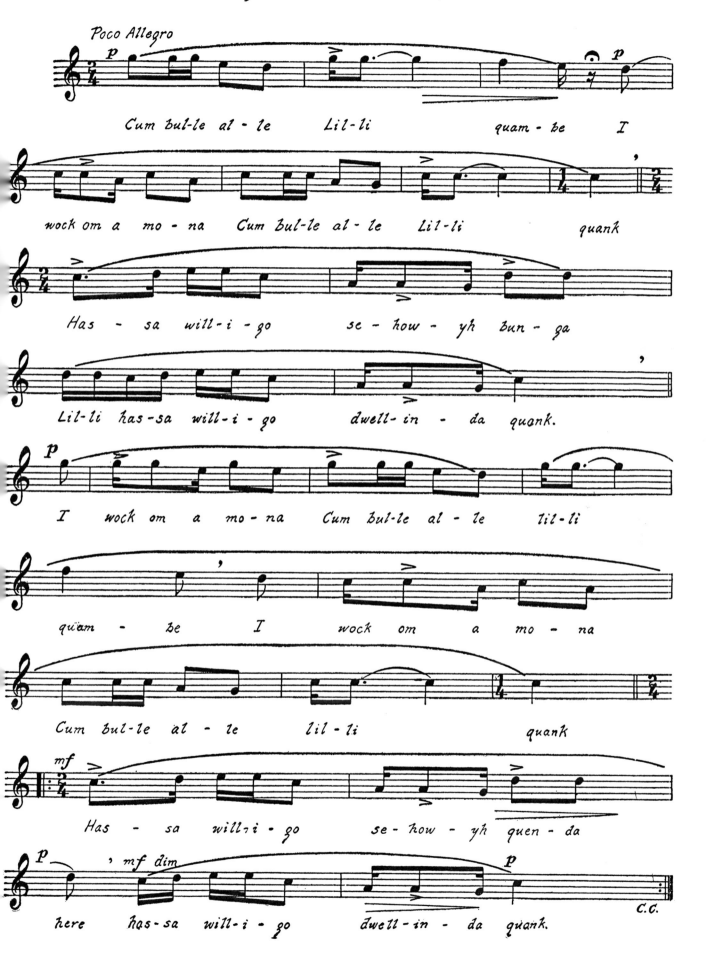

BYUM BY-E

The development of the religious song of the Negro under the influence of the white man's instruction is interestingly shown in this song. A better example could not be found.[54] Nancy Thorpe, of McIntosh County, learned it from her grandmother who, Nancy tells me, "came from Africa and was old in 1862."

It speaks well for Nancy's intelligence that she sings the song as it was taught her, softening certain syllables—just as "Shisha Ma-ley" did—without attempting to correct the English.

The song appears to have originated at the death-bed of "Shisha Shalun," who sang the first melodious verse with calm resignation:

> Fa-le-well Shisha Maley
> Fa-le-well en lay-vun
> Fa-le-well en lay-vun
> An shollen gane en mone
> Shisha har lepentin shu beleven
> Heaven gates are oven
> I love Shisha Maley yes Ah do
> Ah anjum biddum ena cum
> I love my shisha yes Ah do
> Ah anjum biddum ena cum.
> (Repeat, substituting Shalun for Maley)

[54] *The accompanying piano arrangement is by Creighton Churchill.*

4. FA-LE-WELL SHISHA MALEY

Poco Allegro

P semplice

Fal - le - well Shi-sha Ma-ly   Fal-le-well en

lay - vun   Fal-le-well en   lay-vun   An   sholl-en gane en

mone   Shi-sha har le-pen-tin shu be-le-ven   Heav-en gates are

ov - en   I   love Shi-sha Ma-ley yes ah do   Ah   an-jum bid-dum en-a

cum   I   love my shi-sha   yes ah do   Ah an-jum bid-dum en-a cum.

C.C.

When Shisha Ma-ley made her response, grief apparently got the upper hand.
She lapsed into her native tongue as well as the song-form of Africa,[55] and gave vent
to her sorrow in these poignant lines:

> Shisha Shalun gone en lay-vun
> An sholl en gane en moan
>> Lor' Shisha!
> Missa sholl en ganey moan
> U-m-m My-Lor'! Missa-shao
>> Byum by e-e
> U-m-m My-Lor'! Missa-shao
>> Byum by-e
> (Repeat)

[55] In spite of the fact that one verse shows the influence of the white man's hymns while the
other reverts to the African form, there is a homogeneous quality that demonstrates the ability
of the Negro to make the creation his own.

5. BYUM BY-E

Shi-sha Sha-lun gone en lay-vun An sholl en gane en
moan — Lor' Shi-sha Mis-sa sholl en gan-ey
moan Um-m My Lor'! Mis-sa sha-o Byum by-e ___
Um-m My Lor'! Mis-sa sha-o Byum by-e.

"U-m-m," [56] hummed with the lips closed, is a strangely moving tone (rightly named a moan), and in conjunction with the exclamatory words, "My Lor'! Missa-shao!" followed by the roll of the African word, "Byum by-e," gives emotional depth to this unusual song.

"Maum Kate" Wilson of Darien used to sing the following phrase: "Sumanar kusi luki tu," over and over, but no one ever learned what it meant. There are other songs in which half the words are African, but without the music it is useless to give them.

[56] An Anglo-African official tells me that the African side-drum (often called "the hypocrite" from the many different tones it is capable of producing through change of pressure of the arm under which it is held) makes a sound very similar to the hummed "U-m-m-m" so frequently employed in the slave songs. This humming is evidently another African survival. Its use is mentioned by the Denis-Roosevelts as common to the Belgian Congo. Natalie Curtis-Burlin, in Songs and Tales from the Dark Continent, says it is popular among the Zulus: "sometimes . . . a whole chorus will hum together with closed lips."

CHAPTER THREE

Afro-American Shout Songs

There appears to be a difference of opinion regarding the use of the word "shout" in designating the religious ring-dance, which was enjoyed during plantation days after prayer meeting and church service. Formerly writers thought that the Negro used the word because dancing was so sinful that it was wise to avoid even the name. But Dr. L. D. Turner has discovered that the Arabic word *Saut* (pronounced like our word "shout"), in use among the Mohammedans of West Africa, meant to run and walk around the Kaaba. I believe he has provided the right explanation for the difference in the meaning of the word, as used by the whites and the blacks, for I have seen the Negroes do the holy dance around the pulpit in their churches in such a manner.

Shouting appears to be of two types: Along the coast of Georgia and South Carolina the most popular form is the ring-shout, in which a number of dancers move counter-clockwise in a circle. (Illustration 22.) Occasionally individuals are seen in church using the same rhythmic shout step. In North Carolina and Virginia, however, the solo performance is apparently the only form in use, and the ring-shout seems to be unknown.

Those who have traveled in Africa, and have seen native dancing, are convinced that the shout of the American Negro is nothing more than a survival of an African tribal dance, and that the accompanying chants in their form and melody are quite as typical of Africa as the dance itself.[1] It is recognized, of course, that the words of the Old Testament have been substituted by the Negro for those of his native land. When the slaves grew more familiar with the English language, they evolved the more complicated religious songs that are now popularly called spirituals.

[1] *Records Nos. 6 and 10 of the series made in the Belgian Congo by the Denis-Roosevelt expedition are strikingly similar.*

During ante-bellum days shouting was as much a part of the Sunday afternoon service as the sermon. By 1900, however, the more fashionable Negro preachers felt that this mode of worship could not be correct, since it did not conform to the conventional pattern of the white man's service; they began to frown upon the religious dance as they did upon the use of "Amen" and similar responses by the congregation. Even so, the hold of shouting is tenacious, and it is practiced during the Christmas holidays [2] to this day. All the country Negroes enjoy it immensely, though many are unwilling to admit that they know how to do it, as they consider the dance old-fashioned. It was years before I was permitted to see the St. Simon's Negroes indulge in this innocent performance. Why they should have been so secretive about such a pastime I cannot understand, unless—because the style of dancing is unlike ours—they were afraid I might laugh at it.

I shall never forget the night at the hall of the Queen of the South Society when I first saw the ring-shout. Hard board benches were an unimportant matter. Little had I suspected, when Margaret took care of my room at the Arnold House years before, that she could outdo the Ouled Nail Dancers, of Biskra—if she wished. As it was, she wiggled her hips shamelessly, held her shoulders stiff—at the same time thrusting them forward—kept her feet flat on the floor, and, with the usual rhythmic heel-tapping, progressed with real style around the circle—goodness knows how. White folks who attempt the step of the true ring-shout find it difficult exercise. Few young Negroes will do it, and the Big Apple, with the stamp of the white man's approval, has recently been more popular. Should shouting ever achieve the same vogue, its life would be prolonged.

It was good fun telling the St. Simon's Negroes—too self-conscious in earlier years to shout—how a professional performer, Tamiris, seen in New York was dancing spirituals. There is a wide gulf between such a professional and Cornelia, but I am certain that the white artist, no matter how skillful, could learn something in the way of form from this colored woman, whose lean fine frame, beaked nose, and keen eyes bespeak her Arab ancestry—on the male side. As for Edith—who, being a Murphy, is temperamental—every now and then she gives a stylized, angular performance as though copying the poses of the figures in Egyptian decorations. The way she holds her arms and hands is perfect. It positively hurts that I have no moving picture of her statuesque, rhythmic pauses, or the pause Gertrude (Illustration

[2] *Joe Armstrong tells me that before the War Between the States, "Jubilee time began on Monday before Christmas with a big eat of pork and baked yams."*

27) makes with head and shoulders bowed slightly forward, arms held close to her body, elbows bent at right angles, forearms thrust out before her, and palms up-turned in a supplicating gesture. White musicians and dancers have obtained much from these untutored people, who appear to have an inborn gift for rhythm in its many manifestations. Work or play, preaching, praying, music, sculpture, or dancing—all are one to them when it comes to rhythmic expression.

HA'K 'E ANGELS

Deacon Eddy Thorpe, of McIntosh County, who contributed this Watch Night shout, explained that the slaves, when allowed to go to a praise-house that was out of bounds, were given passes with their promise to return before sun-up. On New Year's Eve the service consisted of prayers, religious songs, and a sermon by the preacher. At midnight, different members offered thanks to the Good Lord for the blessings of the past twelve months and implored His aid for the year to come. The shouting then began, and continued until dawn. This shout, which varies little in content or rhythm in Glynn, Liberty, McIntosh, and Camden counties,[3] was the last to be sung as the watcher, appointed for that duty, announced: "Day's a-comin' ":

> Day, day Oh—see day's a-comin'
> Ha'k 'e angels
> Day, day Oh—see day's a-comin'
> Ha'k 'e angels

[3] *In the vicinity of Albany, Georgia, there is a similar version that uses "Yonder Come Day" instead of "Ha'k 'e Angels."*

Day, day Oh—see day's a-comin'
  Ha'k 'e angels
Day, day Oh—see day's a-comin'
  Ha'k 'e angels
Oh look at day (ha'k 'e angels)—Oh Lord
  Ha'k 'e angels
Look out de windah (ha'k 'e angels)—Oh Lord
  Ha'k 'e angels
Look out de windah (ha'k 'e angels)—Oh Lord
  Ha'k 'e angels
See day's a-comin (ha'k 'e angels)—Oh Lord
  Ha'k 'e angels
Look out de windah (ha'k 'e angels)—Oh Lord
  Ha'k 'e angels
Look out de windah (ha'k 'e angels)—Oh Lord
  Ha'k 'e angels
Call my mother (ha'k 'e angels)—Oh Lord
  Ha'k 'e angels
Throw off de covah (ha'k 'e angels)—Oh Lord
  Ha'k 'e angels
Start that a-risin' (ha'k 'e angels)—Oh Lord
  Ha'k 'e angels
Who that a-comin' (ha'k 'e angels)—Oh Lord
  Ha'k 'e angels
Look out de windah (ha'k 'e angels)—Oh Lord

6. HA'K 'E ANGELS

UNTIL I DIE

I am told that this shout was once a favorite at "foreday meetin'," held on Sunday in the neighborhood of five o'clock.

Laura considered it her duty to ring the bell, and get the other members out to church. Since her death, however, nobody has felt the urge to take her place, and on St. Simon's the early service has lapsed:

> I'm goin' tuh set in the humble chair
> > Goin' tuh rock from side tuh side
> > Goin' tuh rock from side tuh side
> > Un-til I die.

Chorus: Un-til I die (leader)
                Un-til I die (basers)
                Un-til I die (leader)
                Un-til I die (basers)
I'm goin' tuh rock from side tuh side 'til I die.
(Repeated several times)

7. UNTIL I DIE

R. Mac Gimsey

Moderately, in steady tempo

Gon tuh sit in nuh hum-ble chah__ Gon tuh rock from side to side__ Gon tuh rock frum side to side__ __ un-til Ah die Un-til Ah die,__ Un-til Ah die__ Un-til Ah die__ un-til Ah die__ Ah'm gon tuh rock frum side tuh side__ til Ah die.__

WHERE WAS PETER

Where was Peter when the church fall down
In some lonesome valley with his head hang down
Oh, where was Peter when the church fall down
In some lonesome valley with his head hang down.[4]

Jesus done lock de lion lion
done lock de lion lion
done lock de lion lion
de lion jaw.
(Repeat three times)

[4] Creighton Churchill adds the following note: "Perhaps the most interesting aspect of this song is its canonical form. In occidental music a canon is a piece in which one voice or part leads off with the theme, and is followed, at given intervals, by one or more harmonizing voices carrying the same melody or musical figure. This song, short and naïve as it is, is actually a canon between the solo voice and the chorus, with perfectly orthodox, foreshortened endings at the finish of each two-measure phrase."

9. *Snooks*

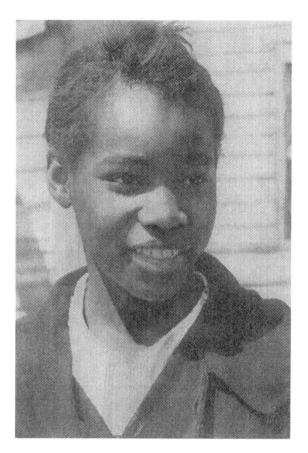

10. Susy

11. Snooks Doing: "Juba Dis, Juba Dat"

8. WHERE WAS PETER

PLUMB DE LINE

There are as many variations in the words of this shout song as there are counties on the coast of Georgia. However, the warning to "Plumb de line" and the tune itself remain the same, while the naming of deacons and plumbers, sisters and members, and the things they must do is made to fit the rhythm as a glove fits the hand:

Members,
      Plumb de line.[5]
Members,
      Plumb de line.
O members,
      Plumb de line.
Want t' go t' Heaven got a plumb de line.[6]
      You got t' sing right
          Plumb de line.
      You got t' sing right
          Plumb de line.
      You got t' sing right
          Plumb de line.
Want t' go t' Heaven got a plumb de line.
      O sister,
          Plumb de line.
      O sister,
          Plumb de line.
      O sister,
          Plumb de line.
Want t' go t' Heaven got a plumb de line.
      You got t' shout right
          Plumb de line.
      You got t' shout right
          Plumb de line.
      You got t' shout right
          Plumb de line.
Want t' go t' Heaven got a plumb de line.

[5] *Julia Walker sings "Plumb de line" an octave higher than the others—as was customary with "high tribbles" in the old days.*

[6] *This line is often sung "You want t'go t'Heaven you got a plumb de line."*

"Dear brother, Plumb de line," continues the song; and the next verse follows the same construction and thought in: "You got t' live right," following which Old Quarterman always put in an effective "Yes Sir!" The above version, used by Katherine, appears to be more modern than that used by Josephine, who gets a far-off look when she sings:

<blockquote>
Deacon deacon,[7]
    Plumb de line.
Deacon deacon,
    Plumb de line.
Deacon deacon,
    Plumb de line.
You can't go t' Heaven till y'u plumb de line.
If you pray fo' me
    Plumb de line.
I pray fo' you
    Plumb de line.
You can't go t' Heaven till y'u plumb de line.
O plumber plumb,
    Plumb de line.
O plumber plumb,
    Plumb de line.
O plumber plumb,
    Plumb de line.
You can't go t' Heaven till y'u plumb de line.
</blockquote>

[7] *The deacon "deacons" a song when he reads it two lines at a time for the benefit of any in the congregation who have not a hymn book or who cannot read. The custom of "lining out" and then singing a hymn was copied from the whites, who sang in this manner a century ago—perhaps later in sections where illiteracy prevailed. When done to short metre it is dreary beyond measure, but long metre sometimes has a barbaric charm.*

9. PLUMB DE LINE

Want to go to H'v'n got a Plumb de line. You got t' sing right

You got t' sing right

Plumb de line

You got t' sing right

Plumb de line

Plumb de line

Want to go to H'v'n got t' plumb de line.

C.C.

10. DOWN TO DE MIRE

Of all the ring-shouts I know, "Down to de Mire" is in more ways than one the most interesting. In the center of the ring, one member gets down on his knees and, with head touching the floor, rotates with the group as it moves around the circle. The different shouters, as they pass, push the head "down to the mire." The several arms reaching out to give a push make an unusually picturesque pattern. The refrain—repeated relentlessly—corresponds in its character and rhythmic beat to that of the drums in a song which accompanied an ominous ceremonial dance seen in *Trader Horn*.[8] One is apparently never too old or too fat to take part in this shout. I saw Quarterman, born in 1844, go "down to the mire" with satisfaction when he was ninety. Josephine, who weighs well over two hundred pounds, thinks nothing of getting down on her hands and knees and, with her head bobbing to the floor, proves the power of mind over matter:

> Sister Emma, Oh, you mus' come down to de mire.
> Sister Emma, Oh, you mus' come down to de mire.
>> Jesus been down
>>> to de mire
>> Jesus been down
>>> to de mire
>> Jesus been down
>>> to de mire
>> You must bow low
>>> to de mire
>> Honor Jesus
>>> to de mire
>> Honor Jesus
>>> to de mire
>> Lowrah lowrah
>>> to de mire
>> Lowrah lowrah
>>> to de mire
>> Lowrah lowrah
>>> to de mire
>> Jesus been down
>>> to de mire
> Sister Josie, you must come down to de mire
> Sister Josie, you must come down to de mire

[8] *I am told that, while the greater part of this film was made in California, "background shots" made in Africa were introduced, for obvious reasons. It is to these shots, naturally, that the above reference applies.*

Jesus been down
    to de mire
Jesus been down
    to de mire
Jesus been down
    to de mire
Honor Jesus
    to de mire
Honor Jesus
    to de mire
Honor Jesus
    to de mire
Honor Jesus
    to de mire
Honor Jesus
    to de mire
You must bow low
    to de mire
You must bow low
    to de mire.

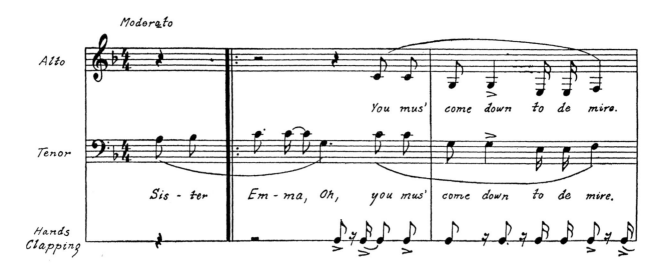

ELI AH CAN'T STAN'

Hate that [9] sin that made me moan
E-li Ah can't stan'!
Repeat:
Chorus: Hay John—John's on nuh [10] islun
Hay John—E-li Ah can't stan'! [11]

*   *   *

John's on the isle uh Pat-te-mos
E-li Ah can't stan'!
Repeat:
Take one brick out Satan's wall
Eli—can't stan'!
Repeat:
Satan's wall come tumblin' down
Eli—can't stan'!
Repeat:
One a these days I'm goin' away
Eli—can't stan'!
Won't be back 'till judgment day
Eli—can't stan'!

[9] *"That" sounds like "tat," and "Ah" sounds very like a short "eh."*
[10] *"The"—following a final "n"—has the sound of "nuh."*
[11] *The chorus is repeated after every two or three verses.*

11. ELI AH CAN'T STAN'

R. Mac Gimsey

Rapidly - steady tempo

Hate tat sin nat made me moan, E - li Ah cah stan.'

Hate tat sin nat made me moan, E - li Ah cah stan.'

Hay____ John____ John's on nuh Is - lun,____

Hay____ John____ E - li Ah cah stan'.

John's on nuh isle of Pat - te - mos, E - li Ah cah stan.

John's on nuh isle of Pat - te - mos, E - li Ah cah stan.'

MOONLIGHT—STARLIGHT

In *Slave Songs of the United States*, the origin of a song similar to "Moonlight—Starlight" is attributed to St. Simon's Island by Colonel Trowbridge, who is quoted as saying "that it was sung at funerals in the night time—one of the most solemn and characteristic customs of the Negroes." Fanny Kemble, in her *Journal*, describes a "buryin'" that took place at the Butler Plantation in 1839:

Yesterday evening the burial of the poor man, Shadrach, took place. I had been applied to for a sufficient quantity of cotton cloth to make a winding-sheet for him, and just as the twilight was thickening into darkness I went with Mr. —— [Pierce Butler, her husband] to the cottage of one of the slaves . . . a cooper of the name of London . . . who was to perform the burial service. The coffin was laid on trestles in front of the cooper's cottage, and a large assemblage of the people had gathered around, many of the men carrying pine-wood torches, the fitful glare of which glanced over the strange assembly. . . . Presently the whole congregation uplifted their voices in a hymn, the first high wailing notes of which—sung all in unison, in the midst of these unwonted surroundings—sent a thrill through all my nerves. When the chant ceased cooper London began a prayer, and all the people knelt down in the sand, as I did also. . . . When the prayer was concluded we all rose, and, the coffin being taken up, proceeded to the people's burial-ground, when London read aloud portions of the funeral service from the Prayer-book. . . . The service ended with a short address from London upon the subject of Lazarus, and the confirmation which the story of his resurrection afforded our hopes. . . . When the coffin was lowered the grave was found to be partially filled with water—naturally enough, for the whole island is a mere swamp, off which the Altamaha is only kept from sweeping by the high dikes all around it. This seemed to shock and distress the people, and for the first time during the whole ceremony there were sounds of crying and exclamations of grief heard among them . . . and so we returned from one of the most striking religious ceremonies at which I ever assisted.

When Margaret, one of my star shouters, was buried a few years ago at Kelvin Grove, in the old slave yard on the marsh, I too was shocked to see the coffin lowered into the water, but in this instance such an occurrence was taken as a matter of course.

Of all the primitive songs this is the most plaintive as well as the most impressive:

> Moonlight—Starlight
> O-o-h [12] Moonlight
> Believer what's the matter?
> John lay the body down!
>   (Repeat)
> John lay the body to the tomb
> O-o-h—let me go!
> John lay the body to the tomb
> John lay the body down!
>   (Repeat)

[12] *Sung with the lips closed. The accompanying piano arrangement is by Creighton Churchill.*

12. MOONLIGHT—STARLIGHT

John lay the bo - dy. to the tomb Oh, let me go

Oh, let me go

John lay the bo - dy to the tomb John lay the bo - dy down.

John lay the bo - dy down.

Repeat Chorus

C.C.

KNEE-BONE

Fanny Kemble, in her *Journal*, describes some shout songs—also used for rowing, through a suitable change of rhythm—in the following words:

I told you formerly that I thought I could trace distinctly some popular national melody with which I was familiar in almost all their songs; but I have been quite at a loss to discover any such foundation for many that I have heard lately and which have appeared to me extraordinarily wild and unaccountable. The way in which the chorus strikes in with the burden, between each phrase of the melody, chanted by a single voice, is very curious and effective, especially with the rhythm of the rowlocks for accompaniment.

But if Fanny Kemble had visited Africa and heard a few of the native songs (such as can now be purchased in gramophone shops specializing in foreign records), she would not have been puzzled by those sung by her husband's slaves.

What was said in 1839 concerning these "unaccountable" songs applies equally well to the songs given in this Chapter. And they are sung today, much as they were then, by descendants of the singers Fanny Kemble mentions. Side by side with these semi-chants you hear songs which show clearly the white man's musical influence. The oldest Negroes say that they shouted after church Sunday afternoons and after prayer meeting at night. Before the shouting began, they sang spirituals and "lined out" hymns. The chances are that all three types were sung from the time the white man concerned himself with the religious instruction of his slaves. In Liberty County the members of the Midway community countenanced a revival in 1838, which lasted two years and was continued by the whites until 1842.

In the shout song, Knee-Bone, curious twists and exotic tones are employed—including the musical, yet nasal "ha-nnn"—that must be heard to be appreciated. None of our musical symbols is capable of suggesting the strange turns used in this, as well as others of the more primitive Afro-American chants. If records are not made soon, the elusive beauty which characterizes this type of singing will be irretrievably lost.

The shouter, in this musical chant, obeys instructions and bends the knee far down with the rhythm of the words "Bend my knee-bone to the ground." The rowing version calls for "knee-bone bend to the elbow bend." "Aye Lord" is often substituted for "Ha-nnn Lord."

12. *The Cabin*

13. *The Author and Susyanna in Front of the School-House*

Knee-bone when I call you
    H-a-nnn knee-bone
Knee-bone when I call you
    H-a-nnn Lord knee-bone bend.
Bend my knee-bone to the ground
    H-a-nnn knee-bone
Bend my knee-bone to the ground
    H-a-nnn Lord knee-bone bend.
Knee-bone Zachaniah
    H-a-nnn knee-bone
Knee-bone Zachaniah
    H-a-nnn Lord knee-bone bend.
Knee-bone when I call you
    H-a-nnn knee-bone
Knee-bone when I call you
    H-a-nnn Lord knee-bone bend.
Knee-bone didn't I call you
    H-a-nnn knee-bone
Knee-bone didn't I call you
    Ha-ah Lord knee-bone bend.
Knee-bone in the mornin'
    H-a-nnn knee-bone
Knee-bone in the mornin'
    Ha-ah Lord knee-bone bend.
Knee-bone in the evenin'
    H-a-nnn knee-bone
Knee-bone in the evenin'
    Ha-ah Lord knee-bone bend.

Creighton Churchill explains to me that when this song was used for rowing it could have had only one rhythmic accompaniment, the oars, since the other two rhythms, the hands and heels, would have thrown the rowers off their beat. To use his words: "The speed of the rowing version must also have been slower, for one could not possibly row to the rhythm of this version. It should be recognized as well that no musical meter known to man can represent exactly the rhythm of oars in their locks; in this song especially, it is something intangible and personal, like the beat of the Viennese waltz. For the sake of simplicity I have represented the rowing rhythm in this transcription as 2/8, 3/8, 3/8, equal to a full measure of time for the voices and other rhythms."

13. KNEE-BONE

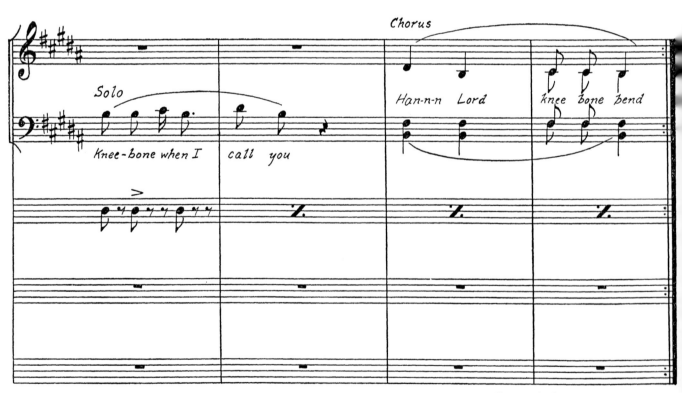

Repeat for verses 2 to 5

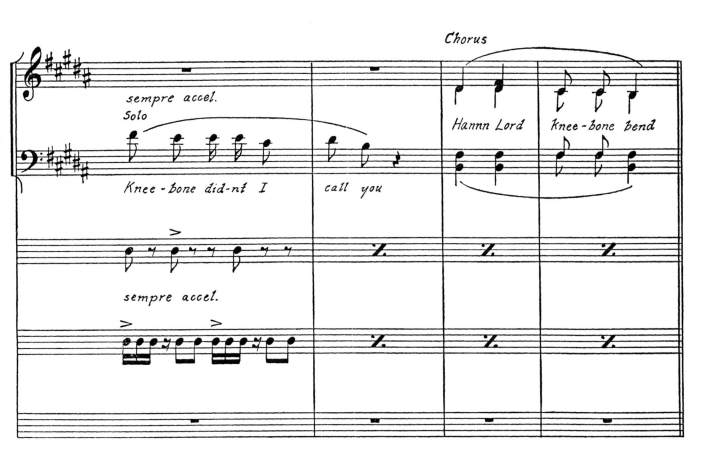

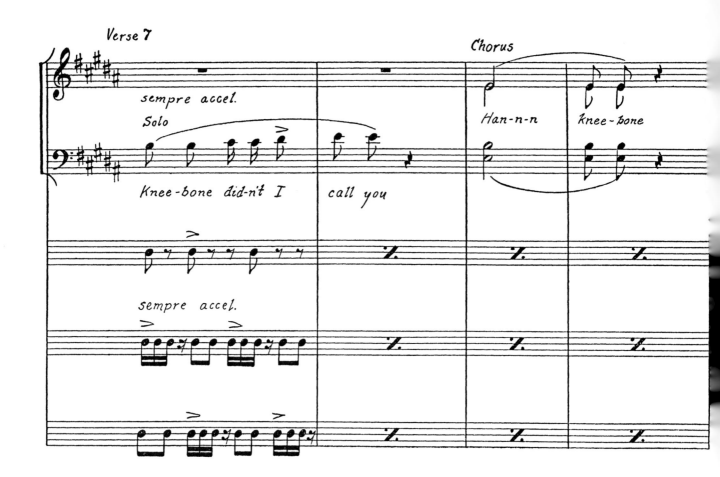

C.C.

OH EVE–WHERE IS ADAM?

In taking down a shout song, you are beset with the difficulty of reconciling the different versions. No leader sings a song twice alike, and no two ever sing exactly the same version; yet the beat, the accent, and the tune remain so stable that leaders are unerringly followed. The words are in truth only the vehicle for carrying along the complicated rhythm. This is beaten out by the heels of the McIntosh County group in a way not approached by any other that I know. Shouters sometimes clap their hands; on St. Simon's they always call for a broom handle, which, when knocked on the floor, provides an extemporaneous tom-tom. In McIntosh County, however, they are so proficient in tapping out the rhythm with their heels that they can dispense with both sticks and hand clapping. With their hands free, they are able to do things descriptive of the text which less skillful groups would not be at liberty to attempt.

The shout:

> Oh Eve—where is Ad-u-m?
> Oh Eve—Adam in the garden
>> Pickin' up leaves.

is a good example of the combination of dancing and pantomime. After swinging deliberately around the circle, singing the slower part of the chant, the dancers, when the time quickens, go through the motion of picking up leaves. With aprons gathered up and bodies bent, the women add greatly to the interest of the dance. All are amusingly industrious, but the men, without the assistance of aprons, are not quite so convincing in following the action indicated by the text.

Since the version I have encountered in Glynn and Camden Counties holds to "pinnin' leaves," I am inclined to believe that some McIntosh shouter took an artist's license and substituted "pickin' up" for "pinnin' " for the sake of more varied, more picturesque action. At any rate, the delightful result justifies the less usual interpretation of the Biblical text.

With "Lord called Adam—pinnin' leaves," the movement is faster. The feet are not supposed to leave the floor or to cross each other, such an act being sinful. The shouting proceeds with a curious shuffling but controlled step which taps out with the heel a resonant syncopation fascinating in its intricacy and precision. Over and over the chant is repeated, the rhythm all-important, always right; the sonorous Old Testament words are just necessary sounds to carry along the melody, and the sequence of thought is nothing to worry about.

The words may be monotonous when read, but are not so when sung: "Adam" is turned into "Ad-u-m," with unusual tones and inflections all through the leading lines, which show surprising invention. It is self-evident that the song belongs to the African question-and-answer type, and bears no trace of European influence in its form:

Oh Eve where is Ad-u-m?
Oh Eve—Adam in the garden
        Pinnin' leaves. (repeat)
Adam in the garden
        Pinnin' leaves. (repeat)

Faster: Lord called Adam
        Pinnin' leaves. (repeat)
Adam wouldn' answer
        Pinnin' leaves. (repeat)
Adam shame'
        Pinnin' leaves. (repeat)
Ad-u-m? (Rising inflection)
        Pinnin' leaves.
Ad-u-m? (Falling inflection)
        Pinnin' leaves.
Where't thou?
        Pinnin' leaves. (repeat)
Adam naked
        Pinnin' leaves. (repeat)
Ain't y'u shame'?
        Pinnin' leaves. (repeat)
Lord I'm shame'
        Pinnin' leaves. (repeat)

14. BLOW GABRIEL

Undoubtedly the greater part of these songs originated under the stress of religious emotion, such as Laura showed when she strode to the middle of my yard and, with a commanding arm lifted high, intoned musically, "Blow, Gabriel!" as though sure of a response. Then she called again—louder this time—"Blow, Gabriel!" and still no answer. She waited a moment before calling at the top of her lungs, "Blow, Gabriel!"—and when nothing happened, she turned, complaining bitterly, gathered up the bunch of white oleanders she had laid beside me, and left as suddenly as she had come. Half chanting to Gabriel, she improvised as she went swiftly down the road, waving the flowers she had probably intended for the grave of her son, who lies in the old slave burying ground at Kelvin Grove.

It seems that earlier in the day she had shrieked and chanted, as is common with those who get this type of religious hysteria. In the old days such excitement was a more usual and respected occurrence than now. The reference in old spirituals to "My head got wet wid de midnight dew" meant that under religious exaltation the individual wandered at night through wood and swamp, as Laura had for several days and nights before I saw her at the locked gate which barred her way to the plantation graveyard.

I called, "Where are you going?" She seemed to waken out of a dream and said, "I forgot." Then she came closer, and impressively declaimed, "Miz' Parris'—I bin sent by God to you. They say I'm crazy, an' they put me in jail nine days—but I'se seen God!" After a long harangue delivered in an impassioned but disconnected way, she told me she had spent Tuesday night in Hell, that she'd been crucified. The blood had trickled down her back, the thorns had pierced her arms. She threw her arms out wide as though to show me. When she noticed they weren't clean, in an abashed aside she apologetically said, "I ain't wash 'em this mornin'." Then she went on, "You needn' tell me that God meant white folks an' colored people to sit down together."

I assured her, when she paused for breath, that I realized the truth of what she said. She told me how she had been out picking berries that morning, and a rattlesnake had charmed her little boy. "I call' to him an' he couldn' move—he jus' look at the snake like this." (She stooped down and stared fixedly ahead of her.) "When I pull' him away, the snake went shzzzz! and the poison went into me." Then it was that she strode into the middle of the yard and called upon Gabriel.

The next morning I was distressed to find that Laura had been taken to jail again. My cook, Julia, and I talked the situation over and decided we would be easier in our minds if we knew she ought to be there. Though noisy the day before, she appeared to be harmless. Dr. Cate, the county physician, kindly took us to the jail at noon, as he also wished to see her. When we reached her cell, he asked, "Well, Laura, what are you here for?" Her reply impressed me very much. "It's not for drinkin' or fightin'—it's a religious affair." But when she went on to say, "I'm havin' a religious war, and I'm puttin' up a dam' good fight," I realized she had better stay where she was until her ardor cooled:

> Blow Gabriel
>> At the Judgment
> Blow Gabriel
>> At the Judgment Bar!
> Blow 'um easy
>> At the Judgment
> Blow 'um easy
>> At the Judgment Bar!
> My Lord call you
>> At the Judgment
> My Lord call you
>> At the Judgment Bar!
> Why don't you answer
>> At the Judgment
> Why don't you answer
>> At the Judgment Bar!
> Ha-Ha angel
>> At the Judgment
> Ha-Ha angel
>> At the Judgment Bar!

MY SOUL ROCK ON JUBILEE

This song was sung and shouted after prayer meeting and after church service
—usually when the church "got a soul":

Chorus: 'N Jubilee—'N Jubilee
         A-a-a-h my Lord![13]
     'N Jubilee—'N Jubilee
         My soul rock on Jubilee!

     Long time talkin' 'bout Jubilee
         A-a-a-h my Lord!
     Long time talkin' 'bout Jubilee
         My soul rock on Jubilee!
     My mother done gone to Jubilee
         A-a-a-h my Lord!
     My mother done gone to Jubilee
         My soul rock on Jubilee!
     I got a right in Jubilee
         A-a-a-h my Lord!
     I got a right in Jubilee
         My soul rock on Jubilee!

        Repeat Chorus:

In reference to the following version, Clara said: "When it gets hot, them
that's on the outside of the church comes runnin' in." I asked what she meant by
"getting hot." "O, you feel good. You know things is warmin' up and you gets
revived":

     I come t' tell you 'bout Jubilee
         O-o-o-h my Lord!
     Come t' shout that Jubilee
         My soul rock on Jubilee!
     That Jud! That Jud! That Jubilee [14]
         O-o-o-h my Lord!
     That Jud! That Jud! That Jubilee
         My soul rock on Jubilee!

[13] *A wild quavering cry given by the "high tribble"—far above the other singers—makes your
"hair riz," as the Negroes say.*
[14] *Faster, with double rap on "That Jud! That Jud!"*

GOOD-BYE EVERYBODY

Certain songs are considered to be peculiarly suitable for specific occasions. This shout has always been the favorite farewell song among the St. Simon's Negroes. At the Cabin, the white folks seem to think the evening cannot end properly without it:

> Good-bye everybody
> Good-bye sing Hallelujah
> Good-bye everybody
> Good-bye sing Hallelujah
> Goin' 'way to leave you, sorry t' tell you
> Good-bye sing Hallelujah.
> Jesus settin' on the Sac'ment Table
> Good-bye sing Hallelujah.
> Handin' the bread an' the wine to the members
> Good-bye sing Hallelujah.
> Good-bye all you deacons
> Good-bye sing Hallelujah
> Good-bye all you deacons
> Good-bye sing Hallelujah

Good-bye is also said to "all you preachers," "all you false-pretenders," "all you hypocrites," and "all you tattlers."

15. GOOD-BYE EVERYBODY

The following verse comes from McIntosh County:

Goin' up in the heaven
Goin' to try on mh garment
Good-bye sing Hallelujah.
Goin' to try on mh garment
See how it fit me
Good-bye sing Hallelujah.

(Illustration 15)

CHAPTER FOUR

Ring-Play, Dance, and Fiddle Songs

Of the ring-play, dance, and fiddle songs, only those accompanying ring-play were countenanced by the church. However, certain solo dances like the Buzzard Lope evaded difficulties by using such religious songs as "Gimme Him" and "Throw Me Anywhere." These solo dances appear to have been "done for fun," and in our section bore no particular classification.[1] But the rags, reels, and fiddle or "sinful" songs were an entirely different matter. They were looked upon by church members with considerable horror as quite beyond the pale. Those of mature years would have nothing to do with them, and even today they are regarded with suspicion. In consequence, innocent as they appear to be, they have been the most difficult to uncover. Perhaps if I were a man or a godless colored woman I might find something as racy as was ever composed or sung in a "jook."

The ring-play songs were totally unknown to me for almost twenty years after I went to St. Simon's. Entirely by chance I learned about them in the Boston Public Library, when I happened on a short account of "Ring-Games from Georgia" by Loraine Darby,[2] and recognized one of the examples as a shanty used by our Negro stevedores in loading lumber. When I returned to Georgia, I asked Julia what that song had to do with ring-games. Again it was brought home to me that we learn from these people, who have no past, only what we first discover for ourselves. She said: "Dear me! It's a ring-play song, but it's so long since I sung one I'd forgotten we ever did." Later I found that I could not have escaped hearing inferior modern versions had I lived near a Negro school, for the children sing them at the top of their lungs.

With such a clue, I have unearthed various stray bits concerning these interesting game songs. Little has been written about them, and that little naturally classes

---

[1] Thomas W. Talley, in *Negro Folk Rhymes*, describes them as "star-danced" by one or two individuals at a time.

[2] *Journal of American Folk-Lore*, 1917.

them with the ring-games of the white people. Undoubtedly there is sound foundation for assuming that they owe something to English originals, for many show it, either in the action, or in certain leading lines. On the other hand, they are more melodious than the game songs of the whites; they employ an amusing variety of dance steps, possess a contagious rhythm, and make use of vigorous hand clapping, which is utterly unlike anything European. These same characteristics are emphasized by Natalie Curtis-Burlin, in *Songs and Tales from the Dark Continent*, and by N. G. J. Ballanta, in his article on "Music of the African Races." Their descriptions of African dance songs might well apply to those of the Georgia Negroes prior to 1900. The similarity indicates that here again we may have such an equal proportion of English and African influence as is found in the other groups of Negro songs.

Not being a scientist, I am privileged to make guesses, and one of them is tied up with the history of our pioneers. In the early years of the nineteenth century, a host of planters, with their families and slaves, moved to the richer lands farther west. The number that went over the Federal Road into Alabama was so great that a lone eastbound traveler reported from Georgia that he was never out of sight of a long line of migrants. A good indication of the extent of the westward movement is given in the fact that the population of Texas increased from four thousand in 1820 to almost twenty thousand in 1830. Most of the settlers were Southerners, who took their slaves with them. In those frontier days the smaller property owners worked with their slaves, and attended the same revivals. Because of this the songs and customs of one were bound to influence those of the other. The more religious pioneers were opposed to dancing, and used these innocent party games, with their accompanying songs, as a substitute at their social gatherings long after they had been discarded by the fashionable planters of the southeastern seaboard, and relegated to the Negroes and children. Original sin of course sees to the preservation of the fiddle songs; we are told that, in the days before railroads provided an easy means of communication with the outside world, social life in the newly-settled territories was "sluggish in some ways and wild in others." In consequence the connection between the worldly songs found on the coast of Georgia and the hill-billy and cowboy songs of the slave states west of the Mississippi River seems to me self-evident.

EMMA YOU MY DARLIN'

This ring-play has been revived by Julia Armstrong, who remembers it from her youth.

Emma you my darlin'
Oh Emma Oh!
You turn aroun' dig a hole in the groun'
Oh Emma Oh!
Emma you duh bad gal
Oh Emma Oh!
You turn aroun' dig a hole in the groun'
Oh Emma Oh!
Emma you from the country
Oh Emma Oh!
You turn aroun' dig a hole in the groun'
Oh Emma Oh!

(Illustration 30)

16. EMMA YOU MY DARLIN'

14. *Farewell Song in the Cabin*

15. *Joe Singing: "Good-Bye Everybody," with Ben in the Background*

16. *Bessie, Deeply Absorbed in the Singing*

GO ROUN' THE BORDER SUSIE

The action in this ring-play is directed by the verses. While the first verse is sung, the players join hands in a circle and swing to its rhythm. In the next verse "That turtle dove started," indicates that a girl has begun to move within the ring. "Out goes the hornet," is the signal for a boy to follow her. With "Hist the windah," the players lift their clasped hands. First the girl weaves in and out of the circle, between the uplifted arms. The boy follows suit. "Don't miss no windah," explains itself, and the last verse, "Close in d' 'semble," means to close the window when the boy and girl are both on the outside. The fun then begins, and the chorus may need to be sung several times while the hornet attempts to catch the turtle dove, who turns in one direction, and then in another, to avoid capture:

Chorus: Go roun' the border Susie
Go roun' the border Susie
Go roun' the border Susie
That long summer day.

Out goes the hornet, shoo down my little one
Shoo down my little one, shoo that day
Out goes the hornet, shoo down my little one
      Shoo down my little one, long summer day.

That turtle dove started, shoo down my little one
Shoo down my little one, shoo that day
That turtle dove started, shoo down my little one
      Shoo down my little one, that long summer day.

Hist the windah, shoo down my little one
Shoo down my little one, shoo that day
Hist the windah, shoo down my little one
      Shoo down my little one, that long summer day.

Don't miss no windah, shoo down my little one
Shoo down my little one, shoo that day
Don't miss no windah, shoo down my little one
      Shoo down my little one, that long summer day.

Close in d' 'semble, shoo down my little one
Shoo down my little one, shoo that day
Close in d' 'semble, shoo down my little one
      Shoo down my little one, that long summer day.

17. GO ROUN' THE BORDER SUSIE

Allegro

Go roun' the bor-der Su-sie Go roun the bor-der Su-sie Go roun the bor-der Su-sie That long sum-mer day. Out goes the hor-net Shoo down my lit-tle one Shoo down my lit-tle one Shoo that day Out goes the hor-net Shoo down my lit-tle one Shoo down my lit-tle one Long sum-mer day.

C.C.

Repeat Chorus: Go roun' the border Susie
Go roun' the border Susie
Go roun' the border Susie
That long summer day.

SANGAREE

This ring-play varies in action wherever I see it done. For that reason I will attempt no description. The tune, however, always remains the same:

If I live
    Sangaree.
Don' get kill'
    Sangaree.
I'm goin' back
    Sangaree.
Jacksonville
    Sangaree.

Chorus: Oh Babe
    Sangaree.
Oh Babe
    Sangaree.
Oh Babe
    Sangaree.
Oh Babe
    Sangaree.

If I live
    Sangaree.
See nex' fall
    Sangaree.
Ain' goin' t' plant
    Sangaree.
No cotton at all
    Sangaree.
    Repeat Chorus:

Chicken in the fiel'
    Sangaree.
Scratchin' up peas
    Sangaree.
Dog on the outside
    Sangaree.
Scratchin' off fleas
    Sangaree.
    Repeat Chorus:

Extra verses are contributed by a Darien singer:

> My husban's got the shovel
>> Sangaree.
> An' I got the hoe
>> Sangaree.
> If that ain't farmin'
>> Sangaree.
> I don't know
>> Sangaree.

> Repeat Chorus:

> If you want t' see a nigger
>> Sangaree.
> Cut the fool
>> Sangaree.
> Let him ride
>> Sangaree.
> A white man's mule
>> Sangaree.

Chorus: Oh Babe
>> Sangaree.
> Oh Babe
>> Sangaree.
> Oh Babe
>> Sangaree.
> Oh Babe
>> Sangaree.

18. SANGAREE

19. IT'S COLD FROSTY MORNIN'

The words of this "play," called "a marchin' piece," are clearly derived from an old English song. With "It's cold!" two and two march; with "There she stands right by your side" they change partners and march again:

It's cold
　　　(It's cold)
It's cold
　　　(It's cold)
It's cold frosty mornin'
In come the farmer drinkin' of the cider
　　It's cold ray-me-oo
An' now where to find her
An' now I lost my lover
An' where shall I find her
　　　(repeat)
There she stan's right by your side
Don't she look jus' like a bride
Hug her an' kiss her an' call 'er your own
Then she'll marry you.

cold ra - ma - o An' now where to find her

Now I lost my lov - er, An' where shall I find her It's

1.

2. where shall I find him

Animato

There she stands right by your side

Don't she look jus' like a bride

Hug her and kiss her and

call her your own Then she'll mar - ry you.

repeat Chos.

C. C.

PRETTY GREEN SHAWL

From the verses of this "play" it can be seen that it is a "promenading piece" and is the Negro counterpart of "It's Cold Frosty Mornin'." Partners are changed after singing the chorus a second time:

> Chorus: Farewell, farewell
> Fare you well my darlin'
> Farewell, farewell
> I love you to my heart
>
> ———
>
> Now choose in another one honey my love
> honey my love
> honey my love
> Choose in another one honey my love
> So early in the mornin'.
>
> O the lady—she wear a pretty green shawl
> pretty green shawl
> pretty green shawl
> O the lady—she wear a pretty green shawl
> So early in the mornin'.
>
> Step gran' (or proud) wid y'r lover, honey my love
> honey my love
> honey my love
> Step gran' wid y'r lover honey my love
> So early in the mornin'.
>
> Repeat Chorus:

FOUR AND TWENTY LAWYERS

The action is spirited, with much hand clapping that encourages those who "lead off." As far as I can see the figures are similar to those of the Virginia reel, with the exception of the beginning, where "Lead off one" is the signal for a man to walk briskly from the top of the line to the foot (men on one side, women on the other, as is usual). "Up and down" indicates the repetition of the short swinging jaunt; at "Lead off next," he takes the hand of the woman on the opposite end and they "Step in a hurry" and go "up and down" twice. The play then proceeds in the familiar way. Unless you have been told beforehand it is difficult to distinguish the words of the response "Lawyer's suit." When it is sung by all, as fast as it should be, and overlaps the leader's last word, a strange twist is given the tune. As can be seen, the words are no more than stage directions, but the rhythm is unusual, with the unmistakable stamp of Africa in the ominous cadence found in "Lawyer's suit."

The chorus is repeated as well as each leading line with its refrain:

> Chorus: There is four and twenty lawyers
> All in a line
> Four and twenty lawyers
> All in a line
> (faster) Lead off one [3]
> Lawyer's suit.
> Up and down
> Lawyer's suit.
> Lead off next
> Lawyer's suit.
> Step in a hurry
> Lawyer's suit.
> Turn that lady
> Lawyer's suit.
> Turn her loose
> Lawyer's suit.
> Don't you hurt that lady
> Lawyer's suit.
> You hurt my heart
> Lawyer's suit.
> She's a very fine lady
> Lawyer's suit.
> Just from the country
> Lawyer's suit.
> Basket of oysters
> Lawyer's suit.

[3] *When another man leads off, the verses change to suit the leader. In place of "Step in a hurry" I have heard "Get in a hurry," then:*
> *Very fine gentleman*
> *Lawyer's suit.*

SHOUT JOSEPHINE SHOUT

Julia remembered this verse from her youth on St. Simon's—with a fragment of another from the same song:

> Josephine! Ma'am?
> Don't you hear y'o' mammy call you
> Why don't you go an' see what she want?
> Josephine! Ma'am?
> Want to shout? Yes, ma'am.
> Shout Josephine—Shout—Shout!
> Shout Josephine—Shout!

> Get a hump on y'o'self you red-eye' devil
> Get a hump on y'o'self you big-eye' coon!

Years later, at Broadfield, I found that the verse given above was the chorus of an amusing play song, with pantomime, which is related to both the ring-play and the solo dances. "Josephine! Ma'am?" is sung first as is usual; the leader then tells where the pain (or ornament) is located and the participants instantly try to place their hands on the spot named:

> Pain in the head—Shout—Shout!
> Shout Josephine—Shout!
> Pain in the back—Shout—Shout!
> Shout Josephine—Shout!
> Pain in the neck—Shout—Shout!
> Shout Josephine—Shout!
> Pain in the hip—Shout—Shout!
> Shout Josephine—Shout!

> Josephine
>   Ma'am?
> Want t' shout?
>   Yes ma'am
> What time?
>   Right now.
> Shout Josephine
>   Shout!

> Pain in the toe
>   Shout! Shout!

Pain in m' leg
  Shout! Shout!
Pain in the heel
  Shout! Shout!
Shout Josephine
  Shout!

That sore toe
  Shout! Shout!
That finger ring
  Shout! Shout!
That water fall [4]
  Shout! Shout!
Shout Josephine
  Shout!

That ribbon bow
  Shout! Shout!
That air ring [5]
  Shout! Shout!
That slipper shoe
  Shout! Shout!
That shiny eye
Shout Josephine
  Shout!
Now shake the baby
  Shake! Shake!
Now shake the baby
  Shake! Shake!
Shake the baby—Shake!

The song is closed off with:

A'n' Jinny hoecake
  Sweet! Sweet!
Take some an' lef' some
  Sweet! Sweet!
A'n' Jinny hoecake
  Sweet! Sweet!
Take some an' lef' some
Sweet! Sweet! Sweet!

[4] An old-time hair-do.
[5] Earring.

THE BUZZARD LOPE—A SOLO DANCE

Since 1915 I have known that such a dance as the Buzzard Lope [6] could be found in the neighborhood of St. Simon's; but the Negroes of that section always told me it was done on some far-off island, such as St. Catherine's or Sapelo. Over ten years ago I asked the same question of a newcomer, as a matter of routine, which I had for years put to the other shouters: "Can you do the Buzzard Lope?" When she said: "Yes'm," I was a bit stunned . . . but she could, to perfection. To my surprise, however, I found that a number who had previously denied such a gift were close seconds. (Illustrations 23 and 26)

This group used an old religious song with narrative lines of a suitable character. In ante-bellum days the slaves called the graveyard "the ole field":

THROW ME ANYWHERE

Throw me anywhere
    In that ole field
Throw me anywhere, Lord
    In that ole field
Throw me anywhere
    In that ole field
Throw me anywhere, Lord
    In that ole field
Members,[7] you want to die, Lord
    In that ole field
Members, you want to die, Lord
    In that ole field
Members, you want to die, Lord
    In that ole field
Members, you want to die
    In that ole field.

[6] *Dances simulating the peculiar characteristics of animals are popular in Africa; and Mr. Herskovits tells me he has seen a similar dance in Dahomey.*

[7] *Deacons, preachers, brothers, sisters, and mother are all mentioned as wanting to die "In that old field."*

20. THROW ME ANYWHERE

C.C.

On Sapelo Island, I found in the Johnson family a combination of the old dance form with rather more modern steps than the original African pantomime warranted. Of the twins, Naomi did the patting while Isaac did the dancing; [8] an older brother rhythmically called out the cues in a sharp staccato, and another one lay on the floor of the wide veranda representing a dead cow. Anyone who has seen turkey buzzards disposing of "carr'on" [9] will recognize the aptness of the following directions. Those who are at all squeamish had better skip this part. The bracketed asides were given for my information:

> March aroun'!   *(the cow)*
> Jump across!   *(see if she's daid)*
> Get the eye!   *(always go for that first)*
> So glad!   *(cow daid)*
> Get the guts!   *(they like 'em next best)*
> Go to eatin'!   *(on the meat)*
> All right!—cow mos' gone!
> Dog comin'!
> Scare the dog!
> Look aroun' for mo' meat!
> All right!—Belly full!
> —"Goin' to tell the res'."

And with an eye to the dramatic exit, Isaac danced into the house.

[8] *In later years I saw the Buzzard Lope done by Isaac's teacher, Reuben Grovenor—a descendant of the Sapelo Bilali who wrote a "diary" in Arabic. Many times have I seen others do this peculiar dance, but Reuben's performance is far and away the most finished. With effortless grace he gives a stylized pattern of the bird's awkward steps, without any attempt at realism. His is indeed a high form of rhythmic approximation, and those who have seen it at the Cabin are fortunate.*

[9] *Miss Kingsley tells us that in West Africa turkey buzzards are called "Jack Crows"—the natives call them "yubu." In the West Indies they are called either "John Crows "or "Carrion Crows."*

GIMME HIM

Another primitive song that offers the proper rhythm sounds slangy, but I am positive that such was not its intent:

Jesus died a happy die
He died fuh sin but not His own
Gimme Him gimme Him Aw sho
Gimme Him gimme Him until I die.
(Repeat the last two lines)
He died on the Roman cross
That we might live
Gimme Him gimme Him Aw sho
Gimme Him until I die.
(Repeat the last two lines)

17. A Combination of African Ideas and American Burial Conventions

18. A Bronze Head Dug up at Ife in 1938   19. Its American Counterpart

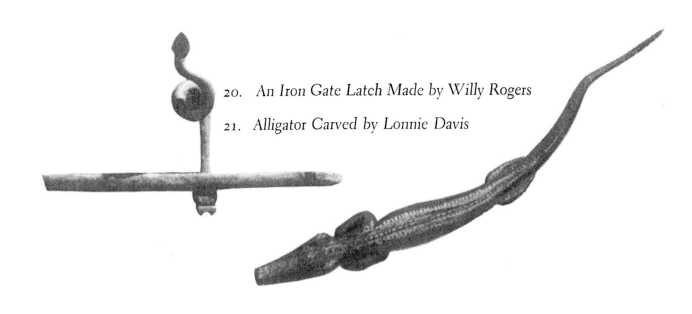

20. An Iron Gate Latch Made by Willy Rogers

21. Alligator Carved by Lonnie Davis

21. GIMME HIM

Moderately fast - with no change in tempo

R. Mac Gimsey

Je - sus died a hap - py die, He died fuh sin but not his own. Gim - me Him, gim - me Him Aw___ sho Gim - me Him, gim - me Him un - til Ah die___ Gim - me Him, gim - me Him Aw___ sho. Gim - me Him, gim - me Him un - til Ah die He died on nuh Rom - an cross that we might live, Gim - me Him, Gim - me Him Aw___ sho. Gim - me Him un - til Ah die.

STICKIT BALL A HACK

Like "Ham Bone," "Ball the Jack" and "Juba dis an' Juba dat," this curious song is half-spoken in a lively fashion, to rhythmical hand clapping. When the verse is finished "Then you kick it off":

> Jack t' the rack back
> Stickit ball a hack
> Low ball high ball
> Scallion jack.

HAM BONE HAM BONE

As is obvious, twelve-year-old Maria's version of these rhythmical lines is modern. Luck was with me when I found George, another twelve-year-old, who could give the older verses which are recited in the same way—alternated with similar patting. The only difference is that Maria balances herself on one foot; with her left hand she holds her cotton skirt tight around the "ham bone" section of her anatomy, places her right foot on the other leg below the knee and with her right hand deftly smacks out the intricate rhythm on her "rusty butt." [10] George, however, takes the line of least resistance, and leans with his back against a wall. However, in that position he is able to lift his "ham bone" a little higher and do a rather more complicated bit of patting. His hand flies back and forth like a shuttle between his chest and his rump.

These are Maria's words:

> Ham bone ham bone pat um on uh shoulder
> 11
> Gimme a pretty girl show y'u how t' hold her
> . . . .
> I went down town one day
> . . . .
> I went with my mother—too.
> . . . .
> My mother bought me a billy goat
> . . . .
> If my billy goat don't butt
> . . . .
> Momma goin' to beat my rusty butt
> . . . .

[10] *The night she wore a corduroy skirt, the patting could not be heard and her performance missed fire.*

[11] *These dots represent patting.*

As far as "I went with my mother—too" the lines are repeated, but when it comes to enumerating what she bought, there is this change:

> My mother bought me a radio
>
> . . . .
>
> If my radio won't play
>
> . . . .
>
> Momma goin' t' beat my NRA
>
> . . . .

George's lines, which are clearly of an older vintage, are given in the time-honored question and answer manner of Africa. Half-way through they merge into an old play song:

> Ham bone ham bone wha's you bin?
>
> . . . .
>
> All roun' the worl' an' back agin.
>
> . . . .
>
> Ham bone ham bone what'd y'u do?
>
> . . . .
>
> I got a chance an' I fairly flew.
>
> . . . .
>
> Ham bone ham bone where you stay?
>
> . . . .
>
> I met a pretty girl an' I couldn' get away.
>
> . . . .
>
> Ham bone ham bone what'd you do?
>
> . . . .
>
> Hopt up to Miss Lucy's doo'.
>
> . . . .
>
> Ax Miss Lucy will she marry me?
>
> . . . .
>
> I wouldn't care if poppa didn't care.
>
> . . . .

At this point George uses the narrative of the old play song: "Brother Froggy went to town—Un hunh!" [12]

> [12] *Brother Froggy went to town—Un hunh, Un hunh!*
> *To buy his wife a weddin' gown—Un hunh, Un hunh!*
> *What y'u goin' t' have de weddin' feas'?—Un hunh, Un hunh!*
> *Two big bread an' not a bit a grease—Un hunh, Un hunh!*
> *Firs' come aroun' wuz Mr. Bug—Un hunh, Un hunh!*
> *He fell in de lemonade tub—Un hunh, Un hunh!*

Nex' come in wuz Mr. Snake

. . . .

Pattin' all round' dat weddin' cake.

. . . .

Nex' cum in wuz Mr. Bug

. . . .

Hoppin' all roun' dat whiskey jug.

. . . .

Nex' come in wuz Mr. Tick

. . . .

He ate so much till it made 'im sick.

. . . .

The youngster said he knew many more verses, but these are more than enough to show how lines of proper length can be utilized.

JUBA DIS AN' JUBA DAT

Juba dis an' Juba dat
An' Juba kill d' yalla cat
An' get over double-trouble
    Juba!
She served d' meal
She gimme d' husk
  Cooked d' bread
She gimme d' crus'
She fried d' meat
  Gimme d' skin
That's 'e way momma
  Took me in
Now Juba! [13]

By rapidly crossing his hands to first one knee and then the other, Snooks pats out an intricate rhythm to the above staccato lines. When he gets to "Now Juba!" he does some clever footwork that matches the coördination of his hands.

(Illustration 11)

[13] Maude Cuney Hare in Negro Musicians and Their Music says that the dance Juba is known to be over a century old. Cable in his "Creole Slave Songs" mentions that "The guiouba was probably the famed juba of Georgia and the Carolinas."

BALL THE JACK

Several of our Negroes "Ball the Jack," as well as the African performer who did a similar serpentine wriggle at a wedding ceremony in the moving picture, "Sanders of the River." [14] Some day, if I ask enough questions, I may discover the original name of the dance—if it had one. Just why it should have been called by a railroad term I can't figure out, unless its African name had somewhat the same sound.

Susy's head and shoulders are stationary and so are her feet (Illustration 10), but there is a flow of undulating rhythm from chest to heels, with a few rotations in the hip region, done to this rhythmic patter:

> Ole Aunt Dinah
> Sick in bed
> Send for the doctor
> The doctor said
> Get up Dinah
> You ain' sick
> All you need
> Is a hickory stick
> An' I ball the jack on the railroad track.

And so on ad infinitum; the words are of no particular moment, only sounds for carrying the rhythm. A box and a stick would do as well.

"Ball the Jack" was brought to St. Simon's about fifty years ago by an "up-country" Negro, and has been performed ever since—to the accompaniment of shrieks of contagious laughter—by the little Negroes in Jewtown. Two white children and their nurse happened along one day. The children's attention was at once riveted, by the severe words of the nurse, on what was being done: "You stop dat while I have my chillen aroun'."

In later years Martha, who weighed over two hundred pounds, went through the performance for me—although, as a neighbor of hers said, "Martha didn't have the figure for it." You could scarcely call it a dance, and I don't wonder "Aunt Lou" did not want her white children copying the contortions which suggest the neck of a chicken attempting to swallow something too big for comfort.

[14] *"Snake Hip" is a far more appropriate nickname.*

FIDDLE SONGS—FRAGMENTS

Ten years ago, when I hunted up the local fiddler, Green Harris, who was already seventy-six, I tried to find out about the tunes he used to play for the "sinful" young Negroes on St. Simon's. He said: "You caught me without my studyin' cap— they jus' gone." He would not even bring out his fiddle.[15] Finally he admitted he had loaned it: "They're holdin' a revival this week an' I don't want it around the house." The implication was that temptation might be too strong for him—besides, it was improper to have a fiddle in your possession at such a time. After two unsuccessful visits I heard him play old-fashioned dance tunes which had been favorites south of the Mason and Dixon Line in ante-bellum days. Here are the harmless, fragmentary verses he gave me:

> Tune my fiddle, tune it good
> The little neighbor in the neighborhood.

> I do I do I tries to do
>   Put on de silver slippers.
> An' I do I do an' I do no mor'
>   Put on de silver slippers.
> I do I do my huckleberry do
>   Put on de silver slippers.
> My ole Miss' promis' me
>   Put on de silver slippers.
> When she die she set me free
>   Put on de silver slippers.
> She live so long till her head got bal'
>   Put on de silver slippers.
> It look like she never die
>   Put on de silver slippers.
> I do I do I do no mor' my huckleberry do
>   Put on de silver slippers.
> Oh how happy I feel
>   Put on de silver slippers.

[15] *Joel Chandler Harris tells us in* The Critic, *December 15, 1883, that "The banjo may be the typical instrument of the plantation negroes, but I have never seen a plantation negro play it. I have heard them make sweet music with the quills—Pan's pipes; I have heard them play passably on the fiddle, . . . and beat . . . on the triangle . . . I have heard them blow a tin-trumpet with surprising skill; but I have never seen a banjo." Cable, himself, grants that the favorite instrument of the negroes of the Southern states is the fiddle.*

Good-bye my honey I'm gwine.
No use grievin'
Got t' do widout me
Good-bye my honey I'm gwine.
I had a little fella
His name was Isabella
He went run awa' wid anudda nigga fella
So bye-bye my honey I'm gwine.
If you ain't got the money
You can' call me honey
Good-bye my honey I'm gwine.

Goin' to the bathin' house
Goin' to the kitchen
My foot slip an' I fell down
I wouldn' go there no mo'.

Choose in the girl with the rosy cheeks
Choose in the boy with the money
Choose in the girl with the coal-black eye
Choose her an' call her honey.

Bu' alligator, alligator come out tonight
Bu' alligator, alligator come out tonight
Bu' alligator, alligator come out tonight
Te-la lallah bam!
Ent a plenty guinea hen here tonight
Ent a plenty guinea hen here tonight
Ent a plenty guinea hen here tonight
Te-la lallah bam!
Ent a plenty pigeon here tonight
Ent a plenty pigeon here tonight
Ent a plenty pigeon here tonight
Te-la lallah bam!

My oldest aunt heard Virginia ex-slaves sing this verse seventy-five years ago:

Went to see my Sally
My Sally wasn't home
I set myself in the big armchair
And I played on the old jaw-bone.

Old Jim Gardiner rapped the bones to the rhythm of the two similar jingles that follow:

> Once I went out huntin'
> I heard de possum sneeze
> I holler back to Susan
> Put on de pot o' peas.
>
> I went down to Missy house
> Missy was in bed
> I took de marrow bone
> An' beat her in de head.

Chorus: Ding dang me one
        Ding dang.
    Ding dang me two
        Ding dang.
    Ding dang me three
        Ding dang.
    Ding dang me four
        Ding dang.

> Toad frog sittin' on the railroad track
> Train come along an' break his back.

Chorus:

BILE DEM CABBAGE DOWN

A St. Simon's Negro called this a "Cracker Dance" and gave me the following verses:

Bile dem cabbage down
Bile dem cabbage down
Look here gal—don' wan' no foolin'
Bile dem cabbage down.

Went to Susy's house
Susy wasn't home
Look here gal—don' wan' no foolin'
Bile dem cabbage down.

My old Missus promis' me
Bile dem cabbage down
When she die she goin' to set me free
Bile dem cabbage down.

She live so long till her he'd got bal'
Bile dem cabbage down
She gib up de idea o' dyin' at all
Bile dem cabbage down.

WAY DOWN IN THE OLE PEEDEE

Julia sang this when she was a little girl—"long time ago":

Chorus:
Way down in the Ole Peedee
Way down in the Ole Peedee
Summer night the moon shine bright
Sally you can see.

I wish that gal was mine
I wish that gal was mine
Summer night the moon shine bright
Sally you can see.

(repeat chorus)

Good-bye mh honey I'm gone
Good-bye mh honey I'm gone
If you call me honey spen' my money
Good-bye mh honey I'm gone.

22. WAY DOWN IN THE OLE PEEDEE

C.C.

JOHNNY COME A LONG TIME

Run 'long muh Lulu
    Johnny come a long time.
Johnny is your master
    Johnny come a long time.

Johnny is your sweetheart
    Johnny come a long time.
Johnny is your sweetheart
    Johnny come a long time.

Run home muh Lulu
    Johnny come a long time.
Johnny is your master
    Johnny come a long time.

Run 'long muh Lulu
    Johnny come a long time.
Run 'long muh Lulu
    Johnny come a long time.

Johnny is your master
    Johnny come a long time.
Johnny is your master
    Johnny come a long time.

23. JOHNNY COME A LONG TIME

Allegro

Run 'long muh Lu-lu | *John-ny come a long time*

John-ny is your mas-ter | *John-ny come a long time.*

John-ny is your sweet-heart | *John-ny come a long time*

John-ny is your sweet-heart | *John-ny come a long time.*

C.C.

I JING-A-LING

Chorus:

I jing-a-ling—jing-a-ling-a-ling
I jing-a-ling—jing jing jing
I jing-a-ling—jing-a-ling-a-ling
I jing-a-ling—jing-a-la-ling

Who killed my dog—jing-a-ling-a-ling
Who killed my dog—jing-a-ling
I kill your cat—jing-a-ling
I kill your cat—jing-a-la-ling

(repeat chorus)

Whose hat is that—jing-a-ling-a-ling
Whose hat is that—jing-a-ling-a-ling

(repeat chorus)

24. I JING-A-LING

CHAPTER FIVE

Religious Songs

About 1830, before "Daddy" Rice popularized the secular songs of the Negro, the music of the slave was considered to be of no more importance than the carvings of his African contemporaries. It was not until certain Northerners—early in the War Between the States—began to write of the beauties of the religious slave songs of the Port Royal section of South Carolina that Southerners awakened to the fact that the Negro race was essentially musical, and that its compositions could be taken seriously.

Up to this period there was very little written concerning the slaves, and anything more must be gathered inferentially from the migrations of the pioneers, who naturally did not leave their slaves behind them. The first expansion of our Southern frontier took place in the neighborhood of 1632 into the Albemarle section of the Carolinas, and thence southward along the coast to Beaufort, South Carolina. In the first years of the nineteenth century the rich lands of the Indians were opened up in West Georgia and Alabama; and at that time began the trek west over the Federal Road, a movement which accounts for the wide distribution of the favorite slave songs of the eastern seaboard. The migration was all in a westerly direction, and it is not reasonable to imagine that the camp-meeting songs and white spirituals, popular in Kentucky and Tennessee at that period, came east against the tide. In fact, investigation in the Bahamas indicates that the slave songs were well established on the mainland by 1776. The loyalists of the Georgia and Carolina coast fled at the end of the Revolutionary War (1782) to the out islands of the Bahamas, and history tells us that the slaves they took with them trebled the black population. I find that the best of the early religious songs are sung on the out islands today, much as they are here in isolated sections.

Since I am a Quaker and am not familiar with the ritual which characterizes

22. Ring-Shout in the Cabin

other denominaticns, I make no attempt to go into a description of usual church observances. My particular concern has been the preservation of the religious slave songs. Those of the Baptist Negroes—the most conservative sect on the Coast of Georgia—give greater evidence than the others of an African background. Coupled as they are with the most picturesque customs, they have come in for special consideration.

Although certain songs are peculiarly appropriate to such occasions as Easter and Communion, they cannot be rigidly classified according to the services which may have inspired them.[1] They were sung at any time, anywhere. The majority of them appear equally suited to church, prayer, and covenant meeting. However, the ceremonies connected with baptism, "settin'-up" with the dead, and burial mean so much to the Negro that a separate section of this Chapter is devoted to each of them. They appear to be connected with customs prevailing a century ago in the section of Africa from which the slaves were obtained. The significance attached to baptism in a river, or immersion on the outgoing tide, may tie up with the initiation rites connected with the river-worship of Dahomey; and anyone who reads what explorers of the eighteenth and nineteenth centuries have to say about the Africans' concern with death will recognize that our Negroes display the same trait.

CHURCH, PRAYER, AND COVENANT MEETING

Patty Gardner [2] used to open the "South End" prayer meeting, held at Deacon Merchant's house, by singing the following song. As the other members joined in, they shook hands ceremoniously with their neighbors assembled in a circle.[3] The younger generation knew nothing of this custom until I had Old Quarterman come to the Cabin and "show them the way."

[1] *Some may have come into existence while the slaves were at work—others were undoubtedly conceived under stress of religious emotion. In the old days a deacon, at the peak of his rhythmically chanted prayer, broke into song, in which those present joined. After a verse or two, he continued the prayer, ending his plea for mercy by singing with the others some appropriate slave hymn. It is unfortunate that this highly effective method of rousing the congregation should have lapsed in most churches. Now, the impassioned exhortation ends with a sudden drop into an ordinary conversational tone—like a dash of cold water in the face.*

[2] *Patty, while singing a religious song at work, would go into a trance-like state. Clarence told me he remembered seeing her moving rhythmically in a circle around her cabin, a dish towel in one hand and a discarded tin can (highly prized in those days) in the other. She dried the can over and over, totally oblivious of time or surroundings.*

[3] *This procedure is mentioned by Sir Charles Lyell in his Second Visit to the United States.*

At one of our singing festivals, Liverpool, who was well over a hundred at the time, became excited as he heard again the old prayer-meeting song, left his seat, joined in the swaying group of sixty-five singers, and gave a demonstration of the "right hand of fellowship" which he performed with the dignity seen in the minuet. First he gave his right hand to the singer on his right; then, bowing sedately, he crossed his left hand over to the same member. Both hands were then shaken as the singers bowed with the rhythim before passing to the next neighbor and repeating the same ceremony.

> 'Tis well an' good I come here tonight
>   come here tonight
>   come here tonight
> Well an' good I come here tonight
> For to do my Master's will.
> O Brother Quarterman show me the way
>   show me the way
>   show me the way
> O my brother show me the way—
> The way to the Promised Land.

At old-time prayer meetings the following song brought out all of the members —one at a time—on the floor, breaking up any tendency to stiffness. Each rose as his or her name was called and moved around the circle, returning to the group when another member's name was about to be called.

This same song was called an "ant'em" on Eleuthera, (one of the Bahamas). When I asked the singer if it was old, she said: "Methuselum sung 'um."

> Oh mh Jesus bin yer
> O He bin yer
> Jesus bless my soul an' gone.
> Jesus bin yer
> O He bin yer
> Jesus bless my soul an' gone.
> Sister Bessie where were you
> My sister where were you
> My sister where were you
> When the Lord was passin' by.

(Illustration 16)

"Covenant meetin'," now called "Pure Mind Meetin'," was formerly held at the last prayer meeting before Communion Sunday, and was of service in keeping track of the members and making sure, from their own words, that they were "livin' in union." No more meetings of this character have been held at the "South End" of St. Simon's since Betty Brown paid the penalty of false testimony. She got up and told the members: "I'm at peace with everybody." Then, as she was leaving the church, she said: "I'm goin' home t' put Josie [her crippled grandson] out the house." She walked to the step, fell, and never reached home alive.

BELIEVER I KNOW

This song, sung on Sapelo by Katie Brown, while sitting under her tall magnolia tree, reflects the peace of her surroundings. Although she was born about 1850, her voice is remarkably true and sweet. She tells me that the record book of the Spalding Plantation has her age as ten years when the War Between the States began, but she believes she was two years older, for she wore a shift [4] at the time her family left Sapelo and "went to the Main" for refuge on the Stephens Plantation in Bryan County. In December, after the "Big War" was over, they walked to Savannah. There Katie's mother, Cotty Grovenor, petitioned the Freedman's Bureau to let her return to Sapelo. "March was comin' and time to plant." She remembers distinctly how sore and swollen her feet were from walking. Cotty had to soak them in warm water each night.

> I know, I know Lord
>   Believer I know
> I know, I know Lord
>   Believer I know
> I know the road so thorny
>   Believer I know
> I know the road is thorny
>   Believer I know

[4] *The slaves count their age by some such event. Katie seemed to be proud of the fact she was old enough to wear a shift. Shad Hall must be younger, for he still wore a "binyan" (apparently an African word), which was the kind of shirt worn by young boys before they wore pants. With a grin, he told me their first pants had no pockets so that it would be less easy for them to steal eggs.*

It's thorny an' ruggy
 Believer I know
It's thorny an' ruggy
 Believer I know
The way to get to Heaven
 Believer I know
Go in the wil'erness
 Believer I know
Fall on your bending [5]
 Believer I know
Fall on your bending
 Believer I know
Cry Lord have mercy
 Believer I know
Cry Lord have mercy
 Believer I know
The way to get to Heaven
 Believer I know
Love everybody
 Believer I know
Love the Christian pastor [6]
 Believer I know
Love everybody
 Believer I know
The narrow road is Heaven road
 Believer I know
Here an' there a traveller
 Believer I know
The broad road is Hell road
 Believer I know
Thousand walk tògether there
 Believer I know
Glory Hallelujah
 Believer I know
I done cross Jurden
 Believer I know.

[5] *Knees are implied.*
[6] *The white minister.*

25. BELIEVER I KNOW

NORAH, HIST THE WINDAH

Norah, hist the windah
Norah, hist the windah
Norah, hist the windah
Hist the windah let the dove come in.

Oh God comman' Brother Norah one day
Oh hist the windah let the dove come in
An' told Brother Norah to build an ark
Hist the windah let the dove come in.

Chorus:　　Oh Norah, hist the windah
Oh Norah, hist the windah
Oh Norah, hist the windah
Hist the windah let the dove come in.

Well Norah commence to buil' his ark
Oh hist the windah let the dove come in
An' he buil' his ark on the ha'd dry lan'
Oh hist the windah let the dove come in.

(repeat chorus)

An' the foolish man come a ridin' by
Oh hist the windah let the dove come in
Well he point his han' an' he scorn at Norah
Oh hist the windah let the dove come in
An' he call ole Norah the foolish man
Oh hist the windah let the dove come in
You buildin' yo' ark on the ha'd dry lan'
Oh hist the windah let the dove come in.

(repeat chorus)

Well, the little turtle dove done droop his wing
Oh hist the windah let the dove come in
An' he gone on Zion's Hill to sing
Hist the windah let the dove come in.

(repeat chorus)

26. NORAH, HIST THE WINDAH

C.C.

THAT SUITS ME

Chorus: Come on Mauma, le's go roun' the wall
                An' that suits me
       Come on Mauma, le's go roun' the wall
                An' that suits me
       Come on Mauma, le's go roun' the wall
       Don' wanna stumble an' Ah don' wanna fall
                An' that suits me.

Well Isa'h lookt up an' 'e saw the chariot comin'
                An' that suits me
Isa'h lookt up an' 'e saw the chariot comin'
                An' that suits me
Isa'h lookt up an' 'e saw the chariot comin'
Step on the wheel an' the wheel keep a turnin'
                An' that suits me.

       Repeat Chorus:

O three more rounds up Jacob' ladder
                An' that suits me
Three more rounds up Jacob' ladder
                An' that suits me

Three more rounds up Jacob' ladder
Every roun' go higher an' higher
                An' that suits me.

       Repeat Chorus:

27. THAT SUITS ME

Moderately - unchanging tempo

R. Mac Gimsey

Come on ma-ma les go roun nuh wall, An that suits____ me. Come on ma-ma les go roun nuh wall an that suits me Come on ma-ma les go roun nuh wall____ Don wan-na stum-ble an Ah don wan-na fall, An that suits____ me. Well Is.- ah lookt up an e saw the cha-riot com-in', An that suits____ me Is ____ ah lookt up an ē saw the cha-riot com-in', An that suits me Is- ah lookt up an ē saw the char-it com-in' step on the wheel an nuh wheel keep a-turn-in', An that suits____ me.

28. WASN' THAT A WONDER

Chorus: Wasn' that a wonder
in the Heaven
Wasn' that a wonder
in the Heaven
Mighty wonder
in the Heaven
That woman clothe with the sun, moon under her feet.

Read about the wonder
in the Heaven
Read about the wonder
in the Heaven
Mighty wonder
in the Heaven
That woman clothe with the sun, moon under her feet.

John saw the wonder
in the Heaven
John saw the wonder
in the Heaven
It's a mighty wonder
in the Heaven
That woman clothe with the sun, moon under her feet.

Well, John' mother may gone before me
But you can't get no higher in Glory
If you get there befo' I do
Jus' tell my Lord I'm comin' too.

Moderately - no change of tempo   R. Mac Gimsey

Wu - dn nat a won - duh   in nuh

Heab-un   Wu-dn nat a   won-duh   in nuh Heab-un   might-y won-

_ duh   in nuh Heab-un   That wo-man clothe

with the sun   moon un - duh her   feet

I HEARD THE ANGELS SINGIN'

Chorus: One mornin' soon
   One mornin' soon
   One mornin' soon
Ah heard the angels singin'.

  All in my room
  All in my room
  All in my room
Ah heard the angels singin'.

Lawd, Ah wuz down on my knees
   Down on my knees
   Down on my knees
Ah heard the angels singin'.

  No dyin' there
  No dyin' there
  No dyin' there
Ah heard the angels singin'.

Ah heard the angels singin' Lawd
Ah heard the angels singin'
Ah heard the angels singin' Lawd
Ah heard the angels singin'.

Well, there's no weepin' there
   No weepin' there
   No weepin' there
Ah heard the angels singin'.

Lawd, it wuz all 'roun' me shine
   All 'roun' me shine
   All 'roun' me shine
Ah heard the angels singin'.

Lawd, it wuz all over my head
   All over my head
   All over my head
Ah heard the angels singin'.

Lawd, it wuz all aroun' my feet
   All aroun' my feet
   All aroun' my feet
Ah heard the angels singin'.

29.   I HEARD THE ANGELS SINGIN'

CAN'T HIDE SINNER

You may run to the rock
 Can't hide
For a hidin' place
 Can't hide
An' the rock cry out
 Can't hide
You can't hide sinner, you can't hide.

You may run to the sea
 Can't hide
For a hidin' place
 Can't hide
An' the sea cry out
 Can't hide
You can't hide sinner, you can't hide.

Oh sinner man
 Can't hide
What you going to do
 Can't hide
In the Judgment day
 Can't hide
You can't hide sinner, you can't hide.

You may run to the grave
 Can't hide
For a hidin' place
 Can't hide
An' the grave cry out
 Can't hide
You can't hide sinner, you can't hide.

You may run to the Church
 Can't hide
For a hidin' place
 Can't hide
An' the Church cry out
 Can't hide
You can't hide sinner, you can't hide.

You may run to the mount'n
 Can't hide
For a hidin' place
 Can't hide
An' the mount'n cry out
 Can't hide
You can't hide sinner, you can't hide.

30. CAN'T HIDE SINNER

C.C.

24. Margaret, on the Left, Demonstrates the Correct Position of Arms and Feet in Shouting

25. *The Younger Generation Doing the Ring-Shout at the Cabin*

JOHN, JOHN

The temptation is strong to tell the clever sayings of Quarterman, but the songs he sang, and not what he said, must take precedence. However, one incident which has a bearing on history must be mentioned. Quarterman's mother was a Butler slave, like Liverpool, but before Quarterman was born she was taken by Roswell King in exchange for services as manager of the Butler estate, and placed on his Liberty County plantation.

The last time that Liverpool and Quarterman were together at my Corner for a "sing," Liverpool made use of the opportunity to deliver his customary eulogy of Pierce Butler and his family. I saw that Quarterman was uneasy and fidgety. The minute that Liverpool showed signs of stopping, Quarterman was on his feet and told the audience what a superior "Maussa" he had had. Shades of Fanny Kemble and all departed abolitionists! The irony of the situation is apparent to those who have read what Fanny Kemble said in her *Journal* about Quarterman's master, "Mr. K." I saw the meeting of "Mr. K.'s" two grandchildren, Miss Julia King and her brother Audley, with Quarterman, and the delight of all three was extremely significant. We read a good deal these days about the way the Negroes "hate" the white people. But let me say that such was not the universal rule in the old days under the patriarchal form of society.[7] The type of education given today, instead of closing the breach between the races, appears to be widening it. I have found only one ex-slave who shows bitterness, and that is toward a distracted mistress who, during war-time, exacted two tasks when one had been the usual requirement.

Quarterman sang many pretty hymns, but in the next breath he sang slave songs that came "out of Maffew. You fine 'em right dere." When I tried to explain that the words did not make the tune, he was puzzled. According to him all you had to do was to go to the Bible and there was your song. There is more to the idea than appears on the surface. You heard a verse read and at once its rhythm fitted something that was sung in Africa. Perhaps this is why the Negroes call the old songs "familiar tunes."

[7] *It is evident from the story of "The Old-Time Negro," by Thomas Nelson Page, that "the relation which once existed all over the South between the old-time Southerner and the old-time darkey . . . still exists where the latter survives."*

Chorus: John, John you will see John
                        Aye John
         John, John you will see John
                        Aye John.

Fiah in nuh Eas' and fiah in nuh Wes'
                        Aye John
Fiah goinah burn out tuh wilduhness
                        Aye John.

                (repeat chorus)

Gawd in nuh wil-d'ness jes begin tuh look out
                        Aye John
Yes, duh ram hohn blow an' nuh childun shout
                        Aye John.

                (repeat chorus)

When Quarterman (Illustration 28) finished singing these verses into my re-
cording machine, he said: "You can't take dat!" And when I played it back to him,
he exclaimed: "O My Missus—de debbil!"

Katherine sings the following verses to the same tune:

        Talk about John but you will see John
                        Aye John
        Talk about John but you will see John
                        Aye John.
        When I get to Heaven goin' to walk all aroun'
                        Aye John
        Angel in the Heaven can't order me down
                        Aye John.

                (repeat chorus)

        When I get to Heaven goin' to sit an' tell
                        Aye John
        Goin' to a'gue with the Father an' chatter with the Son
                        Aye John.

                (repeat chorus)

31. JOHN, JOHN

Moderately fast - steady tempo

R. Mac Gimsey

Chos. mf

John, John you will see John___ Aye___

John. John, John you will see John Aye___

John. Fi - ah in nuh Eas' An Fi - ah in nuh Wes'

Aye___ John Fi - ah gon - na burn out tuh

Repeat Chos. then sing next verse

wil - duh - ness Aye___ John.

Gawd in nuh wil- 'ness jes be - gin tuh look out

Aye___ John Yes duh ram hohn blow an nuh

chil- dun shout Aye___ John.

WHEN I RISE CRYIN' HOLY

Oh my Lord, this is a needed time
Oh my Lord, this is a needed time
Oh my Lord, this is a needed time
In that mornin' when I rise cryin' Holy.

I'm so glad I got my religion in time
I'm so glad I got my religion in time
I'm so glad I got my religion in time
In that mornin' when I rise cryin' Holy.

O Jesus, you promise to answer prayer
O Jesus, you promise to answer prayer
O Jesus, you promise to answer prayer
In that mornin' when I rise cryin' Holy.

Ah'm so glad I got my ticket in my hand
Ah'm so glad I got my ticket in my hand
Ah'm so glad I got my ticket in my hand
In that mornin' when I rise cryin' Holy.

O poo' sinner won't you git down ona y'r knees
O poo' sinner won't you git down ona y'r knees
O poo' sinner won't you git down ona y'r knees
In that mornin' when I rise cryin' Holy.

Julia Armstrong gives me this version of the same song. It was sung during thunder-storms, which were believed to express God's anger:

Oh sister, yo'r robe don't fit you like mine
Oh sister, yo'r robe don't fit you like mine
Oh sister, yo'r robe don't fit you like mine
In that mornin' when I rise cryin' Holy.

Oh Gabriel, blow yo'r trumpet loud
Oh Gabriel, blow yo'r trumpet loud
Oh Gabriel, blow yo'r trumpet loud
In that mornin' when I rise cryin' Holy.

Oh Jesus, don't come that angry way
Oh Jesus, don't come that angry way
Oh Jesus, don't come that angry way
In that mornin' when I rise cryin' Holy.

I'm so glad I got my re-li-gion in time I'm so glad I got my re-li-gion in time I'm so glad I got my re-li-gion in time In that morn-ing when I rise cry-in' Ho-ly

C.C.

33. NO HIDIN' PLACE

Chorus: No hidin' place
No hidin' place
Almos' t' the Judgment Bah
No hidin' place.

'Cause Ah don't know what my sister wan'nuh stay here for

Repeat Chorus:

Ah'm goin' t' run t' the rock for a hidin' place

Repeat Chorus:

Fox got a hole in the groun'
Bird got a nest in the air
There's nare one thing got a hidin' place
But these sinners got none.

Repeat Chorus:

LIVIN' HUMBLE

"Gettin' religion" is a soul-stirring matter with the Negro. When he feels the serious need of salvation he responds to the appeal of the minister to come forward to the "Mou'ners' Bench"—also called the "Anxious" or "Mercy Seat." There, at the bench directly in front of the pulpit, he kneels while the congregation sings an appropriate song. In the old days he wandered at night until he managed to "come through." Many lines in the oldest songs refer to customs that are now practically obsolete. I cannot imagine a young Negro today wandering alone at night until his "head got wet by the mid'l-night dew."

Oh po' moanuh won't chew jus' believe
  Livin' 'umble, livin' 'umble
Oh po' moanuh won't chew jus' believe
  Livin' 'umble, livin' 'umble
Oh po' moanuh won't chew jus' believe
Christ is a waitin' to receive
  Livin' 'umble, livin' 'umble
King Jesus camp in nuh middle uv the air
  Livin' 'umble, livin' 'umble
King Jesus camp in nuh middle uv the air
  Livin' 'umble, livin' 'umble
King Jesus camp in nuh middle uv the air
None but tuh righteous shall git thah
  Livin' 'umble, livin' 'umble
O my head got wet by the mid'l-night dew
  Livin' 'umble, livin' 'umble
My head got wet by the mid'l-night dew
  Livin' 'umble, livin' 'umble
My head got wet by the mid'l-night dew
I pray to my God until I come through
  Livin' 'umble, livin' 'umble
Leave my burden at the foot of the hill
  Livin' 'umble, livin' 'umble
Leave my burden at the foot of the hill
Ever since I been converted
  I been tryin' to live 'umble.

34. LIVIN' HUMBLE

SWING LOW SWEET CHARIOT

From the reference to "Mornin' star was a witness too" and "I heard a voice an' I saw no one," followed by "It mus' be Jesus passin' by," it is apparent that this unusual version of "Swing Low" was another of the songs appropriate to the "comin' through" of "sinners," who had agonized at night in order to achieve the proper exaltation.

Oh swing low—Oh swing low
Oh swing low sweet chariot swing low
Oh swing low—Oh swing low
Oh swing low sweet chariot swing low
It mus' be Jesus passin' by
Oh swing low sweet chariot swing low
Swing low in the Eas'
    swing low
Swing low in the Eas'
    swing low
Swing low chariot
    swing low
Swing low chariot swing low
I heard a voice an' I saw no one
Oh swing low sweet chariot swing low
Swing low in the Wes'
    swing low
Swing low in the Wes'
    swing low
Swing low chariot
    swing low
Swing low chariot swing low
Mornin' star was a witness too
Oh swing low sweet chariot swing low.

35. SWING LOW SWEET CHARIOT

Briskly - with no variation in tempo

R. Mac Gimsey

Oh___ swing low, ___ Oh swing low, _____ Oh

swing low sweet Char-i-ot___ Swing low.

It mus' be Je - sus Pass-in' by___ Oh

swing low sweet Char-i-ot___ Swing low. Swing low in nuh

Eas' swing low swing low in nuh Eas' swing low, swing low char-

-i-ot swing low,___ swing low___ char-i-ot swing low.

WHEN MY LORD CALLS ME I MUST GO

The last time Lady Butler saw Liverpool she told him that he must be here when next she came to America. His reply was: "When my Lord calls me I must go." On one of her yearly visits to Darien, she gave him a rose to wear in his button-hole, and called him "the last flower of the Butler flock." When she saw him again, she found that the rose had miraculously become a perennial from the five and ten cent store. To the paper rose he attached the tribute she had paid him!

Liverpool was loyalty itself to the family of his master, and the same can be said of Dan Wing, who went to England with his mistress, Frances Butler Leigh,[8] when she married the Dean of Hereford Cathedral. Dan and Liverpool, both mentioned in Mrs. Leigh's *Ten Years on a Georgia Plantation* (1866–1876), were keenly interested in what she had said about them. When I asked Liverpool about his display of insubordination, of which she tells, he said—with a chuckle—that his head had been cut by Mr. N., the overseer, because of "back-talk." However, Mrs. Leigh apparently pardoned his outbreak, for he proudly showed me the photograph of herself which she had given him.

No one, least of all the descendants of the slave-owners, could wish for a return of the institution, but a system that could produce such fine characters as the Caters' Dembo, the Kings' Neptun', his son Clarence,[9] the Butlers' Dan and Liverpool, and "Miss Sis" Clifton's Mary Covington—born soon after freedom—and many other Negroes I could name, must have had its redeeming features. I know it will be said the system had little to do with their development, that it was the individual. Maybe so, but after reading everything I can find concerning our ante-bellum Negroes I wonder why there are not more who are outstanding characters today. Per-

[8] *The daughter of Fanny Kemble and the mother of Alice, who became Lady Butler.*

[9] *Clarence's death, a couple of years ago, was a great loss to our community. He was a good man and an excellent singer.*

haps it is true that certain plantation owners were of a superior type and provided a superior example; or was it that the education received by the slaves was better suited to their needs?

I'm goin' to cross that ocean by mysel'
                                                   by mysel'
I'm goin' to cross that ocean by mysel'
                                                   by mysel'
     When my Lord call me I must go

I'm goin' to cross that ocean by mysel'.

     In that lonesome valley by mysel'
                                                   by mysel'
     In that lonesome valley by mysel'
                                                   by mysel'
I'm goin' to weep like a willo' moan like a dove

I'm goin' to cross that ocean by mysel'.

     Weepin' Mary weep no mor'
                                        weep no mor'
     Weepin' Mary weep no mor'
                                        weep no mor'
     When my Lord call me I must go

I'm goin' to cross that ocean by mysel'.

     Doubtful Thomas don't y'u doubt no mor'
                                                        doubt no mor'
     Doubtful Thomas don't y'u doubt no mor'
                                                        doubt no mor'
     When my Lord calls me I must go

I'm goin' to cross that ocean by mysel'.

ZION

Most Negro weddings, in church or out, are conducted, I am told, without music; but when Ben Davis was married, this song was used with telling effect in the Frederica African Baptist Church. Two ushers walked from the altar with lighted lamps in their hands, and met the bridal party at the door. Two little girls headed the procession and strewed flowers in its path. Ben, with the maid of honor, was followed by the bride on the arm of the best man. To the music of "O Zion— when the bridegroom comes," sung by the guests who filled the church, the participants moved to the altar, where the ushers put down their lamps, and Joe Lowman, the preacher, was waiting for them. When Lowman asked Ben: "Will you take this woman to be your wedded wife?" Ben spoke up "good and strong": "Yes suh!" When the same question was asked of Norah, her answer was very weak. This did not satisfy the parson: "Answer as though you mean it. This ain't for today and tomorrow, this is a lifetime business!" Everybody laughed. Lowman, after the usual procedure, offered a prayer and ended the ceremony by telling Ben to "salute the bride."

Besides being used in church and at praise meeting, I find "Zion" was one of the favorite rowing songs of the Butler oarsmen. Tall, lean Liverpool, who looks like an Arab sheik, showed us how he rowed to its rhythm:

Don't you be like the foolish virgin
　　When the bridegroom come
Don't you be like the foolish virgin
　　When the bridegroom come.

Chorus:　　O Zion
　　　　　　　(Zion)
　　　　　　O Zion
　　　　　　　(Zion)
　　　　　　O Zion
　　When the bridegroom come.

Have oil in your vessel
　　When the bridegroom come
Have oil in your vessel
　　When the bridegroom come.

(repeat chorus)

Keep your lamp trimmed and burnin'
    When the bridegroom come
Keep your lamp trimmed and burnin'
    When the bridegroom come.

(repeat chorus)

Five were wise an' five were foolish
    When the bridegroom come
Five were wise an' five were foolish
    When the bridegroom come.

(repeat chorus)

What did the foolish say to the wise
    When the bridegroom come
What did the foolish say to the wise
    When the bridegroom come.

(repeat chorus)

Lend us some of your oil
    When the bridegroom come
Lend us some of your oil
    When the bridegroom come.

(repeat chorus)

We will enter into the marriage
    When the bridegroom come
We will enter into the marriage
    When the bridegroom come.

(repeat chorus)

We will all go out to meet them
    When the bridegroom come
We will all go out to meet them
    When the bridegroom come.

(repeat chorus)

36. ZION

Andante

Don't you be like the fool-ish vir-gin when the bride-groom come, Don't be like the fool-ish vir-gin when the bride - groom come

Oh Zion, Zion Oh Zion, Zion

Oh Zion when the bride - groom come.

C.C.

26. Julia—Who Does the Buzzard Lope

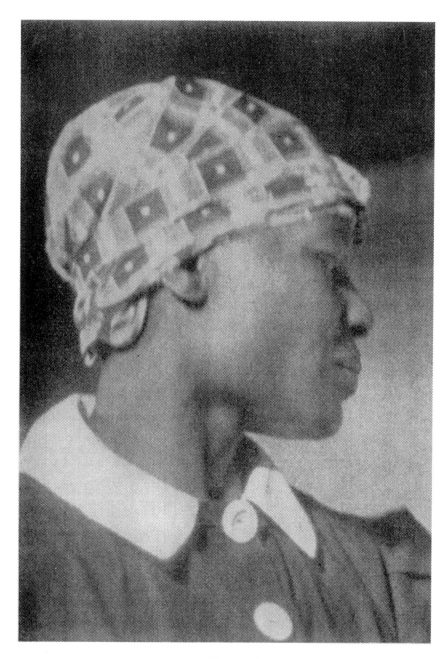

27. Gertrude

MY GOD IS A ROCK IN A WEARY LAND

This song belongs to the exhorting-sermon type which has an African counterpart. The old-time preacher rhythmically chanted his sermon; at effective intervals he broke into song, in which he was joined by the congregation.

> Chorus: My God is a rock in a weary land
> weary land
> in a weary land
> My God is a rock in a weary land
> Shelter in a time of storm.

> Ah know He is a rock in a weary land
> weary land
> in a weary land
> Ah know He is a rock in a weary land
> Shelter in a time of storm.

Stop let me tell you 'bout the Chapter One
When the Lord God's work has jus' begun
Stop and let me tell you 'bout the Chapter Two
When the Lord God's written his Bible through
Stop and let me tell you 'bout the Chapter Three
When the Lord God died on Calvary.

> Chorus: An' Ah know He is a rock in a weary land
> weary land
> in a weary land
> Ah know He is a rock in a weary land
> Shelter in a time of storm.

Stop and let me tell you 'bout the Chapter Four
Lord God visit 'mong the po'
Stop and let me tell you 'bout the Chapter Five
Lord God brought the dead alive
Stop and let me tell you 'bout the Chapter Six
He went in Jerusalem and healed the sick.

(repeat chorus)

Stop and let me tell you 'bout Chapter Seven
Died and risen and went to Heaven
Stop and let me tell you 'bout the Chapter Eight
John seen Him standin' at the Golden Gate
Stop and let me tell you 'bout the Chapter Nine
Lord God turned the water to wine
Stop and let me tell you 'bout the Chapter Ten
John says He's comin' in the world again.

(repeat chorus)

37. MY GOD IS A ROCK IN A WEARY LAND

THE BELL DONE RING

In a collection of *African Music* recorded by Laura C. Boulton a war song [10] is given from the Tuareg tribe of the French Sudan, near Timbuctoo, which is strikingly similar to a sermon song of Henry Shaw's, even to the peculiar reedy quality of tone.[11] The Tuareg singer recites the brave deeds of a chief; Henry recounts the adventures of Jonah.

It has been practically impossible to take down Henry's song as he sings it. When he recites it, he gives an entirely different version. If I ask the meaning of a line, he has to begin all over again—and we never get very far.

Chorus: Live humble, humble, humble your soul
              The bell done ring.
        Live humble little chil'run
              The bell done ring.
        Live humble little soul
              The bell done ring.
        Live humble I say
              The bell done ring.

"Live humble" is sung three more times with the response, "The bell done ring," following each line, and the chorus ends with its first four lines. The gist of the narrative section follows the story of Jonah's tribulations quite literally.

[10] *Vol. I, record 86-A.*

[11] *Our coastal Negroes appear to be musically more closely allied to the Tuaregs than to any other African tribe of whose songs I have been able to secure records. Record 86-B of the same series gives a lullaby sung by a Tuareg woman which—except for the difference in language—might be sung by a grandmother anywhere along this coast. If we knew the period in which certain groups of slaves came to America, and the section of Africa from which they were obtained, we might learn more about their musical background. Two records made by the Denis-Roosevelt expedition in the Belgian Congo indicate that the slaves of South Carolina and Georgia might have come from that region, since their ring-shouts show a similarity to Nos. 6 and 10 in tone, rhythm, and hand clapping. The "sharp exhalation of breath" heard in No. 10 is also demonstrated by some of our ex-slaves, but they do no "stomping," although on two or three occasions I have seen Negroes from the interior do it.*

Lord called Jonah t' Nineveh Lan'
To preach the gospel in de terrible d'man'
Jonah risen an' 'e went on down de Joppa two years started over
      yonda to Tarsha two years to wait 'pon God's comman'
Got on the ship went down to de lowermos' deck
The cap'n of de ship started to sail
Got in de midst o' de middle o' de deep
The cap'n of de ship got de trouble in min'
Search the ship from bow t' stern
The' foun' ole Jonah fast asleep
Wake up . . .

The last two lines, which ended with "tell you now," I could not get. These were followed by the chorus. Further vicissitudes of Jonah were related in two more long verses.

AN' HE NEVER SAID A MUMBLIN' WORD

Last Easter I attended service, by special request, at a makeshift Baptist "tabernacle" far from the highway, in the pine wilderness of Camden County. There was a roof over a part of the one-story shack, but it lacked sides except behind the pulpit. The benches were planks on blocks of wood, and pine slabs were put on the swampy ground to keep our feet dry. In his sermon the minister pointedly stressed the fact that spiritual comfort was infinitely to be preferred over that of the flesh. His earnestness and conviction in describing Christ's appearance before Pilate, and the fortitude with which He bore His sufferings, made the scene too vivid for Phyllis, who became excited, jumped from her seat, and shrieked: "He didn't do nothin'! No He didn't! He was an innocent man! Yes He was!" She was in truth a modern witness for my Lord.

    See how they done my Lord
              done my Lord
              done my Lord
    See how they done my Lord
    An' He never said a mumblin' word.

See how they done my Lord
An' He never said a mumblin' word
    Not a word
    Not a word
    Not a word.
They judged Him all night long
    all night long
    all night long
They judged Him all night long
An' He never said a mumblin' word.
They judged Him all night long
An' He never said a mumblin' word
    Not a word
    Not a word
    Not a word.

The following is a description of what was done to Him: "They led Him from hall to hall. . . . They whipped Him all night long. . . . They nailed Him to the cross." The scene is brought closer with: "Don't y'u hear how the hammer ring?" and the song ends with a verse made out of the phrase: "Wasn't that an awful shame!"

MAY BE THE LAS' TIME I DON'T KNOW

This dirge-like tune is one of the favorites at communion service:

Chorus: I don't know I don't know I don't know
    May be the las' time I don't know.

May be the las' time we eat together
  May be the las' time I don't know
May be the las' time we drink together
  May be the las' time I don't know.

(repeat chorus)

May be the las' time we shout together
  May be the las' time I don't know
May be the las' time we pray together
  May be the las' time I don't know.

(repeat chorus)

Eatin' of the bread an' drinkin' of the wine
  May be the las' time I don't know
It may be the las' time we moan together
  May be the las' time I don't know
I don't know I don't know may be the las' time I don't know
It may be the las' time I don't know.

ONE-A THESE DAYS

This was a favorite song for the close of prayer meeting:

One-a these days
My Sister, one-a these days
My Sister, one-a these days
  When the Lord call me home.

Chorus: Soon shall be done with the crosses
        Soon shall be done with the trouble of the worl'
        Soon shall be done with the crosses
          When the Lord call me home.

Sister Julia, one-a these days
My Sister, one-a these days
My Sister, one-a these days
  When the Lord call me home.

Other "sisters" and "brothers" present are named in lengthening the song.

BAPTISM

On a frosty Sunday morning many years ago, I happened to be on the bank of the Frederica River south of the Fort. From a distance I heard the Negroes singing what sounded like a dirge, but as they came closer I found it was a baptismal song, sung by the procession which had formed, as is customary, at the church a mile away.[12] It was headed by the minister, followed by his assistants, the deacons and other members in pairs, while the "candidates" brought up the rear. The girls were dressed in white, but the boys wore ordinary overalls and work shirts. The solemn dignity of the occasion was impressive. Joe Lowman, one of the assisting preachers, with great earnestness addressed the congregation. He exhorted those of his hearers who had not been baptized to take no chances. In an intimate conversational tone he gave his views on the subject. He wanted it clearly understood that he was not prepared to say, "nobody was going to be saved who had only had his head sprinkled"—but he, for one, was not for disobeying instructions. The Lord ordered us to go down into the water, and that was all there was about it. It was like sending a boy to the store for potatoes; if he brought home turnips it would not be the same thing at all.

After the discourse and the usual prayers,[13] which were punctuated in the African manner with encouraging responses, rhythmically delivered, the officiating minister went down into the river to the spot selected by the deacon, who, with his staff to show the depth, had preceded him. While those on the river bank sang

[12] *Before leaving the church the minister calls his congregation to order, and gives them some last-minute instructions. One cautioned his flock to conduct themselves on the way to the water in an orderly manner befitting the solemnity of the occasion. He said: "Now, I don't want any talkin' or laughin'.—Don' y'u begin to tell about your bean patch an' your peas. This ain' no time for it."*

[13] *In a recent book the assertion is made that our Negroes "pray to the river" when they are baptized. This sounds like an African survival until it is learned that "to" means "beside" in this instance. It is no wonder that those who are unfamiliar with our Negroes and their use of words make curious mistakes.*

"Wade in the Water," the candidates, each escorted by a church member, followed to the water's edge. There the girls' skirts were tied above their knees to prevent undignified billowing, and the assisting deacon led each candidate to the spot where the minister stood in about two-and-a-half feet of water.

The Negroes probably follow the usual procedure of white Baptists; however, I find that no two preachers use precisely the same words, though the substance is always the same: "In obedience to the commands of our Lord Jesus Christ I baptize thee"—and at this point the immersion takes place—"in the name of the Father, the Son, and the Holy Ghost, Amen"—and up comes the sputtering, shivering candidate. When the procession returns to the church, the ones who have just been baptized line up and receive the "right hand of fellowship" from the minister and the church members—and not until then may they consider themselves as safely within the fold.

Although the water was bitterly cold that February morning, the young people behaved very well, and only one squealed a little—which was considered very bad form. If you do not come up like a lamb it is "suspicioned" that your conversion has not been authentic, and the baptism may need to be performed again.

In the old days, when the Negroes were closer to Africa, baptisms in the tidewater section took place punctiliously, no matter how inconvenient the hour, on the outgoing tide.[14] In the interior, of course, where rivers and streams can be depended upon to carry the candidate's sins away from him, a baptism can be safely set for any appointed hour. Now, cement tanks are built in the yards of conventional churches, and another picturesque custom will soon be a thing of the past. Many a time have I gone to the South End or to Frederica, before sunrise, in the hope of learning something new. Something new was not always forthcoming, but the picture in the low morning light was worth going miles to see.

[14] *The stress laid by Negro Baptists upon baptism being performed on the outgoing tide lends support to the theory, held by Melville Herskovits, that the strong adherence to the ritual of baptism among Negro Christians is related to "the great importance of the river-cult in Africa, particularly in view of the fact that, as has often been observed, river-cult priests were sold into slavery in great numbers."* (Handbook of Social Psychology.)

WADE IN NUH WATUH CHILDUN

Chorus: Wade in nuh watuh childun
Wade in nuh watuh childun
Wade in nuh watuh
Gawd's go'nah trouble duh watuh.

If a you don' believe Ah been redeem'
Gawd's go'nah trouble duh watuh
Follow me down to Jurdun stream
Gawd's go'nah trouble duh watuh.

Repeat Chorus:

Who dat yonduh drest in white
Gawd's go'nah trouble duh watuh
Mus' be the childun uv the Isralite
Gawd's go'nah trouble duh watuh.

Repeat Chorus:

38. WADE IN NUH WATUH CHILDUN

SABBATH HAS NO END

In the River uv Jurdun
     I believe
In the River uv Jurdun
     I believe
In the River uv Jurdun
     I believe
  Sabbath has no end.
I went down to the River uv Jurdun
Water caught me to my throat
Jesus Christ was the Captain
An' the Holy Ghos' was my boat.
  I'm goin' cross Jurd'n
     I believe
  I'm goin' cross Jurdun
     I believe
  I'm goin' cross Jurdun
     I believe
  Sabbath has no end.
I went down to the River uv Jurdun
Where John baptize three
Up step ole big man Satan say
  John baptize me.
Look in the Book of Redemption
  There you shall fine
Where Jesus Christ was the doctor
  Turned the water to wine.
  Wasn't that a doctor
     I believe
  Wasn't that a doctor
     I believe
  Wasn't that a doctor
     I believe
  Sabbath has no end.

39. SABBATH HAS NO END

R. Mac Gimsey

"SETTIN'-UP"

The custom of "settin'-up" with the dead still prevails among the Negroes, who even go so far as to ask for such a privilege on the death of a white employer to whom they are devoted. Mrs. Shadman told me that when her grandmother, Margaret Cater, died at Kelvin Grove, her family's ex-slaves came all day "to see the face." At dusk they appeared again and sat up with "Ole Miss" through the night, singing, moaning, and praying until sun-up. When Mrs. Shadman died this year, two young colored men whom she had befriended since childhood continued the custom and sat up with the body.

In some districts a "settin'-up," or "wake," as such a ceremony is now called, is more emotional than in others, and certain families are known to be extremely excitable on such occasions. A man who works for me now and then said he did not like to go to a "settin'-up" because "they holler so much." [15] A wake held at the home of the deceased is likely to be a quieter affair than one held in a church, where the mourners are apt to display a frenzy of grief. When the body is taken from the church, the "hollerin'" begins in earnest. I have always wondered if the stimulation of an audience had anything to do with the difference.

At a private "settin'-up" a big fire of logs in front of the cabin lasts through the night, and rude benches, made of boards laid on sections of a tree trunk, are placed around it. Quantities of coffee in a pot beside the fire, and a large carton of soda crackers help revive the tired mourners and keep them awake.

The Negroes often have a premonition of death. On St. Simon's, Deacon Henry Armstrong, who had been ailing for some months, realized his time was short, and sent for his family and friends. When they arrived he was eating his supper of fish, grits, and coffee. Later, when he stood up, moved about, and began preaching his own funeral sermon, as was sometimes done, his hearers wondered if he was "touched in the head." He called upon one deacon to sing "Old-Time Religion" and then upon another for a prayer. When a member of the group came forward to pray, Henry told him not to proceed, that he was not worthy. A "sister" came to shake his hand and say good-bye; he told her she must go to her father and mother, and beg their pardon for the wrong she had done them. She did as

[15] *Such behavior is in line with established African tradition. In Astley's Collection of Voyages and Travels it is stated that "the cry . . . is sometimes a fortnight or month after the decease. . . . They begin with crying and at night they go to singing and dancing, and so continue till they break-up."*

she was told and Henry said: "Now that is over." That night he died in his sleep.

However, not all premonitions materialize. I was told of an instance on Edisto Island, where a young girl was stricken and believed her last hour had come. Relations were summoned, and the usual rites were conducted. At the last moment, however, when she was expected to make a proper exit, she was overcome with a desire to eat. She clamored for food, and the watchers went home in disgust.

In the old days it was the custom to send messages by the dying to those who had gone before.[16] A friend told me how an ex-slave came to her house just before her father's funeral, and said he wanted to talk to "Marse Jim." She explained to the old man that her father had just died. He said: "I know it. I want to talk to him." Of course he was given permission. How one wishes the conversation could have been overheard!

On the out islands of the Bahamas, the custom of "settin'-up" with the dying is an event enjoyed by the one who is bound for the other world quite as much as by those who come for a last visit. The procedure is practically the same as on the mainland, as is to be expected, since the custom was carried from the States at the end of the Revolution by slaves of the loyalists from South Carolina and Georgia. An acquaintance who spent a winter on one of the Berry Islands gave an account of a "settin'-up" with which she was concerned. A neighboring colored woman, who was very old, decided it was time for her to die, and begged for a certain white dress in which to lie in state. She set the date of her death, and invited her friends from the adjoining islands to be with her on the momentous occasion. She looked very handsome, I was told, and all went well—but twenty-four hours passed, and she did not die. Another day went by, and she still clung to life. When nothing happened on the third day, the guests were obliged to return to their respective homes. In a couple of weeks, however, she sent for them again. This time luck was with her, and she departed according to schedule.

IN THAT OLD FIELD

Susyanna (Illustration 29) learned this lonesome melody from her grandmother, who was a slave. Sung in a minor key, it is one to which the printed word and note can never do justice. It must be heard to be appreciated. "That old field" is the Negro name for a burying ground, and the slave, like his cousins in Africa, was quite as much concerned with the life to come as with that of the moment.

[16] *As exemplified in the song: "Ride on, Conquering King," p. 183.*

Geoffrey Gorer tells us, in *Africa Dances*, that the primitive Negroes "know that the world is entirely spiritual," and "if we are sane" in believing that the physical universe, whether animate or inanimate, is bound by certain laws, which produce certain predictable effects, then "they are just mad. . . . This madness is not always apparent, for superficially Negroes seem to go about the ordinary business of life in a fairly normal way." It is only when you try to persuade them that they are not logical, that you find you cannot influence the most important side of their lives.

In this country the abolitionists seized upon this trait, and made much of it in their writings about the slaves' religious songs. The favorite theme of these writers was that in thinking of the world to come, and singing about it, the slaves found release from the misery of their lot here below—which has always seemed to me like a lot of sentimental nonsense. Their forebears were deeply religious people, and, as Gorer states, "religion is for us a thing apart [like our music]; for the African Negroes their whole existence." Explorers in Africa have told us, times without number, that music is as much a part of the life of the native as breathing—just as it was with our slaves in ante-bellum days. I can imagine Old Elizabeth singing this song until she went into a trance-like state. Gorer mentions that "Negroes can put themselves into very peculiar physical-mental states with extraordinary ease. They will go into trances, or throw fits at the slightest provocation. Even a Negro beating a tom-tom quickly becomes very strange; his pupils dilate and do not focus, he seems to become a rhythmic and unconscious automaton." From first-hand experience, I know that this characteristic survives to a surprising degree among our rural Negroes of the Georgia Coast.

> Throw me any way
> > In dhat ole fiel'
> Throw me any way
> > In dhat ole fiel'.
> I don' care whah you throw me
> > In dhat ole fiel'
> I don' care whah you throw me
> > In dhat ole fiel'.
> Throw me ova hills an' mountains
> > In dhat ole fiel'
> Throw me ova hills an' mountains
> > In dhat ole fiel'.
> Sometimes I'm up sometimes I'm down
> > In dhat ole fiel'
> But still my soul is heaven boun'
> > In dhat ole fiel'.
> Throw my mother out a doo's
> > In dhat ole fiel'
> Throw my mother out a doo's
> > In dhat ole fiel'.

28. *Quarterman*

29. *Susyanna*

40. IN THAT OLD FIELD

Slowly - steady tempo

R. Mac Gimsey

Throw me an-y way In nat ole fiel'

Throw me an-y way In nat ole fiel' All—

—a-roun' nuh val-ley In— nat ole fiel' All—

—a-roun' nuh val-ley In nat ole fiel' Ah

did-n't go to tar-ry In nat ole fiel'. Throw—

—me an-y way In nat ole fiel' Throw

—me out uh dohs In nat ole fiel' Throw

—me out uh dohs In nat ole fiel'.

etc.

JESUS GON TUH MAKE UP MY DYIN' BED

Although this song was brought to St. Simon's after the War Between the States, I am told by an old resident of McIntosh County that it originated in ante-bellum days when there were no colored undertakers, and a certain Negro was appointed on each plantation to make the dead ready for burial.

Chorus: He's a dyin' bed-maker
            Well, well
    He's a dyin' bed-maker
            Well, well, well
    He's a dyin' bed-maker
            Well, well
    Jesus gon tuh make up my dyin' bed.
    Well, in my dyin' room Ah know
    Somebody's gon tuh cry
    All Ah want you to do fuh me
    Jus' to close my dyin' eye.

        (repeat chorus)

In my dyin' room Ah know
Somebody's goin' to weep
All Ah want you to do fuh me
Jus' to fol' my dyin' sheet.

        (repeat chorus)

In my dyin' room Ah know
Somebody's goin' to moan
All Ah want you to do fuh me
Jus' to hear my dyin' groan.

        (repeat chorus)

41. JESUS GON TUH MAKE UP MY DYIN' BED

Moderately fast - steady tempo

R. Mac Gimsey

He's a dy - in' bed mak - er, ___ Well, well, He's a

dy - in' bed mak - er, ___ Well, ___ well, well, ___ He's a

dy - in' bed mak - er ___ Well, well ___

Je - sus gon tuh make up mah dy - in' bed. ___

Verse

Well in mah dy - in' room Ah know Some -

bo - dy's gon ___ tah ___ cry All ___ Ah want them to

do fuh me Jus' to close mah dy - in' eye. ___

___ He's a dy - in' bed mak - er, ___

O DE ROBE

The Irish ditch-diggers, employed in repairing the banks enclosing the rice fields of Glynn County, probably account for the Celtic lilt in this tune.[17] The Negroes have always been great borrowers, musically speaking, but, to my mind, that matters little when they make the material so completely their own that the result is entirely different, and often an improvement on the original. This was clearly the case with the ante-bellum melodies of the white plantation owners. A race which could turn dreary book hymns into living creations deserves great applause, and the less said about the source of its inspiration the better—unless from a desire to call attention to its superior musical gift.

Chorus: O de robe de robe my Lord
              De robe all ready now
        O de robe de robe my Lord
              De robe all ready now.

        My mother gone an' she lef' me heah
              De robe all ready now
        My mother gone an' she lef' me heah
              De robe all ready now.

              (repeat chorus)

        Christian trials just begun
              De robe all ready now
        Christian trials just begun
              De robe all ready now.

              (repeat chorus)

        Ferry boat goin' to carry us over
              De robe all ready now
        Ferry boat goin' to carry us over
              De robe all ready now.

              (repeat chorus)

Joe contributes additional verses:

        You get in trouble
              De robe all ready now
        Write to my Jesus
              De robe all ready now.

        Write to my Jesus t' sen' another angel
              De robe all ready now
        Send another angel t' trouble the water
              De robe all ready now.

[17] *In 1838–39 it was found that the work of digging the canal connecting Brunswick with the Altamaha River—opened its length but never used—was too heavy for the majority of the cotton-field Negroes. Only about two hundred of the original five hundred were retained, and a large number of Irishmen were brought in. From such a contact it can be seen how the word "wake" came to be substituted for "settin'-up," since the two customs—except for the drinking—are quite similar.*

42. O DE ROBE

C.C.

RIDE ON CONQUERING KING

As mentioned elsewhere, this is a good example of the question-and-answer type of song and was used at a "settin'-up" in accordance with the custom of sending messages by the dying to relations and friends in the other world.[18]

If you see my mother
   Oh yes.
Won't you tell her for me
   Oh yes.
I'm a ridin' my horse in the battle-field
I want a see my Jesus in the mornin'.

Chorus: Ride on King
     Ride on King
     Ride on Conquering King
I want a see my Jesus in the mornin'.

[18] *All of them are named in lengthening the song.*

43. RIDE ON CONQUERING KING

Alto

Allegro Moderato

If you see my moth-er   Won't you

Basers

Oh yes

tell her for me   I'm a-

Oh yes

ri - din' my horse in the bat - tle - field   I

Bass Solo

want-a see my Je-sus in the morn - in'____

Chorus

Ride   on   King   Ride   on   King

Ride   on____   Con - quer - ing   King   I

want to see my Je - sus in the morn - in'____

C.C.

AYE LORD, TIME IS DRAWIN' NIGH

Good-bye Mother
   Hmmh [19]
I'm goin' to leave you
   Hmmh
For you can't go with me
   Aye Lord
Time is drawin' nigh.

In the city of Jerusalem
   Hmmh
An' Pentecos' Day
   Hmmh
When the people got the Holy Ghost
   Aye Lord
Time is drawin' nigh.

Good-bye tattlers
   Hmmh
Goin' away to leave you
   Hmmh
You can't go with me
   Aye Lord
Time is drawin' nigh.

[19] *Sung by the basers with closed lips. This odd nasal tone adds attractive variety to a fine piece of melodic construction.*

44. AYE LORD, TIME IS DRAWIN' NIGH

It was interesting to find the tune of this song fitted out in McIntosh County with an entirely different set of words. None but a Negro poet could have created the imagery of the following lines:

> Loose horse in the valley
>   Aye
> Who goin' t' ride 'im
>   Aye
> Nothin' but the righteous
>   Aye Lord
> Time's a drawin' nigh.
>
> Judgment's a comin'
>   Aye
> How you know it
>   Aye
> By the buddin' of the fig tree
>   Aye Lord
> Time's a drawin' nigh.
>
> Don't you hear God talkin'
>   Aye
> He's a talkin' through the thunder
>   Aye
> Then people ona wonder
>   Aye Lord
> Time's a drawin' nigh.

NUMMER ME ONE

Chorus: Nummer[20] me one
          Nummer me one
          Nummer me one
I'm goin' to the Judgment Bar.

> Sen' for my leader here
> Sen' for my leader here
> Sen' for my leader here
> I'm goin' to the Judgment Bar.
>
> Sen' for my preacher here
> Sen' for my preacher here
> Sen' for my preacher here
> I'm goin' to the Judgment Bar.

The song is prolonged by sending for the different members of the family.

[20] *Number.*

45. NUMMER ME ONE

C.C.

FOR I AIN' GOIN' T' DIE NO MO'

The rhythm and tune of this "settin'-up" song suggest an old English ballad. As can be seen, there is nothing religious about the ironic observation in the first two lines. Julia, who taught me the song, laughingly said: "It's true all right. Mighty few visit the sick, but hundreds go to the wake and the buryin'."

> When I'm on my sick bed—nobody visit me
> But now I'm goin' to the graveyard—everybody follow me.
>> My sister won't y'u low my pillow
>>> Low—low—O-h low
>> My sister won't y'u low my pillow
>>> Low—for I ain' goin' t' die no mo'.
>> Somebody goin' to low my pillow
>>> Low—low—O-h low
>> Somebody goin' to low my pillow
>>> Low—for I ain' goin' t' die no mo'.

Janey Jackson, (Illustration 33) one of the most picturesque characters of Brunswick, sang an additional verse of the same song. Janey was born on St. Simon's, in "Nigger House Field" at Kelvin Grove, in 1826. At the age of twelve she was sold by the Caters, with her parents,[21] two sisters and a brother, to Mr. Henry duBignon, of Jekyl Island. She told me her family came over to St. Simon's frequently to see friends and relatives, as it was only a short row at low tide before the channel was deepened. Janey described the Caters' Old Dembo, Neptun' Small, father of Clarence and Cornelia, and Adam Proctor, father of Julia and Willis. No doubt it was on St. Simon's that she learned this verse:

> When I bin in de worl' bin a sin—nobody had nothin' to say
> But now I come into de House of God—everybody got somethin' to say.
>> Carry me an' bring me—in dat returnal day
>> Carry me an' bring me—in dat returnal day.

Under the influence of the duBignons, from whom she also learned to speak French, Janey became a Catholic; and when she went to live in Brunswick, she

---

[21] Janey's father, Jack, was an African prince, but her mother was "country born" (born in America).

always attended early mass. She never married; her sweetheart, Ishmael, belonged to another family, and his owners, thinking he would not be worth much to them in the field if his wife were on another plantation, encouraged a match with one of their own slaves.

To the end of her life, she smoked a pipe, and cooked her food in a black pot over a fire in the yard exactly as she had done in her youth. She must have been very strong, as she rowed a boat, did her half-acre of cotton, and, in her own words, "never knew what it was to be tired." She was a hundred and nine years old when she died in 1936, and evidently came of an exceptionally long-lived family, for her father was a centenarian, her sister lived to be a hundred and eight, and a cousin, also born in 1826, outlived her. Janey was straight and healthy to the last, and the sphinx-like, unwrinkled face in her coffin was like a piece of smooth black ebony. I had not realized in life how handsome she was or how Egyptian were her features. The inexpressible dignity of that dark mask so impressed me that I went back three times to make sure I would not forget it.

"BURYIN' "

Old residents of St. Simon's tell me that before the days of automobiles, when even horses [22] and wagons were luxuries, a Negro "buryin' " was an impressive affair. The mourners sang as they walked from the church, where the service was held, to the graveyard a mile away. The singers could be heard the minute they left the church, for at that time "they opened their mouths. They weren't like the young people today—too proud to sing." [23]

The home-made coffin, lined with "paper cambric" and covered with black calico or darkened with lampblack, was placed in the "rough box" and carried on a one-horse wagon. Only the preacher rode with the driver. The men walked single file on one side of the road and the women on the other.

When the minister could not come to the island for the church service, it was not held until his next visit—possibly in three weeks, sometimes in three months. In the days when "Reverend" Andrew Neal officiated, if he was urgently needed to

[22] *After the War Between the States only a vicious stallion, belonging to the Coupers, was left on St. Simon's. It was necessary to hobble him before he could be used. There were plenty of ponies, called "tackies," living on the salt marshes; but Joe tells me they were wild, like deer, and it never paid to buy one.*

[23] *It was said of Adam and Neptun' Small and MacWilliams that they could be heard a mile —than which, according to slave standards, there was no higher praise.*

"preach the funeral," [24] the St. Simon's Negroes would row all the way to Savannah —over eighty miles—to get him. They landed at Frederica, where the First African Baptist Church was located.

At Aaron's funeral Laura gave the time-honored dramatic touch by growing hysterical, throwing up her arms, and screaming: "Good-bye Aaron—y'u gone forever." While the clods were shoveled upon the coffin, singing providentially kept us from hearing the sound. Different men, headed by the undertaker, took turns filling in the grave. The way they joked and laughed as they worked rather shocked me. I understand, however, that Africans show the same levity after distressing occasions.

M. H. Kingsley, in *Travels in West Africa*, mentions the intense love of the African for funerals, and, according to the descriptions given by other explorers, there is a striking similarity in the burial customs of the natives and their rural American cousins. In Africa it is believed that the position of the ghost in the other world requires that the funeral be as expensive as the family can possibly provide. Furthermore, without a fitting ceremony the departed spirit cannot reach its final destination, but lingers among the living, making conditions very uncomfortable for them. The Negroes of our Southern states show the same feeling about funerals. They spare no expense in making them elaborate affairs. One that took place on St. Simon's years ago will long be remembered: "Why, Mrs. Parris', it cost four hundred dollars. They sent to Savannah for flowers, and she was buried in new white slippers that cost six dollars . . . !" I notice that the American Negro, no matter what the work or business in hand, puts it aside for such an event. To pay the cost of a funeral that will be a credit to the corpse as well as his family, the survivors will mortgage what property they may have, if they have not been so provident as to take out an insurance policy, join a "Bury League," or pay to some society or lodge dues which range from ten to twenty-five cents a week.

[24] When Quarterman's son-in-law died, his daughter said to me: "Tell the old man my husband died three weeks ago and the funeral will be preached next Sunday." Then she asked me if I would please give her a black hat. A Northern friend frequently sent me boxes of summer hats in the autumn. If the original owners could have seen them in winter on the dusky wearers, they would have been surprised. The fun of fitting out the singers with becoming hats has always made me wonder if I hadn't missed my calling.

31. "Cap'n" Joe

IN SOME LONESOME GRAVEYARD

In Charleston, where I was so ill-advised as to ask a member of the white Society for the Preservation of Spirituals why this work was not done by the Negroes, I was tartly told that they no longer sang the old songs. In spite of that statement, when a friend called her cook into the dining room, and summoned an old flower woman from the street, I heard the two sing songs which were perfectly familiar.

I asked for "In Some Lonesome Graveyard." They tittered and said: "You know dat one? Dat's real ole." After singing three verses, the cook, with an instinct for a dramatic exit, threw her apron over her head, and retreated sobbing to the kitchen. She probably remembered she had something in the oven that required her attention.

Willis tells me he learned the song as a small boy from his father, Adam Proctor, while planting corn.

> U-m-h, u-m-h,[25] I hear' a mighty moanin'
> U-m-h, u-m-h, I hear' a mighty moanin'
> U-m-h, u-m-h, I hear' a mighty moanin'
> In some lonesome graveyard.

> Mother, Mother, don't let your daughter condemn you
> Mother, Mother, don't let your daughter condemn you
> Mother, Mother, don't let your daughter condemn you
> In some lonesome graveyard.

> U-m-h, u-m-h, I hear' a mighty moanin'
> U-m-h, u-m-h, I hear' a mighty moanin'
> U-m-h, u-m-h, I hear' a mighty moanin'
> In some lonesome graveyard.

Fathers are warned about their sons, preachers about their members.

[25] *Sung with the lips closed.*

46. IN SOME LONESOME GRAVEYARD

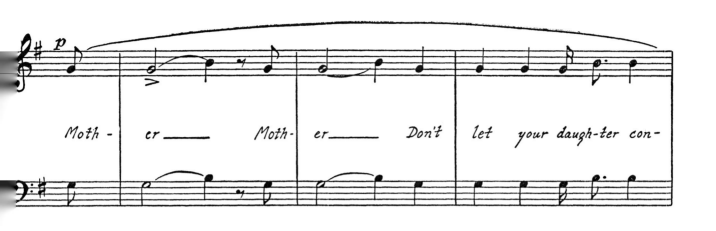

Moth - er _____ Moth - er _____ Don't let your daugh-ter con-

demn you Moth- er _____ Moth- er _____ Don't let your daugh-ter con-

demn you Moth- er _____ Moth- er _____ Don't let your daugh-ter con-

demn you In some lone - some grave - yard.

C.C.

I GOT TO LAY IN YONDER GRAVEYARD

It is a pity that the music of these touching lines is not available.

I got to lay in yonder graveyard
  I got to lay there fo' myself
Nobody here can lay there fo' me
  I got to lay there fo' myself.

I got to stan' my trial in the Judgment
  I got to stan' there fo' myself
There's nobody here can stan' there fo' me
  I got to stan' there fo' myself.

I got to give an account in the Judgment
  I got to give it fo' myself
Nobody here can give it fo' me
  I got to give it fo' myself.

I got to cross that river o' Jurden
  I got to cross there fo' myself
Nobody here goin' to cross there fo' me
  I got to cross there fo' myself.

I got to pray in that lonesome valley
  I got to pray there fo' myself
Nobody here goin' to pray there fo' me
  I got to pray there fo' myself.

I got to weep at Zion's Court House
  I got to weep there fo' myself
My dear mother can't weep there fo' me
  I got to weep there fo' myself.

CHAPTER SIX

Work Songs

In the old days, before Negroes rode to work in automobiles, they sang as they walked, and most of their tasks were lightened with song. One of my pleasantest memories is of hearing them singing in the early morning and at sundown, and—during the heat of the day—calling to each other across wide fields. The call was peculiar, and I always wondered how they came by such a strange form of vocal gymnastics, since I never heard a white person do anything like it. Years later I ran across a description of the trick in Natalie Curtis-Burlin's *Songs and Tales from the Dark Continent*. The author, in speaking of a Bantu rain song, calls attention to a passage which contains "an upward break in the voice, something like a Swiss yodel." Such field-calls are rarely heard today, although I am told they are still in use in the vicinity of the Okefenokee Swamp.

In the late eighteen-eighties, the Negroes in my home neighborhood—southern New Jersey—began to pattern their behavior after that of the silent white folk, and from that time on, little of their singing was heard. Farther south, this racial characteristic was later in disappearing. In 1901, Georgia Bryan Conrad tells us that, in her youth, "the Negroes were always singing," but adds regretfully: "Nothing is in greater contrast to that time than the quietness of the Negroes now." [1] However, there are remote places where they still sing at work. In factories where large numbers are employed in such monotonous jobs as shucking oysters or picking crabs and shrimp, rhythmic songs are used to relieve dullness. They are also sung wherever work is heavy, and concerted effort is required. In Brunswick, vessels are still loaded to the musical chant of "Sandy Anna"; freight cars at the sugar terminal are shunted for short distances to the rhythm of "Old Tar River," and the cabin in front of my house was moved on rollers from Kelvin Grove to the significant tune of "Pay Me My Money Down!"

[1] "Reminiscences of a Southern Woman," Southern Workman, 1901.

On the Mobile waterfront, where many of the "shanties" [2]—as they are called by the dock-hands—are supposed to have originated, I was told that machines are now used in loading vessels in place of the singing stevedores: "that type of labor was too inefficient." Their songs will soon be a thing of the past. The loss is the more regrettable since they are the most characteristic of all the work songs. (Illustration 32)

This fact was recognized as early as the Civil War period by a Delaware gentleman whose account of the stevedores' singing is quoted in the preface of *Slave Songs of the United States*, published in 1867. In writing the editors, he said:

We must look among their non-religious songs for the purest specimens of negro minstrelsy. It is remarkable that they have themselves transferred the best of these to the uses of their churches—I suppose on Mr. Wesley's principle that "it is not right the Devil should have all the good tunes." . . . Some of the best *pure negro* songs I have ever heard were those that used to be sung by the black stevedores, or perhaps the crews themselves, of the West India vessels, loading and unloading at the wharves in Philadelphia and Baltimore. I have stood for more than an hour, often, listening to them

[2] *There appears to be a difference of opinion as to the derivation of the name "shanty," which is given in the Oxford Dictionary as first appearing in print in 1869. In Roll and Go, Joanna C. Colcord tells us that Sir Richard Runciman Terry "thinks it is derived from the shanties in which the negroes lived who originated so many of these songs, or from the drinking shanties along the Mobile water-front where the sailors picked them up."*

On the other hand, Miss Colcord's conclusion that they might have come out of the Maine woods, where the word "shanty-man" was synonymous with "lumberman" is not compatible with what she has to say about the development of shanty-singing, and the superiority shown by the American Negroes—"the best singers that ever lifted a shanty aboard ship." She tells how this development was affected by the rise in the cotton trade between Liverpool and the Southern states and the gold rush around the Horn. It seems improbable that the woods of Maine had anything to do with giving a name to the work songs of the stevedores in a land where "Cotton was King," and where the forests of yellow pine, particularly those of Georgia, furnished more of the lumber product, in 1900, than any other part of the country.

Such being the case, it seems to me that Terry's explanation of how the name might have originated is the more likely one. In The Shanty Book, he tells how he lived for some years in the West Indies, and "in addition to hearing them [shanties] in West Indian seaports, aboard Yankee sailing ships and sugar droghers . . . also heard them sung in Antigua under rather curious conditions. West Indian shanties are movable wooden huts, and when a family wishes to change its venue it does so in the following manner: The shanty is levered up on a low platform on wheels to which two very long ropes are attached. The ropes are manned by as many hands as their length will admit. A 'shanty-man' mounts to the roof of the hut and sits astride it. He sings a song which has a chorus, and is an exact musical parallel of a seaman's 'pull-and-haul' shanty. The crowd below sings the chorus, giving a pull on the rope at the required points in the music, just as the sailors did when hauling at sea."

as they hoisted and lowered the hogsheads and boxes of their cargoes; one man taking the burden of the song (and the slack of the rope) and the others striking in with the chorus. They would sing in this way more than a dozen different songs in an hour; most of which might indeed be warranted to contain "nothing religious"—a few of them, "on the contrary, quite the reverse"—but generally rather innocent and proper in their language, and strangely attractive in their music; and with a volume of voice that reached a square or two away. This plan of labor has now passed away, in Philadelphia at least, and the songs, I suppose, with it. So that these performances are to be heard only among black sailors on their vessels, or 'long-shore men in out-of-the-way places, where opportunities for respectable people to hear them are rather few.

Something of the African background of these *"pure negro songs"* may be gathered from a description of the work songs of West Africa, given by N. G. J. Ballanta, who tells us: "Music in Africa is not cultivated for its own sake. It is always used in connection with dances or to accompany workmen. The rhythmic interest of the songs impels them to work and takes away the feeling of drudgery." He goes on to say that work songs are "—mainly rhythmic—short phrases mostly of two or three bars; solo and chorus follow each other instantly; the chorus is in many instances composed of two or three ejaculatory words, answered by the workmen. Tempo moderate." This summary fits so many of the songs used by our stevedores that the connection is unmistakable.

The similarity between the songs of African workmen and those of their cousins in this country is also illustrated in some examples from the shipping docks of Beira, given by Natalie Curtis-Burlin. One of them, used by laborers in pushing or pulling heavy things, might have been sung on the docks of Brunswick. Another, like so many of the work songs of the American Negroes, was suggested by the particular job in hand, in this case, the literal translation runs: "Dawn—with freight—Yes, yes!—Dawn—with freight—Look for the label!"

Among the Negroes, any song with the proper rhythm is used to accompany whatever work requires its help. While those of a religious character have always been the greatest favorites in our section,[3] the type of work is necessarily the determining factor. It is unlikely that a shanty could be used for rowing, or a rowing song for beating rice. In the old days, if no suitable verse came to mind for a particular task, one was made up then and there out of slender material. Fanny Kemble,

[3] *It is interesting to notice that the religious songs used by the stevedores and other workmen are vastly superior to those heard in church and prayer meeting. The reason is self-evident: the latter have been dressed up to conform to the white folks' fashion.*

in her *Journal*, gave several illustrations which show how anything was grist for the Negroes' song-mill. With the rivers affording the only means of travel, it was natural that she should hear rowing songs of all kinds; and on one occasion she had the unique privilege of hearing her own praises extemporaneously chanted by her two Negro boatmen. They described her personal attractions, and amused her intensely by their repeated references to her "wire waist." [4]

Today the Negroes are less inventive, and generally confine themselves to a substitution of names or familiar lines in the old songs, but we can still hear examples of the way they utilized incidents or phrases that struck their fancy. If a captain said: "It's rough going 'round the Horn," the Negroes made up a song about the statement, and we had: "Go 'round the Horn, Yalla gal, Go 'round the Horn!" "Ragged Leevy," a waterfront character of Brunswick, was described in the shanty that bears his name. "Little Johnny Brown, fines' cap'n on Doboy Sound," was so popular among the stevedores that he figured in one of their jolliest shanties; and "Yonder come that *Hessie*" always brings a regretful feeling to those of us who remember the "good old days" on St. Simon's when the *Hessie* was our means of communication with the outside world, and the captain obligingly did our errands.

In our machine age it is inevitable that these work songs should pass. Before they have entirely disappeared, records should be made of the few examples that have survived.

SHANTIES

If anyone needs more information about the use of these shanties, I suggest that he apply to either Joe Armstrong or Henry Merchant of St. Simon's Island. Both were at one time leaders of stevedore crews, and both have told me the uses to which the different songs were put. Since I am a land-lubber and more interested in music than in the mechanics of loading lumber and stowing cotton, details concerning the latter have not stuck, while the tunes have—to the last note. Any mistake in describing their application is mine, not Joe's or Henry's.

In the early days of the lumber industry, great rafts of logs were nailed together, and—with two or three men in charge—were drifted down the Altamaha to the mills at its mouth. [5] Ships from everywhere came for the sawed lumber. Julia once

[4] *African explorers with more knowledge of the native dialect than their boatmen realized were often entertained in the same manner, but their defects—not their charms—were derisively enumerated.*

[5] *Fanny Kemble mentions in her Journal that on one of her boat-trips from Darien she saw "The river . . . covered with Ocone [river] boxes." She describes them as monstrous square*

told me she had seen as many as thirty-five vessels lined up at The Mills in the days when the Hilton-Dodge Lumber Company was at the peak of its production. There was the *Waltham*, a three-masted schooner, under Captain Bartow—remembered as "the bad-luck ship." The *Annie Bishop* was also a three-masted schooner, the *Irene* was a brig, and there was one called the *Hope Sharewood* which brought forth many a pun. As many as twenty-five Negroes would "roll ballast"—which means, as can be imagined, that the stones with which the windjammers came loaded were landed at a temporary dock, and rolled in wheelbarrows to waste land. A geologist with a bit of curiosity might find it of interest to examine the contents of the small islands of ballast in the marsh between St. Simon's and Brunswick. They represent calling cards from all over the world. I have always wondered what the handsome white bark *Regina*, from Archangel—which I saw at The Mills in 1913—could have brought to these shores.

The *Waltham* probably came loaded with the New Engand granite that provided the owner of Hamilton Plantation with a rock garden in a rockless land. Some years ago chunks of flint from the chalk cliffs of England were plentiful on the banks of the river beside Fort Frederica, but Boy Scouts have no doubt found them useful —as my children did—for they are no longer abundant.

Floyd White and Henry Merchant, among others, have given me lively shanties, and they both employ the old-fashioned falsetto tones which are so effective when heard in the open. It is a curious fact that most dark-colored men now appear to be baritones; yet a hundred years ago Fanny Kemble said that tenors predominated on St. Simon's.[6] I remember from my youth the high tones of the Negro

---

boxes, "made out of rough planks put together in the roughest manner possible to attain the necessary object of keeping the cotton dry. Upon this great tray are piled . . . cotton bags, to the height of ten, twelve and fourteen feet. . . . These Ocone boxes are broken up at Darien, where the cotton is shipped either for the Savannah, Charleston, or Liverpool markets and the timber of which they are constructed, sold." This chance reference to the sale of timber indicates the beginning of the lumber industry.

[6] "The only exception that I have met with yet among our boat voices to the high tenor which they seem all to possess is in the person of an individual named Isaac, a basso profundo of the deepest dye." The situation she describes holds to this day. We have only one true bass on the island, but he does not appear to enjoy hearing his voice as we do. I cannot get him to use it, although I try every means—praise, bribery, and the opposite tack are all of no avail. A pity; singing in unison needs the substance given by such a voice, as well as the variety provided by the interpolations of the "high tribble" and tenor. It was interesting to find in Northern Haiti that our yard boy would sing a verse in a high falsetto; the next would be in his natural baritone—from which I gathered that such a procedure might be traditional.

men, and the odd break on the top note before the singer suddenly dropped a whole octave. These must have been conventions, for since 1890 I have not heard anybody except these two men use them. Floyd sings "Free at Last" with all the ancient frills, and tells me the tune was used for "blockin' timber." Joe mentions such technical lumber-loading terms as "wing-tier," which probably means just what the word implies, and "kelson knees," which the Oxford Dictionary defines as "a line of timber placed inside a ship along the floor timbers and parallel with the keel." The "beam-dog" is, I gather, a grappling-iron with a fang which clutches the log or piece of timber to be handled. "Block and tickle" means a system of pulleys by which this work was done. Joe learned such work as "narrow trunkin' "—stowing lumber in a peculiar way—from colored men who had been taught by Irish steve-dores. The head stevedore was a white man who contracted to load a vessel for so much per thousand feet. Big ships employed four colored stevedores called "head-ers," [7] and used derricks; schooners needed only three headers—one outside and two inside. Short lumber went into the hatch, but for long lumber you had to "knock out the port," which was generally in the bow. In stowing cotton, the bale, as far as I could figure out, was lowered into the hold in a sling with three hooks attached, something like an ice-hook with an extra prong. Then it was rammed tightly into place by what "Cap'n" Joe [8] (Illustration 31) calls a "snilo"—a post against which the cotton jack was placed. "Pullin' lumber" meant shoving it on a long greased skid, waist high, made up of a series of carpenter's horses. There were generally four men at one end, and the same number at the other.

There are many shanties of which only fragments remain. One about the menu of the captain indicates, as Miss Colcord tells us, that it might have originated on a slave ship in tropical waters:

> What do you think he had for dinner?
> Monkey soup an' gray molasses.
> Blow, my bully boys, blow!

Floyd says it was used to "hist the gaff when the cap'n was ready to go to sea." He remembers another fragment which runs like this: "Clear the track an' let the bullgine back," and another:

[7] *The "headers" were the stevedores responsible for the proper loading of a vessel.*

[8] *In plantation days the most important Negro slave was the "driver." His distasteful task was to see that the orders of the white overseer were carried out. As can be imagined the very name "driver" was unpopular, and after emancipation the Negro who had charge of a gang of laborers was called "Cap'n," and the old term is no longer heard.*

O bring me a 'gator
O gal when you come off the islan'.
A ring-tail' 'ator
O gal when you come off the islan'
A Darien 'gator
O gal when you come off the islan'

Let us hope that more of these rollicking songs can be retrieved. They have a flavor that is unique.

CALL ME HANGIN' JOHNNY

This song was used in loading lumber, when six men on each side of the rope hauled on the block and tackle in putting a great "stick" [9] in place on board a vessel.

Call me hangin' Johnny
    O hang boys hang.
You call me hangin' Johnny
    O hang boys hang.
Yes, I never hang nobody
    O hang boys hang.
I never hang nobody
    O hang boys hang.
O we'll heave an' haul together
    O hang boys hang.
We heave an' haul forever
    O hang boys hang.
They hang my ole Grandaddy
    O hang boys hang.
They hang him for his money
    O hang boys hang.
O they hang him for his money
    O hang boys hang.
They hang him for his money
    O hang boys hang.
They call me hangin' Johnny
    O hang boys hang.
O I never hang nobody
    O hang boys hang.

[9] *This is Joe's way of referring to a piece of timber 16″ x 16″, and 40′ long.*

47. CALL ME HANGIN' JOHNNY

C.C.

48. KNOCK A MAN DOWN

Johnny Brown was captain of a tugboat called *The Dandy*, which towed to open water the sailing vessels coming to Doboy Sound for lumber. The stevedores agreed he was "the fines' cap'n of 'em all."

Whoever heard talk about Little Johnny Brown
Oh Ho knock a man down.
Knock a man down from London town
Oh gimme some time to knock a man down.

Knock a man down bullies an' kick him aroun'
Oh Ho knock a man down.
Knock a man down from London town
Oh gimme some time to knock a man down.

Y'u ever heard talk about Little Johnny Brown
Oh Ho knock a man down.
Fines' cap'n on Doboy Sound
Oh gimme some time to knock a man down.

SANDY ANNA

Seaman, what's the madda?
Hoo-ray 'o-ray
Seaman, what's the madda?
Hooray, Sandy Anna.
Seaman stole my dolla'
Hooray 'o-ray
He stole it in Savannah
Hooray, Sandy Anna.
He spend it in Havana
Hooray 'o-ray
I caught 'im in his colla'
Hooray, Sandy Anna.
I shake 'im till he holla'
Hooray o'-ray
Seaman stole my dolla'
Hooray, Sandy Anna.

49. SANDY ANNA

Seaman, what's the madda? Hoo-ray-o- - ray Seaman, what's the madda? Hoo-ray, Sand-y-an-na. 2) Sea-man stole my dol-lah Hoo-ray-o- - ray He stole it in Sa-van-nah Hoo-ray, Sand-y-an-na.

C.C.

PAY ME MY MONEY DOWN

Pay me, Oh pay me
                    Pay me my money down
Pay me or go to jail
                    Pay me my money down.
Oh pay me, Oh pay me
                    Pay me my money down
Pay me or go to jail
                    Pay me my money down.

Think I heard my captain say
                    Pay me my money down
T'morrow is my sailin' day
                    Pay me my money down.

(chorus)

Wish't I was Mr. Coffin's son
                    Pay me my money down
Stay in the house an' drink good rum
                    Pay me my money down.

(chorus)

You owe me, pay me
                    Pay me my money down
Pay me or go to jail
                    Pay me my money down.

(chorus)

Wish't I was Mr. Foster's [10] son
                    Pay me my money down
I'd set on the bank an' see the work done
                    Pay me my money down.

[10] Mr. Foster was the "Big Boss" at the Hilton-Dodge Mills on the west side of St. Simon's, and the ex-stevedores tell me they always sang this verse when they saw him coming.

50. PAY ME MY MONEY DOWN

Leader (Tenor): Pay me, Oh pay me Pay me my mon-ey down Pay me or go to jail Pay me my mon-ey down. Oh Pay me, Oh Pay me Pay me my mon-ey down Pay me or go to jail

Pay me my mon-ey down | Think I heard my Cap-tain say

Pay me my mon-ey down | T'mor-row is my

Sail-in' day | Pay me my mon-ey down.

C.C.

DEBT I OWE

Debt I owe, Lord, debt I owe
I ain' gonna pay no debt I owe
Debt I owe, Lord, debt I owe
I ain' gonna pay no debt I owe
Debt I owe in Brunswick sto'e [11]
I ain' gonna pay no debt I owe
O Mister Watchman don't watch me
I ain' gonna pay no debt I owe
Watch that nig'ah right behine that tree
I ain' gonna pay no debt I owe.

[11] To sustain interest the shanty leader always introduced an element of surprise into his lines. To this day we feel cheated when Floyd fails to include "Jewtown Sto'e" and "St. Simon's Sto'e" when he sings about the debts he "ain' gonna pay," but then, that may be part of the game.

51. DEBT I OWE

Debt I owe, Lord, Debt I owe, I ain' gon-na pay no debt I owe Debt I owe in Bruns-wick sto'e I ain' gon-na pay no debt I owe. Oh Mis-tah watch-man don' watch me, I ain' gon-na pay no debt I owe Watch that nig'-ah right be-hin' that tree, I ain' gon-na pay no debt I owe.

C.C.

RAGGED LEEVY

Ragged Leevy! Oh — Ho!
Do ragged Leevy
Ragged Leevy! O boy!
You ragged like a jay bird!
Mr. Sipplin! Ha-n-nh
Goin' to buil' me a sto'e fence [12]
In the mornin'—Oh — Ho!
Soon in the mornin'.
Hos' an' buggy—Oh — Ho!
Hos' an' buggy
Hos' an' buggy—O boy!
Dey's no one to drive 'um.
Mr. Sipplin! Ha-n-nh
In de mornin'
When I rise
I goin' to sit by de fire.
In de mornin' Oh — Ho!
O soon in de mornin'
In de mornin'
When I rise I goin' to sit by de fire.
Mauma Dinah Oh — Ho!
Do Mauma Dinah
Mauma Dinah
O gal I can't suppo't you.
Mr. Sipplin! Ha-n-nh
Do Mr. Sipplin
Walkin' talkin'!
O buil' me a sto'e fence.
Sweet potato Oh — Ho!
Sweet potato
Sweet potato O boy
There's two in de fire.
Mr. Sipplin! Ha-n-nh
Goin' to buil' me a sto'e fence
In de mornin' Oh — Ho!
When I rise I goin' to sit by de fire.

Used when "blockin' heavy timber."

[12] Store fence.

52. RAGGED LEEVY.

R. Mac Gimsey

Rather Slow - steady tempo
mf

Rag - ged Lee - vy, Oh Ho Do rag-ged Lee - vy

Rag - ged Lee - vy, Oh boy You's rag-ged lak a Jay bird.

Sip - lin. Ah'm gon - nah buil' me a sto'e fence

In nuh mawn - in' Oh Ho soon in nuh mawn - in.

In nuh mawn - in' When Ah rise Ah'm gon-nah set by duh fi - ah.

In nuh mawn - in'. Oh ho soon in nuh mawn - in'.

In nuh mawn - in' When Ah rise Ah'm gon - nah set by duh fi - ah.

Sip - lin. Ah's gon - nah buil' me a sto'e fence

Sip - lin Ah's gon - nah buil' me a sto'e fence

Rag - ged Lee - vy. Oh Boy You's rag-ged lak a Jay bird.

GOOD-BYE MY RILEY O

Riley, Riley, where were you?
O Riley, O man!
Riley gone an' I'm goin' too
Goodbye my Riley O!
Riley, Riley, where were you?
O Riley, O man!
Riley gone to Liverpool [13]
Good-bye my Riley O!
You Democrat Riley
O Riley, O man!
You Democrat Riley
Good-bye my Riley O!
Riley, Riley, where were you?
O Riley, O man!
When I played that nine spot through
Good-bye my Riley O!

[13] *London Town* and *Mobile Bay* are the other spots where Riley is supposed to have gone.

53. GOOD-BYE MY RILEY O

C.C.

OLE TAR RIVER

Chorus: O, On the ole Tar river

O—e-e-e [14]

O, On the ole Tar river
Lord, Lord, the ole Tar river.
Tar river goin' run tomorrow

O—e-e-e

Tar river goin' run tomorrow
Lord, Lord, the ole Tar river.

Tar river run black an' dirty

O—e-e-e

Tar river run black an' dirty
Lord, Lord, the ole Tar river.
Tar river goin' to water my horses

O—e-e-e

Tar river goin' to water my horses
Lord, Lord, the ole Tar river.

Ole Tar river is a healin' water

O—e-e-e

Ole Tar river is a healin' water
Lord, Lord, the ole Tar river.
Ole Tar river run free an' easy

O—e-e-e

Ole Tar river run free an' easy
Lord, Lord, the ole Tar river.

Chorus: Way down, way down in the country

O—e-e-e

Way down, way down in the country
Lord, Lord, the ole Tar river.

[14] *In some sections such a refrain is called a howl. In Seaboard Slave States, Olmstead calls it "Jodeling" or "The Carolina Yell" and describes its use by a group of Negro laborers. "Suddenly one raised such a sound as I never heard before; a long, loud, musical shout, rising and falling, and breaking into falsetto, his voice ringing through the woods, in the clear, frosty night air, like a bugle call. As he finished, the melody was caught up by another, and then another, and then by several in chorus." Olmstead goes on to say that a similar response was sung by this group of Negroes as they put their shoulders to a bale of cotton and rolled it up an embankment:*

*"Come bredern, come; let's go at it, come now, eoho! roll away
eeoho-eeoho-weeioho-i!"*

A different example, sung by Negro boat hands, is given in another chapter by this observant gentleman:

*"Ye see dem boat way dah ahead . . .
Oahoiohieu . . .
Dey's burnin' not'n but fat [wood] an' rosum
Oahoiohieu."*

54. OLE TAR RIVER

SHILO BROWN

Shilo Ah wonduh what's tuh mattuh?
  Shilo, Shilo Brown.
Shilo Ah wonduh what's tuh mattuh?
  O Shilo, Shilo Brown.
  Stivedore's in trouble
    Shilo, Shilo Brown.
  Stivedore's in trouble
    O Shilo, Shilo Brown.
Take yo' time an' drive 'um
    Shilo, Shilo Brown.
Take yo' time an' drive 'um
    O Shilo, Shilo Brown.
Shilo gone to ruin
    Shilo, Shilo Brown.
Shilo gone to ruin I know
    O Shilo, Shilo Brown.

55. SHILO BROWN

Moderately – in steady tempo   R. Mac Gimsey

Shi - lo   Ah   won - duh   what's tuh   mat - tuh?

Shi - lo, Shi - lo__   Brown Shi - lo Ah won - duh what's tuh mat - tuh?

Shi - lo, Shi - lo   Brown.   Ste - ve - do'es   in   trou - ble,__

Shi - lo Shi - lo Brown,   Ste - ve - do'es   in   trou - ble,__

Shi - lo, Shi - lo   Brown.   Take yo' time an' drive 'em,

Shi - lo, Shi - lo Brown. Take yo' time an' drive 'em,   Shi - lo, Shi - lo   Brown.

THIS TIME ANOTHER YEAR

This time another year
I may be gone
In some lonesome graveyard
O Lord how long!
My brother broke the ice an' gone
O Lord how long
My brother broke the ice an' gone
O Lord how long!

Befo' this time another year
I may be gone
In some lonesome graveyard
O Lord how long!
Mind my sister how you walk on the cross
O Lord how long
Your right foot slip an' y'ur soul get los'
O Lord how long!

HAUL AWAY, I'M A ROLLIN' KING

Haul away, I'm a rollin' king
Haul away, haul away
I'm boun' for South Australia.
Yonder come a flounder flat on the groun'
Haul away, haul away
I'm boun' for South Australia.
Belly to the groun' an' back to the sun
Haul away, haul away
I'm boun' for South Australia.
Ain' but one thing worry me
Haul away, haul away
I'm boun' for South Australia.
I leave my wife in Tennessee
Haul away, haul away
I'm boun' for South Australia.
Haul away, I'm a rollin' king
Haul away, haul away
I'm boun' for South Australia.

SUNDOWN BELOW

This tune was sung at the end of the day as a hint to the captain, when the hold was too dark for the stevedores to see what they were doing:

Sun is down an' I mus' go
Sundown
Sundown below.
Sun is down in the hole below
Sundown
Sundown below.
I hear my captain say
Sundown
Sundown below.
Sun is down an' I mus' go
Sundown
Sundown below.

MY SOUL BE AT RES'

One a dese mornin's—it won't be long
My soul be at res'.
One a dese mornin's—it won't be long
My soul be at res'.
Be at res'—goin' be at res'
My soul be at res'.
Be at res' till Judgment Day
My soul be at res'.
It won't be long—it won't be long
My soul be at res'.
Be at res'—till Judgment Day
My soul be at res'.
One a dese mornin's—it won't be long
My soul be at res'.
Goin' t' hitch on my wings an' try the air
My soul be at res'.
One a dese mornin's—it won't be long
My soul be at res'.
You a'ks fo' me an' I'll be gone
My soul be at res'.

ANNIEBELLE

Of all the shanties, this concerning Anniebelle appears to be adaptable to the most varied uses, and to be the most widely distributed. Joe tells me he learned it over forty years ago from the stevedores who loaded lumber on the vessels at the Hilton-Dodge mills, but its main use was for "spikin' steel" on the railroads. I notice, however, that he puts the song to equally good use in chopping wood or swinging the weed cutter. In the mines it is called a "hammerin' song."

Anniebelle

          Hunh!

Don't weep

          Hunh!

Anniebelle

          Hunh!

Don't moan

          Hunh!

Anniebelle

          Hunh!

Don't go

          Hunh!

Leave home.

          Hunh!

When I throw

          Hunh!

My head

          Hunh!

In the bar

          Hunh!

Room doo'

          Hunh!

I'll never

          Hunh!

Get drunk

          Hunh!

No mo'.

          Hunh!

Don't want t' hurt nobody

          Hunh!

O-h no
>Hunh!

O-h no
>Hunh!

Dis ole hammer [15]
>Hunh!

Kill John Henry
>Hunh!

Laid him low buddy
>Hunh!

Laid him low.
>Hunh!

At this point Joe interpolated rhythmically: "Stan' by for another verse."

Ain't no hammer
>Hunh!

In this mount'in
>Hunh!

Ring like mine buddy
>Hunh!

Ring like mine buddy.
>Hunh!

Several years ago I heard the following version sung by Boogaloo, one of Darien's happy-go-lucky Negroes, as he cut weeds on the highway shoulders in front of Josephine's house. It was amusing to read in a recent issue of *Time* a letter from Mary J. Phillips telling of the explanation of the present war Boogaloo had given her husband. Mrs. Phillips quotes Boogaloo as saying: "Boss, I tells you what I thinks about this here war. Germany, some back, she starts a crap game, threw an eight, then falls off. Now she wants her money back and starts grabbing." I imagine that Boogaloo's speech was more consistent all through, but the thought is clearly his.

This is the hammer that kill John Henry
Tell 'im I'm dead, buddy, tell 'im I'm dead
Cap'n Smith what you reckon?
Ten-pound hammer kill John Henry
Kill' my buddy, Lord, but 'e can't kill me.

[15] *Sometimes he specifies "nine-poun' hammer."*

56. ANNIEBELLE

33. *Janey Jackson, Born at Kelvin Grove, St. Simon's, in 1826—Died in 1936*

34. *Milly Polecat, the Witch Doctor*

RICE SONGS

Growing rice was a thriving industry along the Ogeechee, Altamaha, and Satilla rivers a century ago, but today it is difficult to find even a handful of grain to demonstrate how it was beaten. At Hofwyl Plantation, the last in Glynn County to grow rice to any extent, I asked Jerry Rutledge about the songs that were used for planting rice, and getting it ready to eat. He gave me these appropriate lines:

> John say you got to reap in the harvest what you sow
> John say you got to reap in the harvest what you sow
> If you sow it in the rain, you got to reap it jus' the same
> You got to reap in the harvest what you sow.

He explained how the rice sheaves, about a foot through, and tied with a twist of straw, were whipped with "frails"; they were laid in parallel rows on a large sheet on the floor with the butt ends out. When two Negroes "t'rashed" together, they always sang as they faced each other. The short part of the flail which flew in the air in a seemingly reckless fashion was called a "bob," and it was rather important to have its gyrations rhythmically controlled. As soon as one side of a sheaf was clear of rice it was turned over and the other side whipped. By the time the string was broken the grain was in a long row in the middle.

Julia Walker, born near Riceboro in Liberty County, gave me precisely the same description of the work, and sang the following song as she demonstrated how the "frail" was used. Frankly, I was skeptical of the strength of the rawhide that attached the bob to the stick, and kept well out of range:

> Turn sinner turn—sinner wouldn't turn
> Turn sinner turn—sinner wouldn't turn
> My Lord call you—wouldn't come
> I know sinner too late, too late
> O too late I know, sinner, too late.
> Church bell ring—you wouldn't come
> Preacher preach—an' you wouldn't come
> My Lord call you—an' you wouldn't come
> I know sinner too late, too late
> O too late, sinner, too late.

Julia said that when only a small amount of rice was to be thrashed, the grain was stripped from the straw by hand, and put on a good clean floor. With a quick and effective dance step, the outer husk was scuffed off. On Sapelo the work was done to a similar step, with these words:

> Peas an' the rice done done
>   Higho—Higho!
> Beaufort boat done come
>   Higho—Higho!
> How do you know—done heard it blow
>   Higho—Higho!

On St. Simon's, Julia Armstrong sings still another version:

> New rice an' okra—Nana—Nana! [16]
> Eat some an' leave some—Nana—Nana!
>   Beat rice to bum-bum
> Eat some an' leave some.

I am told that Old Adam Proctor hoed rice to the tune of:

> Way over yonder in that new bright worl'
> Poo' sinner got a home at las'

and tied up the sheaves to:

> Do Lord remember me—Do Lord remember me
> Way over in Beulah Lan'—Do Lord remember me.

A shout song was often used for the rice dance. The following lines indicate how the rhythm changed. While walking around in a circle with a preliminary scuffle, the "t'rashers" sang the slow part as in shouting.

> Sheep know his shepher's voice
>   Yes Lord, I know the way.
> Sheep know his shepher's voice
>   Yes Lord, I know the way.

[16] *According to Dr. Turner, "nana" means grandmother.*

You know the way an' you wouldn't come home
Yes Lord, I know the way.
Every sheep know his shepher's voice
Yes Lord, I know the way.

The faster part was sung as two hops were made on one foot while the other did the scuffing.

Make a jump, jump for joy!
Make a jump, jump for joy!

This phrase was repeated over and over, with the variation:

Sheep jump, jump for joy!

The planters believed that rice was only good when freshly beaten,[17] and the sheaves kept for family use were put in a well-ventilated mouse-proof loft. The commercial rice was threshed in a mill, but the husks were left on, and even in cities, in the South, the rice was beaten fresh every day. The mortars were generally hollowed out of cypress or hard pine logs and used upright, although on Sapelo I have seen some made of immense pieces of squared timber laid flat so that the beating took place against the grain. The pestles had two ends, one sharp for bruising the husks and removing them, the other flat for whitening. Boys or women generally did the beating. They would grasp the pestles in the middle, raising and letting them fall so quickly and evenly, to the rhythm of what was more like a chant than a song, that the task was not considered difficult.

[17] *William Ellis in his* History of Madagascar, *1838, makes it clear that our early rice planters got their ideas about the culture and preparation of rice for the table directly from Madagascar. In* Seed from Madagascar *Duncan Clinch Heyward tells us that the seed of the Carolina Gold rice was brought from that land by a sea captain about the year 1685, but Mr. Ellis furnishes the African end of the picture. After describing planting and harvesting methods, he explains the laborious process by which rice was made ready for cooking. "The rice, which is kept in the husk in a sort of granary, is made ready for use in such quantities only as the daily consumption of the family may require." In minute detail he explains that it is then beaten in a mortar by two people using large wooden pestles, about five feet in length, so as to break and remove the outer husk without breaking the grain. The rice is taken out, and separated from the husk by winnowing; it is then beaten in the mortar a second time for the purpose of taking off the inner skin. The process is repeated a third time; tossed again in the winnowing-fan, then washed and cooked. It was reported by Francis Moor that on the West Coast of Africa men worked the corn ground, and women and girls the rice ground. Jobson, another West African traveler, says: "the wives do all the hard labor such as cleaning and pounding rice . . . which is done in mortars with great staves." One explorer mentioned that rice was so plentiful in Kongo and Angola that it hardly bears any price.*

DO REMEMBER

The rhythm of this song, like that of "Peas an' the Rice," is all-important. The words themselves mean little except that their syllables lend themselves to the flat-footed hopping steps which are utilized to scuff off the outer husks of the rice on the floor. When this tune is used for shouting, there is an interminable number of lines given over to "Do remember me," with emphasis on "do" in the first line, and on "me" in the second. When ready to sing the chorus again—after repeating "Do re-member me" eighteen or twenty times—the performers give a stamp on the next to the last "me"—with a perceptible pause.

Chorus: Old broom sweep my floor
New broom scratch my floor
O—do remember
Do remember me.
  (repeat)
Do remember
    Do remember
Do remember
    Do remember
Do remember
    Do remember
Do remember
    Do remember
Do remember
    Do remember
Don'cha 'member
    Do remember
Don'cha 'member
    Do remember
Do remember
    Do remember me.

57. DO REMEMBER

PEAS AN' THE RICE

In her youth, Julia Walker employed these rhythmic lines to help in thrashing rice on the floor.[18]

> Peas an' the rice, peas an' the rice
> Peas an' the rice done done done done
> Peas an' the rice, peas an' the rice done done done done.
> New rice an' okra, eat some an' lef' some
> Peas an' the rice, peas an' the rice done done done done.

[18] *James A. Grant in a Walk across Africa tells of many interesting things he saw in 1861 on the way from Zanzibar to Uganda. "On the third of April the rice harvest was being gathered. . . . The reapers consisted of negro women and girls, who sang pleasantly. . . . The thrashing of the rice was novel. A quantity of ears was placed upon a cow's hide, slaves in irons were made to work it with their toes and feet, and winnow it in the wind; and after being thoroughly sun-dried upon a clear space of cow-dunged ground, it was fit for the process of shelling in the large pestle and mortar. If a considerable amount was to be thrashed, a bludgeon answered the purpose of the negroes' feet. . . . If our Seedees had to clean rice in the wooden mortar, a dozen hands would set about the work of two. It could not be done without those who worked beating time with the pestle to their song, the lookers-on clapping hands and stamping their feet. The work and song never ceased till the rice was pounded almost into dust—such joyous reckless creatures are these simple Africans!" To the Southerner of the nineteenth century this account presents a familiar picture.*

58. PEAS AN' THE RICE

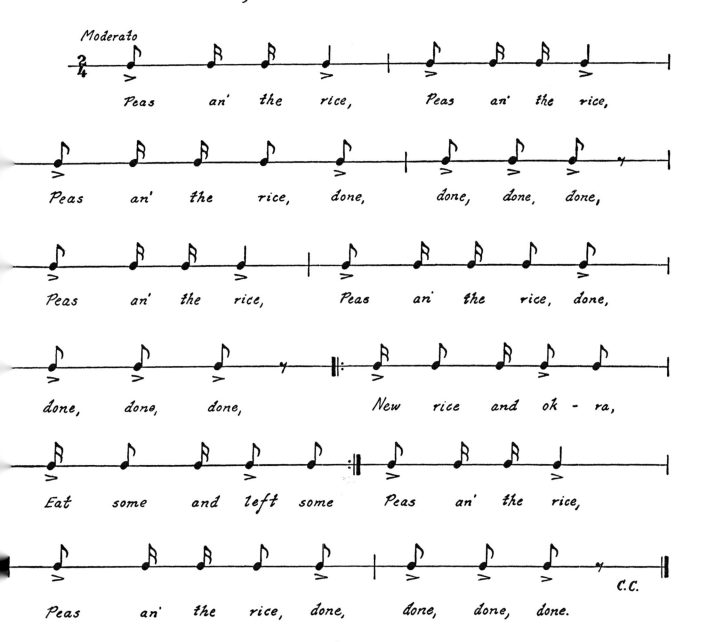

Moderato

Peas an' the rice, Peas an' the rice,

Peas an' the rice, done, done, done, done,

Peas an' the rice, Peas an' the rice, done,

done, done, done, New rice and ok - ra,

Eat some and left some Peas an' the rice,

Peas an' the rice, done, done, done, done.

C.C.

HARD TIME IN OLE VIRGINNY

On Sapelo, in hunting up Emma Johnson's twins, I came upon such a picture as must have been common in plantation days. Under the immense live oaks, two boys were beating rice in a home-made mortar. Chickens were all about, picking up stray grains. A couple of fanners were on the ground ready to fan the rice as soon as the hulls were loosened in the mortar. Fanning, as can be imagined, is done by jumping the rice in the flat basket and letting the wind do the rest; [19] but I noticed that Emma was thrifty, and the rice hulls—which looked like bran—fell on oilcloth laid on the ground. She told me they were to be fed to the pigs. The boys were "shamed" and stopped singing when I came up, but there was no shyness about Emma. She seized one of the pestles in the middle and sang a combination of the shanty, "Hard Time in Ole Virginny," the religious song, "Aye Lord, Buddin' of the Fig Tree," and a dance song, "My Ole Missus Promise Me."

> Summer comin' again
> 　Hard time in ole Virginny.
> Comin' in the rainbow
> 　Hard time in ole Virginny.
> Comin' in the cloud
> 　Hard time in ole Virginny.
> My ole missus promise me
> 　Hard time in ole Virginny.
> When she die she set me free
> 　Hard time in ole Virginny.
> She live so long
> 　Hard time in ole Virginny.
> Her head got bald
> 　Hard time in ole Virginny.

[19] *If there is no wind, the one who does the fanning whistles for it.*

A. B. A. B. A.

The rhythm of this nonsensical Butler Island song enables the rice beaters to do work which would otherwise be extremely tiresome.[20] It continues as long as the work lasts, with no change in rhythm and very little in the words.

Uncle July mortal man, stan' right by de doo'

An' see how y'r rice done mash.[21]

An' A. B. A. B. A.

An' A. B. A. B. A.

An' A. B. A. B. A. B. A.

Go A. B. go

Go A. B. go

July'll cut y'r win'.

A. B. A. B. A.

A. B. A. B. A.

An' July'll cut y'r win'.

July de mortal man

July cut y'r win'.

A. B. A. B. A.

An' A. B. A. B. A.

Go Lizzy go, Billy goin' t' cut y'r win'.

Go Emma go, Gally goin' t' cut y'r win'.

[20] *Mrs. Cate tells me that each plantation had its particular songs for beating rice, just as its rowing songs were unlike those of other plantations.*

[21] *The footnote on page 232 suggests that the "reckless" Africans pounded rice in the same careless fashion.*

I GWINE T' BEAT DIS RICE

"J. P." learned this half-chanted composition from his grandfather, Old Quarterman. He never sings the words twice alike, but the rhythm is always the same.

> I gwine t' beat dis rice
> Gwine t' beat 'um so
> Gwine t' beat 'um until the hu'ks come off
> Ah hanh hanh (nasal)
> Ah hanh hanh.
> Gwine t' cook dis rice when I get through
> Gwine t' cook 'um so
> Ah hanh hanh.
> Ah hanh hanh.
> Gwine f' eat mh belly full
> Ah hanh hanh
> Ah hanh hanh.

ROWING SONGS

A hundred years ago, when boats offered the most comfortable and convenient mode of transportation, and provided the sea islands of South Carolina and Georgia with their only means of communication with the mainland, the rowing songs were an important adjunct to the work of the oarsmen. English travelers rarely failed to mention them. Captain Basil Hall in his *Travels in North America* (1827–28) tells of leaving Darien—"A neat little village"—and proceeding down the current to St. Simon's Island "in a canoe, some thirty feet long, hollowed out of a cypress tree. The oars were pulled by five smart negroes, merry fellows and very happy looking. . . . They accompanied their labor by a wild sort of song not very unlike that of the Canadian voyageurs, but still more nearly resembling that of the well-known Bunder-boatmen of Bombay." [22]

Fanny Kemble frequently mentioned the singing of the Butler Island oarsmen in her *Journal*, written ten years later. In 1845, Sir Charles Lyell [23] tells of being met at Darien by Mr. Hamilton Couper, who came down the river from Hopeton "in a

---

[22] *The editors of Slave Songs of the United States say that "Mr. E. S. Philbrick was struck with the resemblance of some of the rowing tunes at Port Royal to the boatmen's songs he had heard upon the Nile."*

[23] Second Visit to the United States.

long canoe, hollowed out of the trunk of a single cypress and rowed by six negroes, who were singing loudly and keeping time to the stroke of their oars." He went on to say: "For many a mile we saw no habitations, and the solitude was profound; but our black oarsmen made the woods echo to their song. One of them taking the lead, first improvised a verse, paying compliments to his master's family, and to a celebrated black beauty of the neighborhood, who was compared to the 'red bird.' The other five then joined in the chorus, always repeating the same words. Occasionally they struck up a hymn, in which the most sacred subjects were handled with strange familiarity, and which, though nothing irreverent was meant, sounded oddly to our ears, and, when following a love ditty, almost profane."

Lyell's account of his canoe trip from Hopeton to visit Mr. Couper's summer residence on St. Simon's Island, fifteen miles distant, is of interest for several reasons. In describing the Negro houses on Butler Island, where the party landed on their way, he tells us they "were neat, and whitewashed, all floored with wood, each with an apartment called the hall, two sleeping rooms, and a loft for the children" —which is contrary to what Fanny Kemble had written about the selfsame houses a few years earlier. He also mentioned seeing ricks of rice raised on props five feet high, to protect them from the sea, which, during hurricanes, has been known to rise five or six feet. His observations on the mental development of the slaves are particularly significant: "It is evident that on these rice farms, where the negroes associate with scarcely any whites, except the overseer and his family, and have but little intercourse with the slaves of other estates, they must remain far more stationary than where, as in a large part of Georgia, they are about equal in number to the whites, or even form a minority. . . . In Glynn County, where we are now residing, there are no less than four thousand negroes to seven hundred whites,[24] whereas in Georgia generally there are only 281,000 in a population of 691,000 or more whites than colored people."

I give these figures because they explain why more distinctive slave songs can be found in the rice swamps and cotton plantations of the adjoining sea islands than in the Piedmont section where Anglo-Saxon influence has always predominated. In all probability we have the malaria mosquito and the absentee landlords to thank for this. In Africa the black race had developed an immunity to malaria—which they

[24] *About the same ratio as when I first went to St. Simon's. Charles Spalding Wylly states that in 1810 almost every acre of arable land on St. Simon's was under cultivation. There were fourteen plantations and a slave population of about 1200.*

are now losing—and the resistance of the slaves to "the miasma of the rice fields" enabled them to take care of the crop during the "pestilential season" with the minimum of white supervision. In consequence, all white residents who could leave [25] fled at nightfall to the "salts"—as the sea marshes were called—or to the dry and higher pine land, whichever might be nearer, and the Negroes were left very much to themselves. It requires no stretch of the imagination to assume that the beloved rhythms and dances that had been brought from Africa were kept alive in just this way. For which let me say—God be praised! I have never been able to believe that all virtue was vested in the white man or his music.

Another statement of Lyell's is so accurate that it should be given here. He tells us that "The slaves identify themselves with the master, and their sense of their own importance rises with his success in life." Mrs. Shadman, who knew all the ex-slaves on St. Simon's, told me that Maum Rhina at Cannon's Point was heard to say: "I hol' my head jus' as high as my Missus. I'se a Wylly nig'ah." The Wylly Negroes always felt they were superior to those of the Hazzards, who lived on the adjoining plantation. The feeling of animosity that has persisted for more than a century among the descendants of the slaves of the two plantations may be because of the duel over a boundary dispute, in which young Wylly was killed by his neighbor, Dr. Hazzard.

In spite of the Negroes being passionately fond of music and dancing, the activity of the Baptist and Methodist missionaries was such before 1845 that Lyell tells us: "On the Hopeton Plantation above twenty violins have been silenced." The ban on secular music was the same in the vicinity of Beaufort, South Carolina. The editors of *Slave Songs of the United States* reported that they never saw a musical instrument among the Port Royal freedmen, and mentioned that the last violin, owned by a "wordly man," disappeared from Coffin's Point in 1861. They expressed regret that they could not obtain enough secular songs to make a division by themselves, and went on to say: "It is . . . already becoming difficult to obtain these songs. Even the 'spirituals' are going out of use on the plantations, superseded by the new style of religious music, 'closely imitated from the white people.'" The statement made by the editors that "The same songs are used for rowing as for shouting," holds true on the coast of Georgia, and it is interesting to find that the identical tunes were favorites the length of the sea-island chain between the Peedee and the Satilla Rivers. (Map, page xxxii.)

The similarity of the speech, customs, and music of the Gullah Negroes through-

[25] The terms of the overseer's contract required his presence on the plantation except under urgent circumstances.

out this section is not surprising to those who have studied its social and economic conditions at first hand—or have carefully read *Seed from Madagascar* by Duncan Clinch Heyward. This gentleman's words are authoritative. He learned planting methods and the management of Negro labor at first hand on the Combahee swamp plantations of his paternal ancestors in South Carolina and at the Clinch Plantation, called Refuge, on the Satilla River in Georgia, where his maternal ancestors were also rice planters.

In *American Humor*, Constance Rourke quotes a traveler as saying in 1795 that "The blacks are the great humorists of the nation." She goes on to tell us how Negro humor has always been abundant, and how, from it, early minstrels drew as from a primal source. She also says that many minstrels had lived in the South and West and knew the Negro at first hand. One of them saw an old peddler of watermelons with a donkey cart in a Georgia town, and followed him about until he had mastered his lingo, cries, and snatches of song, which may account for the similarity of our Negro secular songs to those of the minstrel stage. Few of the white singers, however, gave credit where it was due. Miss Rourke states that "Plantation owners on the Mississippi had crews of black oarsmen who sang as they rowed and improvised good-natured verses to match the occasions of the day. . . .[26] A western poet declared that 'among the earliest original verses of the West were sundry African melodies celebrating the coon hunt and the vicissitudes of river navigation.' The Negro was to be seen everywhere in the South and in the new Southwest, on small farms and great plantations, on roads and levees. He was often an all but equal member of many a pioneering expedition. He became, in short, a dominant figure in spite of his condition and commanded a definite portraiture."

Because of his position in democratic communities it is readily seen why the songs of the Negro have left their stamp on those of the hill-billy and the cowboy; and when he attended the same revival meetings as the whites—as he frequently did —his mode of singing undoubtedly exerted as much influence upon their religious songs as his secular music does today upon our radio singers.

[26] *They carried on a tradition that was characteristic of the South Carolina and Georgia coast. Liverpool, who was stroke oar of the Butler Island crew of ten men, told me they rowed a cypress dugout, thirty-three feet long, made from one immense log. His favorite rowing song was "Zion," but others preferred "Knee-bone." Mrs. G. V. Cate tells us, in Our Todays and Yesterdays, "there was a spirit of rivalry among the planters to have the best boat . . . and a desire on the part of the slaves to sing the best songs. The oarsmen of one plantation would never sing the songs belonging to another plantation," and when a boat passed at night it would be known from the song to what plantation the singers belonged.*
In A Walk across Africa, Grant describes a very large canoe—hollowed out of an immense tree—that carried a ton and a half.

OH WHEN I COME TO DIE

When Willis was a child and went to Lonesome Point for fish and oysters with his father, Adam Proctor, this is the song they often used to make the rowing easier. It is recognized, of course, that the rhythm had to be readjusted to the stroke of the oar. Josephine Young says the song was also used "down on our knees, for watch night 'n prayin'." Needless to say, she would have left off the final g in "dying."

Chorus: O when
(O when)
O when
(O when)
O when I come to die
Give me Jesus.

When I am dying
When I am dying
When I am dying my Lord
Give me Jesus.

(repeat chorus)

When the doctor give me over
When the doctor give me over
When the doctor give me over my Lord
Give me Jesus.

(repeat chorus)

When my friends forsake me
When my friends forsake me
When my friends forsake me my Lord
Give me Jesus.

(repeat chorus)

When trouble is over
When trouble is over
When trouble is over my Lord
Give me Jesus.

(repeat chorus)

59. OH WHEN I COME TO DIE

dy-in' my Lord give me Je-sus Oh when Oh

dy-in' my Lord give me Je-sus Oh— when

Solo Chos. Solo

Oh when Oh

when Oh when I come to die give me Je-sus.

Oh— when Oh when I come to die— give me Je-sus.

Chos.

when

C.C.

MISCELLANEOUS WORK SONGS

By this time the reason for placing this chapter at the end of the collection must be obvious. Practically any of the foregoing songs were utilized in one kind of labor or another. The shout songs were peculiarly adapted to rowing; and certain of the religious songs were suited to the stevedore's need of a swinging tune in work that was continuous. There were, however, other tasks which required a special rhythm, dependent oftentimes upon the mood of the laborer, and these occasions were likely to bring forth extemporaneous compositions. Mrs. Shadman told me that laundresses generally sang while ironing, and this is one of the improvisations she had heard:

> Do tu'key buzzard len' me y'u wing
> T' fly ova yonda t' see Miss Geo'gia King.

She had also heard churning done to these coaxing words:

> Come budda come, Missus want e budda, come budda come.

But it was over the wash-board that a singer gave free scope to a religious turn of mind. Some years ago a Northern Negro composer, unfamiliar with the traditional songs of his race, heard the following spiritual sung by a washerwoman while at work. She claimed she had made it up; he innocently believed her, and told reporters that new spirituals are born every day. No one wishes more sincerely than I that such might be the case, but this particular song was sung in Glynn County long before he was born. It is Joe's favorite for swinging the weed cutter:

> By an' by-e I'm goin' t' see the King
> By an' by-e I'm goin' t' see the King
> By an' by-e I'm goin' t' see the King
> Lord, I wouldn' mind dyin' if dyin' was all.
>
> Wouldn' mind dyin' but I got t' go by myself
> Lord, I wouldn' mind dyin' but I got t' go by myself
> O Lord, I wouldn' mind dyin' but I got t' go by myself
> Lord, I wouldn' mind dyin' if dyin' was all.[27]

[27] *A variation of this verse is expressed in these words:*
> *Wouldn' mind dyin' but I got t' lay in the grave so long*
> *Lord, I wouldn' mind dyin' if dyin' was all.*

After death I got to stan' a tes'
After death I got to stan' a tes'
Oh Lordy, after death I got to stan' a tes'
Lord, I wouldn' mind dyin' if dyin' was all.

Dishwashing is another of the monotonous jobs which invite the accompaniment of flowing song. In my own kitchen I have heard dishes disposed of to a tune which, surprisingly enough, has an Algerian counterpart. I heard it first, from my hotel on the heights of Constantine, played on a primitive pipe in the little Berber village at the base of the cliff far below. It was repeated over and over—that is why I am familiar with it. Apparently, the tune bothered a cow, for her bellowing frequently gave me a respite. The air is lovely, but when heard by the hour it is not so enjoyable.

I want a die easy when I die
O when I die.
I want a die easy when I die
I want a die easy when I die—Shout salvation as I fly
I want a die easy when I die.

Until after the War Between the States stoves were unknown in the South, and cooking was done mostly in large fireplaces with cranes and hooks for hanging pots and kettles over the heat. Meat was roasted in "tin kitchens" placed in front of the fire, although the remains of an enormous brick oven at Cannon's Point indicate the part it played in the large-scale hospitality of the Couper family. Cooking, in fact, was one of those interrupted jobs which required undivided attention, and for that reason, perhaps, I never heard of a good cook who sang.

On St. Simon's and Jekyl Islands great quantities of cotton were grown. The best description of the process was given by Captain Basil Hall in 1828. He tells how the "task" varied with the heaviness of the work. In describing the "listing" of the ground—breaking it with a broad cotton-field hoe—he said that "a full hand lists half an acre." Janey Jackson must have been a full hand, for she told of doing her half-acre and thinking nothing of it. She and Floyd White's parents belonged to the Caters, and both sang a tune which was a favorite for hoeing cotton. They agreed that "June month was a ha'd month": the weeds grew fast and the sun was hot.

What y'u gwine t' do fo' June month? Jerusalem Jerusalem.
Pull off y'u coat an' go t' work—Jerusalem Jerusalem.
June month's a ha'd month—Jerusalem Jerusalem.
Jersualem in de mornin'—Jerusalem Jerusalem.

Floyd sang several variations of the central theme, but as he said himself, "This is enough!" Janey's song was practically the same except that she substituted "Zion" for "Jerusalem."

You mus' pray ha'd—June a ha'd month
June month a sailin'—Oh, Zion O Zion.
    What y'u do fo' June month?
Y'u pull off y'u coat an' go t' work—Oh, Zion O Zion.

In her "Reminiscences" Mrs. Conrad tells how meal was ground on Broughton Island in a Biblical handmill: "Large stones with a hole in the uppermost one that connected it with the roof of the shed in which it stood,[28] held a stout pole. The women would take hold of this piece of wood and turn the stone with a celerity and ease that was surprising. I can shut my eyes now at any time, and hear the whirring of the stones, the soft rustle of the meal as it fell in the basket placed to receive it and the sound of the women's voices singing at the mill." However, from this scanty description, I could not visualize how the mill worked until Belle Murray of St. Simon's explained that a large block of wood supported the stones; that the lower stone was held in place through the use of a bar of iron called a "spindle"—about one and one-half inches square and eighteen inches long—and that it fitted into an auger hole in the timber underneath. It appears that after the square piece of iron had made the lower stone secure, it abruptly ended in a half-inch bolt, about three inches long, which went through a round hole in a rectangular piece of iron, about two and one-half inches by three and one-half inches and half-an-inch thick, called a "frog." The corn was fed into the round hole in the stone above the frog; three holes of varying depth and width—chipped out of the top stone only about three inches from its rim—regulated the fineness or coarseness of the meal through shifting the pole from one hole to another. A wedge was also put under the stones to tilt them when one wanted the mill to run more easily. According to Mrs. Conrad,

---

[28] *In all probability a hole in an overhead beam engaged the upper end of the pole at the time its lower end—on a slant—was moving the stone with "celerity and ease."*

the meal fell into a basket, but I still cannot see how this was possible when the stones were circular. Belle says that her mill was set up in a box and the meal fell into it.

I go into detail because no one has told me so clearly as Belle how the work was done. She obligingly sold me the mill that came from Butler's Point where she was born, and said: "I wish I.had a dollar for every mess of grits I've ground in it." Lonnie Davis says he knows how to set it up, and soon I hope to be grinding enough meal at the Cabin to supply Belle's needs and mine.

A colored man who used to be a "shack-rouser" at a railroad camp on the Georgia Central Line sang these warning lines before he gave the rat-a-tat-tat, with a stick, on the different doors.

> Wake up buddy
> An' sit on the rock
> It ain't quite day
> But it's four o'clock
> Rata-tat-tat!

Next door:
> Hey buddy
> It's hard but it's fair
> You had a good home
> But you wouldn't stay there
> Rata-tat-tat!

And the next:
> I had a little kitten
> He grow to be a mouser
> Yonder come
> That cruel shack-rouser
> Rata-tat-tat!

Shad Hall, who lives on Sapelo, showed me how the conch was blown in olden times to get the hands out to work before day. It was a joy to find that the musical note I had heard on the Riviera was used in this country in spite of Thomas Spalding's dislike of music. His antipathy was such that he banned all instruments—except one fiddle which was retained for dancing. It is just possible that Mr. Spalding's attitude resulted in the same reaction among the Sapelo Negroes as was seen among those of the Quaker community in which I was born. In neither section did the Negroes hear much of the white folks' music, and for that reason, perhaps, they relied upon their traditional tunes more than they would have otherwise.

Quarterman told me that when the Negroes "suspicioned" someone was telling tales to the driver to get one of them a whipping, they would sing a song like the following while at work in the field:

> O Judyas he wuz a 'ceitful man
> He went an' betray a mos' innocen' man.
> Fo' thirty pieces a silver dat it wuz done
> He went in de woods an' e' self he hung.

A Negro "stump-knocker"—as itinerant preachers without a regular charge used to be called—frankly told me he wasn't much on preaching, but when it came to singing he always got his people—and a meal. Another preacher of this class, with a remarkable flow of rhythmic words and a fine grasp of the dramatic build-up—not necessarily connected with ideas—boasted to me of his ability to get his congregation "goin'."

FIVE FINGERS IN THE BOLL

When I asked Josephine what the words "five fingers in the boll" meant, she explained that in the shade at the bottom of the stalk of cotton the bolls are likely to be rotten; they come off in the hand, and "y'u can't make any time grabbin' de cotton out uv 'em." "Fingers" are the compartments holding the white fiber. The song has reference to the variety that contains five in a boll, but I am told that some have three, and others four. I confess I never noticed how many there were.

> Way down in the bottom—whah the cotton boll's a rotten
> Won' get my hundud [29] all day
> Way down in the bottom—whah the cotton boll's a rotten
> Won' get my hundud all day.
> Befo'e I'll be beated—befo'e I'll be cheated
> I'll leave five finguhs in the boll
> Befo'e I'll be beated—befo'e I'll be cheated
> I'll leave five finguhs in the boll.
> Black man beat me—white man cheat me
> Won' get my hundud all day
> Black man beat me—white man cheat me
> Won' get my hundud all day.

[29] *Ninety pounds of cotton was looked upon as the least a hand should pick in a day.*

60. FIVE FINGERS IN THE BOLL

DRINKIN' OF THE WINE

The swinging rhythm of the communion song, "Drinkin' of the Wine," made it a favorite with the chain-gang for cutting weeds along the highway. The afternoon I heard it sung by convicts in front of my house, there were no chains to be seen or heard. When I asked the guard the reason, he told me they were used only to enforce camp discipline. The prisoners had been on their good behavior that week, and the chains had been left off.

I mentioned the incongruity of wearing stripes [30] and singing spirituals. He laughed and said the prisoners got very religious while in camp. It is a fact, however, that the Negro takes his religion very seriously, and, given time for meditation—enforced though it be—quite naturally reacts in this way. Then, too, he apparently has a different concept of morality from white people, and in consequence the idea prevails among us that he does not put his religion into practice. But, for that matter, who does? Each race seems to have its own particular blind spot, and inability to recognize the sanctity of property appears to the white man to be the hereditary weakness of the Negroes in this country, as in Africa. Before the white man meddled with their lives, it was considered legitimate business for the inhabitants of one community to steal from another. Up to the time of the Emancipation Proclamation, I am told, many a slave held the ingenious idea that property could not steal from property. It is possible that this notion, coupled with the viewpoint inherited from Africa,[31] may account for the tolerance still shown by the Negro toward the light-fingered members of the race who run afoul of the law.

According to a *London Morning Post* correspondent at Nairobi, capital of Kenya: "To the native mind there is nothing morally wrong in thefts of stock from other natives and from European farmers." This is possibly the reason why it is hard to get our primitive Negro to see that it is wrong to take a chicken from the roost when he is hungry, or a shirt off the clothes-line when he is half-naked. The same

---

[30] *The "lifers" wear a plain drab suit and the lesser offenders, stripes. It should be the other way about. When convicts escape, as they often do, protective coloration gives the advantage to those who should not have it.*

[31] *In Astley's Collection, John Leo is quoted as saying that the Negroes on and between the Senegal and Gambia rivers lived in common. They had no property in land, but supported themselves in equal state, upon the natural produce of the country. Seagrave also comments on the fact there is no property in ground. The king's license is obtained and the people then go out in troops, and first clear the ground from bushes and weeds which they burn, "and so continue to work in a body for the public benefit, till every man's ground is tilled and sowed."*

correspondent goes on to tell of the difficulties encountered by the Governor of Kenya in stamping out what we consider crime. "Imprisonment is found to be no deterrent. Nor among the Kikuyu does an ex-convict lose caste in the tribe. After he is released from jail the sacrifice of a single goat puts everything right. A new suit of a white tunic and shorts is thoroughly enjoyed by native prisoners for theft in East Africa. Fines are not always a success because the native, well-fed, housed and clothed at government expense, actually enjoys his term as a vacation."

Our own prison camp in Glynn County formerly offered an example of the same problem. A colored convict whose time was up pleaded with Mr. Higgenbotham—who was the court of last appeal at the camp—to be allowed to stay. A living being hard to get nowadays, he figured he could not provide for himself as well as the county did.[32] But the authorities were firm, and he was obliged to move on. Of course, he knew how to get back if times were too hard. It is the same with us, as in Africa, when it comes to any stigma being attached to a Negro who has served a term in jail or spent time on the chain-gang. Ex-convicts assume the same status in their community as they enjoyed before the county forcibly detained them.

Today the chain-gang is a thing of the past, and our roadsides and drainage ditches are neglected. No one need tell me that prison walls and ball-playing are proper substitutes for the healthy outdoor life that our convicts formerly led. There is a great deal of sentimentality connected with the discouragement of crime, and the abolition of the chain-gang is one of its manifestations. Of course there were abuses, but they also occur within prison walls—only there they are not so readily found out.

> Chorus: Drinkin' of the wine—wine—wine
> Drinkin' of the wine
> O—yes—my Lord.
> I oughta bin to Heaven ten thousand years
> Drinkin' of the wine.

[32] *My corner was for years the favorite resting-place at noon for the convicts when they worked on the island. I saw the substantial rations served them, and it is no wonder the discharged convict felt he could go farther and fare worse. I also observed that the model prisoners were well treated. One day I overheard a guard say very hospitably to one of my Negro singers, who was working for me: "Want to come back?" With a good-humored chuckle, the man replied: "No, thank you." It seems that he had been mixed up in a drinking affair in which a knife had figured. He told me he had run away, but had found the world a hard place to live in—so he had come home, surrendered, and taken his medicine. The guard said he had been a star prisoner.*

Eatin' of the bread—bread—bread
Eatin' of the bread—O yes my Lord.
I oughta bin to Heaven ten thousand years
　　Drinkin' of the wine.

　　　(repeat chorus)

If my mother ask for me
Tell her Death done summon' me.
I oughta bin to Heaven ten thousand years
　　Drinkin' of the wine.

　　　(repeat chorus)

If y'u get there before I do
Tell my Lord I'm comin' too.
I oughta bin to Heaven ten thousand years
　　Drinkin' of the wine.

　　　(repeat chorus)

Ain' but one thing I done wrong
Stayin' in the wilderness mos' too long.
I oughta bin to Heaven ten thousand years
　　Drinkin' of the wine.

　　　(repeat chorus)

WHEN I'M GONE TO COME NO MO'

Nobody but a Negro could employ such entrancing elaborations as occur in the singing of "Gone—gone—gone," and no transcription could possibly give it. Our musical method is opposed to that of the Negro, and, try as we may, we cannot achieve his strange inflections, nor place emphasis as he does. A song may appear perfectly simple, but try to learn it, and the simplicity vanishes.

The first time I heard this song, a gang of Glynn County convicts was using its rhythm to heave great clods of black earth out of the tide-water creek behind my house. The leader was such an excellent singer that I asked the guard how soon he was due to be free. The man did not have much more time to serve, his record on the gang was good, and his last offense was nothing more than taking a stool he fancied from an office; but he was a repeater. He just could not leave other people's property alone. Even though I coveted his voice, obligation to the community would not permit me to encourage his presence on the island:

Chorus: When I'm gon-ne—gon-ne—gon-ne
When I'm gone to come no mo'
Church I know y'u're goin' to miss me
    When I'm gone.

Y'u're goin' to miss me—for my walk
Y'u're goin' to miss me—for my talk
Church I know y'u're goin' to miss me
    When I'm gone.

Y'u're goin' to miss me—for my prayer
Y'u're goin' to miss me—for my song
Church I know y'u're goin' to miss me
    When I'm gone.

Y'u may see me goin' along so
I have my trouble here below
Church I know y'u're goin' to miss me
    When I'm gone.

Done been up—done been tried
Dat ain't all—got more beside
Church I know y'u're goin' to miss me
    When I'm gone.

B for the Bible—it's a good old book
Fin' God's word wherever you look
Church I know y'u're goin' to miss me
    When I'm gone.

Batimas he born blin'
Couldn' keep the Lord God out of his min'
Church I know y'u're goin' to miss me
    When I'm gone.

A Selected Bibliography

I SLAVE SONGS

Allen, Ware, and Garrison, *Slave Songs of the United States*, New York: 1867.

Ballanta, N. G. J., *St. Helena Island Spirituals*, New York: 1925.

Barton, W. E., *Old Plantation Hymns*, Boston: 1899.

Curtis-Burlin, Natalie, *Negro Folk Songs*, Hampton Series, New York: 1918–19.

Fenner, Thomas P., *Cabin and Plantation Songs*, New York: 1874.

Hallowell, Emily, *Calhoun Plantation Songs*, Boston: 1907.

McIllhenny, Edward Avery, *Befo' de War Spirituals*, Boston: 1933.

Murphy, Jeannette Robinson, *Southern Thoughts for Northern Thinkers*, New York: 1904.

Seward, Theo. F., *Jubilee Songs As Sung by the Jubilee Singers of Fisk University*, New York: 1872.

    Spiritualles. Sung by the Carolina Singers (Fairfield Normal Institute), 1872–73.

Talley, Thomas W., *Negro Folk Rhymes*, New York: 1922.

II. MINSTREL AND WORK SONGS—SINGING GAMES

Colcord, Joanna C., *Roll and Go. Songs of American Sailormen*, Indianapolis: 1924.

    Minstrel and Plantation Songs, Boston: 1882.

    Minstrels, Lucy Neale's Nigga Warbler, Philadelphia: 1838 (?).

Porter, Grace Cleveland, *Negro Folk Singing Games*, London: 1914.

Terry, Richard Runciman, *The Shanty Book*, London: 1921.

    White's New Illustrated Melodeon Song Book, New York: 1848.

III. AFRICA

Astley, Thomas, *Collection of Voyages and Travels*, London: 1745.

Bender, C. J., *Proverbs of West Africa* (E. Haldeman-Julius, Blue Book, No. 505), Girard, Kansas: (?).

Curtis, Natalie, *Songs and Tales from the Dark Continent*, New York: 1920.

DuBois, W. E. Burghardt, *The Negro*, New York: 1915.

Egerton, F. Clement C., *African Majesty*, New York: 1939.

Ellis, William, *History of Madagascar*, London: 1838.

Gorer, Geoffrey, *African Dances*, New York: 1935.

Grant, James A., *A Walk Across Africa*, Edinburgh: 1864.

Guillaume, Paul, and Monro, Thomas, *Primitive Negro Sculpture*, New York: 1926.

Herzog, George, and Blooah, Charles G., *Jabo Proverbs* (Liberia), University of Chicago: 1930.

Hodgson, W. B., *Notes on North Africa, the Sahara and Soudan*, (?).

Kingsley, Mary H., *Travels in West Africa*, London: 1897.

Kingsley, Mary H., *West African Studies*, London: 1899.

Maran, René, *Batouala*, New York: 1922.

Mayer, Brantz (Editor), *Captain Canot or Twenty Years of an African Slaver*, New York: 1854.

Park, Mungo, *Travels in the Interior Districts of Africa (1795–97)*, Philadelphia: 1800.

Rattray, Capt. R. S., *Ashanti Proverbs*, Oxford: 1916.

Sweeney, James J., *African Negro Art*, New York: 1935.

Tillinghast, J. A., *The Negro in Africa and America*, New York: 1902.

Zayas, M. de, *African Negro Art, Its Influence on Modern Art*, New York: 1916.

IV. NORTH AMERICA—MISCELLANEOUS

Ames, Mary (Clemmer), *From a New England Woman's Diary in Dixie in 1865*, Norwood, Massachusetts: 1906.

Ames, Susie M., *Studies of the Virginia Eastern Shore in the 17th Century*, (?) 1940.

Bartram, William, *Travels in North America*, London: 1792.

Bassett, J. S., *The Southern Plantation Overseer*, Northampton, Massachusetts: 1925.

Benedict, David, *An Abridgement of the General History of the Baptist Denomination in America*, Boston: 1820.

Beckwith, Martha, *Black Roadways in Jamaica*, Chapel Hill, North Carolina: 1929.

Cate, Margaret Davis, *Our Todays and Yesterdays*, Brunswick, Georgia: 1930.

Christensen, (Mrs.) A. M. H., *Afro-American Folk-Lore, Sea Islands of South Carolina*, Boston: 1892.

Edwards, C. L., *Bahama Songs and Stories*, Boston: 1895.

Featherstonhaugh, G. W., *An Excursion through the Slavery States*, (?) 1834.

Hall, Capt. Basil, *Travels in North America (1827–28)*, London: 1829.

Harris, Joel Chandler, *The Story of Aaron. The Son of Ben Ali*, Boston: 1896.

Henry, H. M., *The Police Control of the Slave in South Carolina*, Emory, Virginia: 1914.

Herskovits, Melville J., *Acculturation*, New York: 1938.

Heyward, Duncan Clinch, *Seed from Madagascar*, Chapel Hill, North Carolina: 1937.

Higginson, Thomas Wentworth, *Army Life in a Black Regiment*, Boston: 1870.

Jones, C. C., *Religious Instruction of the Slaves*, Savannah: 1842.

Jones, Charles Colcock, Jr., *Negro Myths from the Georgia Coast*, Boston: 1888.

Jordan, Lewis G., *Negro Baptist History in the United States*, (?) 1930.

Kemble, Frances Anne, *Journal of a Residence on a Georgia Plantation (1838–39)*, New York: 1863.

Kennedy and Parker, *Official Report of the Trials of Sundry Negroes (Negro Plot)*, Charleston, South Carolina: 1822.

Kingsley, Z., *Treatise on the Patriarchal System of Society (3rd Edition)*, (?) 1833.

Leigh, Frances Butler, *Ten Years on a Georgia Plantation (1866–76)*, London: 1883.

Letters and Diary of Laura Towne (1863–84), Cambridge: 1912.

Letters from Port Royal, 1862–68, Edited by Elizabeth Ware Pearson, Boston: 1906.

Lyell, Sir Charles, *A Second Visit to the United States*, New York: 1849.

Olmstead, Frederick Law, *A Journey in the Seaboard Slave States (1853–54)*, New York: 1856.

Puckett, Newbell Niles, *Folk Beliefs of the Southern Negro*, Chapel Hill, North Carolina: 1926.

Rippton, John, Editor, *The Baptist Annual Register*, London: 1790–91–92.

Rourke, Constance, *American Humor*, New York: 1931.

Smedes, Susan Dabney, *A Southern Planter*, Baltimore: 1887.

Steward, William, and Steward, Rev. T. G., *Gouldtown: A Very Remarkable Settlement of Ancient Date* (Negro), Philadelphia: 1918.

   Two Centuries of the First Baptist Church of South Carolina, 1683–1883.

Whaley, Marcellus S., *The Old Types Pass*, Boston: 1925.

Wylly, Charles Spalding, *Memories and Annals*, Brunswick, Georgia: 1897 and 1916.

   The Seed That Was Sown in Georgia, New York: 1910.

V. SELECTED MAGAZINE ARTICLES AND PAMPHLETS
(Abbreviation: JAFL = *The Journal of American Folk-Lore.*)

Ames, Mrs. L. D., "The Missouri Play-Party," JAFL, 1911.

Ballanta, J. N. G., "Music of the African Races," *West Africa*, London: June 14, 1930.

Barrow, David C., "A Georgia Corn Shucking," *Century*, October, 1882.

Bascom, William R., "The Legacy of an Unknown Nigerian 'Donatello,'" *Illustrated London News*, April 8, 1939.

Backus, Mrs. Emma M., "Folk Tales From Georgia," JAFL, 1900.

Benjamin, S. G., "The Sea Islands," *Harpers*, November, 1878.

Bennett, John, "Gullah: A Negro Patois," *South Atlantic Quarterly*, October, 1908 and January, 1909.

Bergen, (Mrs.) Fanny D., "On the Eastern Shore," JAFL, 1889.

Brown, John Mason, "Songs of the Slave," *Lippincott's*, December, 1868.

Cable, G. W., "The Dance in the Place Congo," *Century*, February, 1886.

   "Creole Slave Songs," *Century*, April, 1886.

Chamberlain, Alexander F., "Negro-English or Yoruba Proverbs," JAFL, Vol. 17.

Clark, M. O., "Song Games of Negro Children in Virginia," JAFL, 1890.

Conrad, Georgia Bryan, "Reminiscences of a Southern Woman," *Southern Workman* (Hampton, Virginia) February, March, May, June, July, 1901.

Darby, Loraine, "Ring Games From Georgia," JAFL, 1917.

Edwardes, Charles, "Negro Church Service," (Jacksonville) *MacMillan's Magazine*, 1884.

Field, M. J., "Gold Coast Food," *The College Press*, Pamphlet No. 5, Achimota, West Africa.

Fletcher, Inglis, "A Bootleg Dance Among the Ma-Nganja," *Asia*, September, 1930.

"Florida Game Songs," JAFL, 1902.

Furness, Clifton J., "Communal Music Among Arabians and Negroes," New York: 1930.

   "Mysticism and Modern Music."

Glave, E. J., "Fetishism in Congo Land," *Century*, April, 1891.

Greenberg, Joseph H., "The Decipherment of the 'Ben Ali Diary,' a Preliminary Statement," *Journal of Negro History*, July, 1940.

Hamilton, Goldy M., "The Play-Party in Northeast Missouri," JAFL, 1914.

Harris, Jack, "The Position of Women in a Nigerian Society," *Transactions of the New York Academy of Sciences*, Series II, Vol. 2, No. 5.

Harris, Joel Chandler, "Plantation Music," *Critic*, December 15, 1883.

Haskell, Marion Alexander, "Negro Spirituals," *Century*, August, 1899.

Herskovits, Melville J., "What Has Africa Given America?" *New Republic*, September 4, 1935.

Herskovits, Melville J., "Social History of the Negro," Chapter 7, *Handbook of Social Psychology*, Clark University Press, Worcester: 1935.
    "Kru Proverbs," JAFL, 1930.
Higginson, Thomas W., "Negro Spirituals," *Atlantic Monthly*, 1867.
Hussey, L. M., "Homo-Africanus," *American Mercury*, January, 1925.
Isham, Caddie S., "Games of Danville, Virginia," JAFL, 1921.
Kahn, Morton C., "Where Black Man Meets Red," *Natural History*, May, 1936.
Lawrence, J. B., "Religious Education of the Negro in the Colony of Georgia," *Georgia Historical Quarterly*, Vol. 14.
Leiding, Harriette Kershaw, "Street Cries of an Old Southern City," Charleston: 1910.
McGrady, Edward, XXVIII.—"Slavery in the Province of South Carolina, 1670–1770," Charleston, South Carolina: 1895.
Miles, Emma Bell, "Some Real American Music," *Harper's Magazine*, 1904.
Moore, Francis, "Voyage to Georgia," *Georgia Historical Society Collections*, Vol. 1, 1840.
Moore, Ruby A., "Superstitions from Georgia," JAFL, 1894.
"Negroes and Negro Melodies," *American Art Journal*, 1894.
"Negro Minstrels," *Saturday Review*, London: June 7, 1884.
"Notes on Negro Music," JAFL, Vol. 16.
Page, Thomas Nelson, "The Old-Time Negro," *Scribners Magazine*, November, 1904.
Pendleton, Louis, "Notes on Negro Folk-Lore and Witchcraft in the South," JAFL, 1890.
Perkins, A. E., "Spirituals from the Far South," JAFL, 1922.
Pierce, Edward L., "The Freedom at Port Royal," *Atlantic Monthly*, September, 1863.
Redfern, Susan Fort, "Songs from Georgia," JAFL, 1921.
Smiley, Portia, "Folk-Lore from Virginia, South Carolina, Georgia, Alabama, and Florida," JAFL, Vol. 19.
Smith, Reed, "Gullah," *Bulletin of the University of South Carolina*, No. 190. Columbia: November, 1926.
    "Songs of the Blacks," *Dwight's Musical Journal*, November 15, 1856.
Spalding, H. G., "Under the Palmetto," *Continental Magazine*, August, 1863.
Spalding, Thomas, "Life of Oglethorpe," *Georgia Historical Society Collections*, Vol. 1, 1840.
Spenney, Susan Dix, "Ring Games from Raleigh, North Carolina," JAFL, 1921.
Turner, Lorenzo D., "West African Survivals in the Vocabulary of Gullah."
    "Wandering Negro Minstrels," *The Leisure Hour*, London: September 16, 1871.
Ward, W. E., "Music of the Gold Coast," *The Musical Times*, London: August, September, and October, 1932.
Waring, Mary A., "Mortuary Customs and Beliefs of South Carolina Negroes," JAFL, 1894.
Wood, H. C., "Negro Camp-Meeting Melodies," *New England Magazine*, March, 1892.
Woodson, Carter G., *Journal of Negro History*, Vol. 19, a Review of *White Spirituals in the Southern Uplands*, by George P. Jackson.
Work, Monroe M., "Some Geechee Folk-Lore," *Southern Workman*, 1905.

Printed in the United States
150420LV00001B/5/A